From Skisport to Skiing

From Skisport

The University of Massachusetts Press

AMHERST

E. JOHN B. ALLEN

to Skiing

One Hundred Years
of an American Sport,

1840–1940

Copyright © 1993 by
The University of Massachusetts Press
All rights reserved
LC 93-9224
ISBN 0-87023-844-2; ISBN 1-55849-047-7 (pbk.)
Designed by James F. Brisson
Set in Galliard Roman

Library of Congress Cataloging-in-Publication Data
Allen, E. John B., 1933–
    From skisport to skiing : one hundred years of an
American sport, 1840–1940 / E. John B. Allen.
      p. cm.
    Includes bibliographical references and index.
    ISBN 0-87023-844-2 (alk. paper);
    ISBN 1-55849-047-7(pbk. : alk. paper)
    1. Skis and skiing—United States—History. I. Title.
GV854.4.A4 1993
917.3—dc20   93-9224
                                        CIP

British Library Cataloguing in Publication data are available.

This book is published with the support and cooperation of the
University of Massachusetts at Boston.

CONTENTS

LIST OF ILLUSTRATIONS/ ix

PREFACE/ xi

P A R T 1 THE SKISPORT, 1840–1920

1/The Skisport: An Introduction/ *3*

2/California Gold Rush Snow-Shoeing/ *13*
Utilitarian Skiing/ 14
Mail Service/ 16
Recreational Skiing/ 20
Race Meetings/ 21

3/Utilitarian Skiing and Ludic Enthusiasms/ *29*
Hunting/ 30
New England/ 32
The Northwest/ 33
The Rocky Mountains/ 34
Washington and Oregon/ 36
Mail Service/ 37
U.S. Military/ 39
Skis as Artifacts/ 40
Recreational Enthusiasms/ 44

4/Foundation of the Skisport/ 47
Nansen and Idraet Influences/ 47
Problems of Idraet: Cross-Country/ 54
Problems of Idraet: Jumping/ 55
The Decline of Idraet: Professionalism/ 59

5/Controlling the Skisport/ 63
Efforts to Control the Skisport/ 64
The Lure of Record Breaking/ 65
Ski Manufacturing/ 70

6/The New Enthusiasts/ 75
The Educated Sportsmen/ 75
The Clubs/ 81

PART 2 THE MECHANIZATION OF SKIING, 1920–1940

7/Post–World War I: Prelude to Skiing/ 89
Challenges to the Skisport/ 90
The Challenge of Skiing to the Skisport/ 96

8/The Mechanization of Skiing/ 104
Ski Trains/ 104
Ski Tows/ 109
Ski Trails/ 114

9/The Sport of Skiing/ 117
Alpine Instruction and Terminology/ 119
Downhill and Slalom Racing/ 123
International Racing and the Olympics of 1936/ 126
The National Ski Patrol System/ 129
Tuckerman and the Inferno Races/ 132

10/Western Idylls/ 135

11/The Economics of Pleasure/ 145
  The New Consumer/ 146
  The Equipment Market/ 150
  Skiing in Style/ 156
  Getting There and Getting Up: Development of the
    Ski Center/ 159
  Politics and Development in the Depression/ 164
  Publicizing Skiing/ 165
  The "Take-Off" Phase/ 167

12/Epilogue: To the Future/ 171

NOTES/ 175

SELECTED BIBLIOGRAPHY/ 219

INDEX/ 227

ILLUSTRATIONS

1. Drawing of John A. "Snowshoe" Thompson   17
2. Broadside for the 1869 Alturas Snow Shoe Club Meet   22
3. Four abreast at "a mile a minute"   24
4. Earliest drawing of a race scene, 1874   27
5. Illustration from the journals of Major John Owen   30
6. Hunting on skis in Colorado   31
7. To town on skis, Colorado, 1902   32
8. Gold miners on skis in Colorado   36
9. Idaho mailman with his dog team, c. 1900   38
10. U.S. Cavalry on skis, Yellowstone Park, 1886   40
11. Typical turn-of-the-century skis   42
12. Norden Club of Ishpeming, Michigan, 1887   51
13. Second National Ski Tournament, Michigan, 1906   52
14. Torger Hemmetsveit jumping, 1893   56
15. Ole Feiring jumping, Duluth, 1907   60
16. Somersault, 1913   61
17. U.S. Olympic Team, St. Moritz, 1928   70
18. Early ski manufacturing, New Richmond, Wisconsin, 1923   72
19. Frank Merriwell on skis, 1913   77
20. Skiing in advertising, 1921   80
21. Lake Placid, 1927   82
22. Winter Olympic Games, Lake Placid, poster, 1932   94
23. The Arlberg crouch, 1934   97
24. Boston and Maine snow train poster, 1930s   105
25. Early rope tow   110
26. Experiments with first chair lift for Sun Valley   112
27. Arlberg stylist's *Vorlage,* 1936   118
28. Hannes Schneider ski school poster, New Hampshire   120
29. Finish of first U.S. National Downhill Championship, 1933   124
30. National Ski Patrol poster, 1930s   130

31. Spring skiing poster, Tuckerman headwall, New Hampshire   133
32. Alta, Utah, 1940   136
33. Timberline Lodge, Oregon, commemorative postcard, 1986   142
34. Ski fashion advertisement, 1937–38   154
35. Ski wear advertisements, 1936   157
36. *American Boy* cover, 1937   160
37. Indoor ski jump, Boston Garden   168

PREFACE

The history of the ski would be a wonderful record of
events could it be fully told.

—*Taylors Falls* [Wisconsin] *Journal,* 1888

My academic life took a new direction on 10 February 1976. I was four
chapters along in a manuscript I was writing on Renaissance diplomacy
when I saw a small exhibit of old skiing prints in Innsbruck. On the instant,
I decided to become a collector, but four-hundred-year-old woodcuts are
far too difficult to find and out of the reach of an academic salary. I settled
for an old postcard or two and some ski manuals from the 1930s. "Two
players ski diagonally towards one another until they collide," I read in a
1938 booklet, *Games to Play on Skis,* "the player with the least falls wins."
Here was a vastly different skiing world from my own, yet one that was still
within reach, and I wondered if I could find anyone who had played
"Collision." This fascination with the 1930s was only the beginning; what
skiing was like before that and how it took shape on the North American
continent lured me into serious research. A number of years have gone by
since that exhibition, and here is a social history of American skiing.

I do not claim that this is a story "fully told." That it can be told at all is
due to the nearly two hundred people with whom I have talked. I cannot
list everyone who has reminisced with me, so let me mention the two oldest
(now departed) as representatives of all who have helped me understand
skiing's past: Otto Mason was on skis in 1905 and Dorothy Clay, in 1910.
Their oral testimony has brought a human aspect to archival research.

Ski material (even the precious stuff of archives) is stashed away in
closet, attic, and barn across the country—the Nansen Club Constitution
and Minutes were rescued from the rafters above a commercial garage—
and in many small museums. I should like to thank the curators of the
Bodie, Bridgeport, Downieville, Eureka Park, Kentucky Mine, and Plumas

County museums, all in California; the Historical Society, Aspen, and the Colorado Historical Society, Denver; the Adirondak Museum in Blue Mountain and the Adirondack Research Center in Schenectady, New York; Vesterheim Museum in Decorah, Iowa, and the New Sweden Historical Society in Maine. The most important repositories in the United States, however, are the four major ski museums. I greatly appreciate the unfailing courtesies which their administrators and curators have shown me over the years: Bill Clark of the Western Skisport Museum, Boreal Ridge, California; Michelle Cahill of the Colorado Ski Museum, Vail, Colorado; Burton Boyum, Ray Leverton, and Ken Luostari of the National Ski Hall of Fame, Ishpeming, Michigan; and, especially, Linda Gray and Dick March of the New England Ski Museum, Franconia, New Hampshire.

American skiing owes much of its early equipment and technique, as well as the values people attached to it, to an immigrant foundation, so my research sent me to European archives and museums as well. For their help and hospitality, I should like to thank: Manfred Lämmer of the Institut für Sportgeschichte of the Deutsche Sporthochschule, Cologne, Germany; Ekkehart Ulmrich of the Deutsche Skimuseum, Planegg, Germany; Franz Klaus of the Zdarsky Archiv, Lilienfeld, and Hans Heidinger of the Wintersport- und Heimatmuseum, Mürzzuschlag, both in Austria; Max Triet of the Schweizer Sportmuseum, Basel, Switzerland; Elisabeth Hussey of the Ski Club of Great Britain, London, England; Karin Berg of the Holmenkollen Skimuseet, Oslo, Norway; Kenneth Åström of the Svenska Skidmuseet, Umeå, Sweden; Merja Heiskanen of the Hiihitomuseo, Lahti, and Pekka Honkanen of the Suomi Sportmuseo, Helsinki, both in Finland. In Austria, the staffs of the Heimatmuseum in St. Anton am Arlberg and the University of Innsbruck library were most courteous, as was the staff of the Oslo University library.

I have tried out various aspects of this history at conferences in this country and in Europe, and I am grateful for critiques, particularly at the sessions of the British and North American Societies of Sports History. Two colleagues, David Switzer and William Taylor, have commented on other sections, and Frumie Selchen critiqued an early draft. I owe special thanks to Allen Guttmann and Stephen Hardy for a critical reading of a later version. Paul Wright and Pam Wilkinson of the University of Massachusetts Press have brought the final manuscript to print. I am responsible for ideas, interpretations, and any errors.

Dr. Johnson believed that the greatest part of an author's time was spent in reading in order to write. Much of my reading was made possible by Joyce Bruce of Plymouth State College and Robert McDermand, now of San Jose State College, who did the heavy duty, interlibrary loaning and I acknowledge with gratitude their efforts and those of their counterparts—regrettably nameless—at the other end of the requests. Judy Hart and Barbara Robinson did much of the early typing. To both I owe thanks, as I do to Plymouth State College for various small grants.

Three other people deserve special mention: Bill Berry of Reno, Nevada, who in the most unselfish and generous way sent me an early draft of his manuscript on California skiing now published as *Lost Sierra: Gold, Ghosts and Skis*. Richard W. Moulton, director of the documentary film, *Legends of American Skiing*, with whom I worked for four years, was in large measure the person who forced me—although neither he nor I realized it at the time—to refine my ideas on ski history and make them presentable to the public. And last, I owe most to my long-time skiing friend and one of the most graceful skiers on any mountain, my wife, Heide: trenchant critic, sympathetic translator, flawless typist, and game traveling companion who, thank goodness, also thinks ski history is both important and fun. It is to her that this book is dedicated.

1

THE SKISPORT,

1840–1920

1 / The Skisport: An Introduction

I cannot think of an outdoor sport which is more conducive
to health, ambition, and cheerfulness than skiing. From my
own experience, I can recall very often, when depressed
both in mind and body how a cross-country run on skiis has
stimulated my body and brightened my mind and soul, so
that the perplexing problems before me became easy to
solve and the world appeared like a brilliant ray of sunlight.

—G. C. Torguson, President of the
National Ski Association, 1922

Skiing!—What images flash to mind? Perhaps first that wretched fellow
we watch week after week cartwheeling off a jump in the introductory tape
to ABC's "Wide World of Sports." Maybe the sleekly spandexed and hel-
meted high-tech racer we see flashing down a well-defined course—well
defined that is by many strategically positioned cameras—to the accompanying dazzle of rapidly changing hundredths of seconds on the digital
display and the rising and falling pitch of the announcer's voice cuing us to
the skier's relative speed on the course. The images for those who ski are
probably a kaleidoscope of memories, at once exhilarating and painful—
the stuff of tall tales told far from the actual activity—combined with a
private question or two about the next season: Will the old legs stand up to
another year on the slopes?

These images are strong but they have little to do with the sort of skiing I
shall discuss in this book. I wish there were a different, commonly accepted
word to describe the skier in the years before the Second World War. In fact
quite a number were in use at the time—*skister, skee-man, snow skater*—but
they gave way to *skier,* so we are stuck with that term. These early terms are
graphic; writers of skiing matters from between 1850 and 1920 had to
describe the actions because the majority of people had little or no knowledge of skiing. When skiing became well known, from the turn of the
century on, the vocabulary of winter sporting included a skier as one who
skis, compared with, say, a skater or tobogganist.

Although the skiers were very different in the period from 1840 to 1940
from what they are today, I will argue that they also could exhibit or at least

adumbrate all the attributes of modern skiers: love of speed, enjoyment of winter out-of-doors, sociability, one-upmanship, and fashion. With a jargon to bind a like-minded community together, they thought of themselves as special people.

The neatness of the exact one hundred years considered in this study is not a concoction of the historian's penchant for order. As early as 1841 the record shows that one Gullick Laugen was on skis in the Beloit area, just over the Wisconsin line from Chicago. By 1940 all the component parts of skiing that we recognize as modern had emerged, just as war interrupted the sport's evolution. Modern skiing, per se, is therefore a post–1945, postwar phenomenon, and this study is an analysis of what made skiing into a modern sport, an analysis of the "becoming" rather than the actuality. The year 1940, then, is not a purely arbitrary date with which to end this book.

Although the story I tell is roughly chronological, it breaks into two major parts. The first covers the nineteenth-century period into the 1920s, the second, the 1920s to 1940. The mid to late twenties are important because those were the years when the new attraction and sport that we today call Alpine skiing emerged, as opposed to the earlier Nordic cross-country skiing and jumping. In the 1920s skisport gave way to skiing. The reasons for the decline of the Scandinavian sporting *Idraet* ideal and the growth of Alpine disciplines constitute a major part of the analysis. The late 1920s and early 1930s were also the years when skiing became mechanized.

Despite this chronology and its natural division, the thrust of the book is in the analysis of how and why skiing became a modern sport, and my argument and exposition owe a debt to Allen Guttmann's *From Ritual to Record: The Nature of Modern Sports.* His thesis is the most important theoretical mark against which I have tested my ideas. Guttmann posits seven distinguishing characteristics of modern sport: secularism, equality of opportunity to compete and in the conditions of competition, specialization of roles, rationalization, bureaucratic organization, quantification, and the quest for records. Guttmann is quite aware that these characteristics are easy to name, but that "their implications, ramifications, mutual relations, and ultimate significance require precise and somewhat extended analysis."[1] It is just such an involved analysis for skiing that I attempt in this book, and I show where and why skiing differs from Guttmann's paradigm.

We should remember that Guttmann examines and analyzes all sport over all time, swooping from the Maori *Teka* to Vince Lombardi with astonishing ease and erudition. In the present study we are bound mostly to the winter months and to areas in the United States (and, occasionally, Canada) that are covered by natural snow. We should also remember that various traditional, historical, social, economic, political, and technological threads are woven together to make the fabric of modern skiing. Indeed, only in an extended analysis can we unravel them. I hope to show in detail just what created the modern sport of skiing. In the Weberian sense, developments that made skiing modern were the same as those that changed American society, thus the nexus between modern society (or sectors of it) and modern skiing is delineated.

The history of the formative years of skiing exhibits a generally acknowledged reorientation of American culture at the end of the nineteenth century.[2] The generation before the First World War experienced a crisis of authority. The consequent rise of antimodernism was expressed in many different ways, mostly by the very people who benefited from an industrial society. By the 1880s and 1890s the United States was in the flush of a materialistic, achieving ethos. Immigrants who had left traditional societies like Norway found themselves hard put to retain the old ways to the extent they wished in the face of increasing pressures engendered by the American way of life. Many sports changed in this period. As the skisport modernized it paralleled a changing America. Immigrants held on to their cultural ideals and traditional values but they exulted in increasing competition in which higher, further, and faster (and money) were the recognized measures of success. Then privileged college students took to skiing as a recreation and sport. They kept its Norse foundation but modified it to suit their leisure-oriented, romantically inclined youth. Fitness, they believed, would stave off the malaise of a society that seemed more urban and artificial than countrified and true.

The first half of this book shows skiing as part of this reorientation of American culture. Skiing provided a healthy and cheap simplicity at the same time that the United States was being caught up in the efficient machine age. Those who skied, although they enjoyed the advantages of materialistic America, were uneasy about its urban, over-civilized quality. Skiing provided an antidote and offered young men authentic experiences in nature's boundless winter snows. Thus, besides being healthy, skiing was moral. Because industrial America had removed much of the effort that had been part of day-to-day existence, "manly" individuals could find the "strenuous life" famously extolled by Teddy Roosevelt in the simplicity of the great outdoors.

As winter entertainment, skating and tobogganing, both spatially limited and socially popular, lacked the heroic quality that skiing provided. Numbers of young men registered the miles they skied during an entire season and kept track of mountains they climbed on skis. One of the most influential men to formulate these ideas was Richard Hovey, appropriately at Dartmouth College in New Hampshire. He captured the romantic idealism of a youth culture, for example, in the school song "Men of Dartmouth."[3] The students made their own strenuous life, skiing in the woods and mountains of the Granite State. They fashioned the skisport to their own manner and after graduation kept up their activities in clubs, many of which continued a collegiate ambience.

Other factors affected the thinking of the well-to-do in the 1890s. First, the economic crisis led some to realize that the be-all and end-all of life was more than the accumulation of goods. The crisis also engendered strikes and walkouts, often believed to be the seditious work of urban immigrant workers—principally the Irish and eastern Europeans. The discrimination experienced by these ethnic groups was seldom felt by the Scandinavians who, for the most part, lived in rural areas and were not associated with such goings-on. If anything, quite the reverse was the case: Social Darwinists believed the Nordic race to be superior, and there was interest in such cultural artifacts as the Norse sagas. Since descendants of those same Norsemen were guardians of all that was sacred to the culture of skiing, the skisport remained strongly Norse in detail and ideal.

In the days before these skiing clubs and efficient transportation, skiing was localized. Skiing was first popular in the mining camps of California, but gold rush skiing had no effect whatsoever because it did not spread from the Sierra to the rest of the country. Only foot and wagon transportation provided possible connections to the West until the Union Pacific's golden spike joined east and west in 1869. Early Californian skiing was a separate entity, and I treat it as such, both its utilitarian and its sporting aspects, in Chapter 2.

Geographical settlement patterns also dictated developments in skiing. Scandinavians settled large sections of generally flat and wooded lands which they turned into farm communities in what was called at that time "the Northwest."—(I shall use this term in Part 1 to refer to today's Michigan, Wisconsin, Minnesota, and Iowa.) In winter immigrants in these regions founded ski clubs and held jumping tournaments.

The differences in the woods and hills of New England, the flat central plain, and the mountainous West and Far West geographically influenced the development of American skiing. Railroad transportation favored New Hampshire rather than Vermont because New England looked to Boston for its skiing clientele in the 1930s; natural routes led to the White Mountains. A resort like Sun Valley in Idaho owed its very existence to a railroad spur. The more efficient transport became, the less marked the geographical differences. Even before 1940, a few skiers were flying from Boston to the Rockies.

I have used the words *ski, skier,* and *skiing* as a jumping event, race, memory, occasion, means of transportation, sport, as well as something that is geographically and ethnically oriented. It is time to state their meanings as clearly as possible.

When people first slipped winter boots through leather straps and slid across the snow on ten-foot boards, skiing was an individual pursuit, carried on for communication and other utilitarian purposes. Only when there was some time for leisure did people begin to think of skiing as something enjoyable in itself. In my third chapter, "Utilitarian Skiing," I argue that such skiing was essentially secular in character as well, to use Guttmann's first point, thus combining part of the thesis with chronological development. There was no organization to this sort of skiing. Indeed, one could consider only its usefulness were it not for a few exceptions, where skiing was indulged in as a ludic activity, as playful fun.

Skiing as a sport, however, is decidedly different because it is highly organized. Believing that physical all-round capability would produce not only a healthy person but a moral citizen too, immigrant organizers of the skisport soon discovered that American achievement and materialism combined to give skiing a different orientation. In the early years, as clubs were formed, rules devised, prizes offered, and many people became involved in the whole paraphernalia of the performance of an event, the old ideals found less acceptance. Chapters four, five, and six analyze the organization of the skisport and look at how the challenges of an industrializing society were met.

The second part of this book, "The Mechanization of Skiing," analyzes the modernizing tendencies associated with downhill and slalom skiing. These Alpine disciplines, experimental in the 1920s, were cultural, sporting activities from the European Alpine countries. Downhill and slalom required a different way of skiing and a different way of thinking about skiing. It was the wealthy who after the First World War both broke with the traditional concepts of skiing and learned to ski in a different fashion. Globe-trotting Americans transplanted what they had learned abroad back to their own skiing venues and a Germanic ambience came to define the right way to ski and to think about skiing.

Any understanding of the modernizing development of skiing, the "skisport" as it was called in the early days (remembered presently in the title of the Western Skisport Museum), requires a linguistic history and analysis of the terms used. Following the morphological construction of a given term, sometimes taken over entirely from another language, its use became common enough to express real meaning first to the initiated and then to a larger interested public: a new gemeinschaft was in the making. Some words and expressions became talismanic to certain groups, some disappeared, and others changed radically from the time they were first used until the Second World War. The following analysis will show something of the link between society and its attitudes toward the sport of skiing.

There was no word *ski* in the English language! The word *snowshoe* was used for *ski* throughout the mountain West. "The celebrated 'Norwegian snow-shoes,' or 'Norway skates,'" wrote Charles W. Hendel, "are from 8 to 12 feet long, 3½ to 4 inches wide, and 1¼ inches thick in the center . . . with a spring worked in so that without weights they rest on the heels and the points." They were concave and grooved on the underside which was also burned with tar to a mahoganylike finish. For racing, the shoes were 10½ to 13½ feet in length, from 3¾ to 4¼ inches in width, wider on the front part than on the back. "So great have been the improvements during the past few years . . . that they now appear to have reached perfection." Hendel is a reliable witness; he was a surveyor and mining engineer who traveled Plumas and Sierra counties in the gold rush years.[4]

Hendel used the adjective *Norway* or *Norwegian* to describe the long boards. Although Swedes and Finns were among the immigrants who skied, by the late nineteenth century skiing had become part of the Norwegian national culture in a different way than elsewhere in Scandinavia. Therefore, when Scandinavians arrived in ski country, it was only natural that skis were described as "Norwegian." That terminology also distinguished them from the racquet snowshoes, only used at lower altitudes. William Brewer in his journal for 1862 noted, "The only way of getting about is on snowshoes, not the great broad Canadian ones . . . but the Norwegian ones."[5]

Norwegians themselves, however, used two words for a long time because it was customary to have unequal lengths of skis. The *Ski* was for gliding and the *Andor,* shorter and pelt-covered, was for pushing. *Andor* rarely appeared in the literature on this side of the Atlantic, and to date only in New Sweden, Maine, have makers of unequal lengths of skis been found.[6]

For the general reading public, however, it was only necessary to distinguish the ski from the snowshoe. At the turn of the century, Teddy Roosevelt carefully explained the two sorts of snowshoes to his readers in *Wilderness Hunter.*[7] Members of the Denver Snowshoe Club, founded in the spring of 1901, were all on skis.[8] In reports of early skiing activities, skis are often referred to simply as *shoes.* One race reporter described how "Metcalf's shoes darted by and led the way to the pole winning by about fifteen feet."[9] Skis were explained to a British audience in 1883 in the same way, and as late as 1909, in a manuscript being prepared for publication, naturalist E. R. Warren felt it necessary to explain that he inspected his traps in Colorado "on snowshoe or skis." In his diary and in the manuscript he preferred the word *snowshoeing* for his activities, even though by then he had been skiing for more than twenty years.[10]

The description of skis as *skates* is perhaps not so strange as it may first appear. Before skis were known in western Europe or North America, they were often described as skates. Travelers reported on a number of Russian tribes, the Ostyak for example, who used short skilike contraptions for moving across the snow. They could maneuver them both in a sliding ski style and in skating fashion. An article in an English magazine was entitled "The Skating Soldiers of Norway" and described Norwegian ski troops.[11] The facility with which Norwegians twisted and turned on their skis was similar to the possibilities on skates; it is not surprising that expressions like "the Norwegian snow skate" appear in this country as early as 1853 and remain in use to the end of the nineteenth century. *Crofutt's New Overland Tourist and Pacific Coast Guide,* published in 1882, described the snow skate of Sierra country, and one of William Thayer's "marvels" ten years later was the snow skate "designed for skating upon hard snow."[12]

But the word *ski* became ubiquitous about 1900. Although the Europeans did not accept the Norwegian term without serious debate, there was little controversy in the United States and *ski, skis,* and the verb *to ski* were adopted and variously spelled: *skee, skeer, skiis, skeys, skeeing, skeed,* and *skiied.*[13] *Ski,* in its present form, became the usual spelling around the turn of the century but other varieties continued until 1920. Writers often used both spellings. In his diary, Fred Harris, the founder of the Dartmouth Outing Club, suggested a club for "skiing" on 17 December 1908 and took a trip on "skees" two days later.[14]

Two other terms described those who skied. *Skidor* and the much longer-lasting *ski runner. Skidor* is the Swedish term for skier. The first American ski catalog, which doubled as an instruction booklet, was published by the Theo. Johnsen Company of Portland, Maine, in 1905. Whenever *skier* was intended, *Skidor* was used. It needed no explanation: "Any *Skidor,* novice or expert, will tell you skeeing is most exhilarating."[15] The term never caught on; historians agree that Swedish immigrants were assimilated easily into the American milieu and that may account for the short life of *Skidor.*

Ski runner is quite different. The term describes both a person and a style of skiing associated with cross-country skiing. The Norwegian *løbere* may be directly translated as runner, and because the Norwegian immigrants had such an influence in early American skiing, the immediate translation sufficed at first. And it was exactly the right word. Skiing in the Northwest in the 1840s and 1850s was necessary for winter communication and hunting, and it really did involve running across the snow on skis. When organized racing and club activity began in the 1870s and 1880s, *ski running* was exactly the correct term for competition too. Early college ski meets were similar to track contests with dashes as well as longer distances, hence the term *ski runner* was maintained. It was only when "down-mountain" racing began, as early Alpine events were frequently termed, that *ski runner* gave way to *skier; ski running* changed first to *ski-ing,* then to *skiing.* The Ski Club of Great Britain, which had great influence in Alpine matters, officially abolished *ski runner* on 13 July 1933 and replaced it with *skier.*[16]

The Alpine discipline of "downhill" has a linguistic history divided between the "straight race" and the "down-mountain race." In the 1930s both gave way to "downhill." Into the 1920s, the ideal of the good skier in the European Alps was the person who sliced a straight track. As speed became increasingly valued, "taking it straight," redolent of the fox hunt, became the mark of an admired ski runner. The straight path tracked directly down the mountain, so races became "down-mountain races." This was all very well on the Alpine meadows above tree line in Europe. In the eastern United States, where down-mountain racing was first adopted, trails had to be cut through woods, and the ideal of the straight race continued in New England. The first racing trail cut in 1932, the Richard Taft, is as straight as a die for the first half mile.

The modern term *slalom* for a race requiring many twisting, high-speed turns through a set of flagged gates has a checkered linguistic history. One of the many nineteenth-century Norwegian races was the *Slalaam* (a *Laam* is a track) which led the contestant curving around natural obstacles.[17] The Austrian pioneer Mathias Zdarsky had tried what he called a "Gate Race" as a "testing run [*Prüfungsfahren*] for swinging around obstacles" and not for achieving speed. In the 1920s, in much the same way, Arnold Lunn, influential British arbiter of many facets of Alpine skiing, first tried his slalom—small boughs were stuck into the snow to simulate trees—to provide practice for ski mountaineers for their descent on skis through the woods to their inn on the valley floor. But almost immediately speed was the measure of success and the slalom became a recognized Alpine discipline.[18] It is an indication of the continuing Norwegian influence, though, that the British and all other skiing nations of Europe called the new race *slalom* and so it remains today.

Skisport, the all-encompassing term for skiing as a recreation, sport, and business, has the most involved linguistic history. The term came to the United States from Scandinavia in the nineteenth century. The Norwegian and Swedish word was not *sport*—the word did not exist in those languages—but *Idraet* (Norwegian) and *Idrott* (Swedish). *Idraet* meant outdoor physical exercise in which "strength, manliness and toughness" were the goal.[19] By 1834 it included the idea of striving to perfect the individual soul as well as the body, and ideally would develop "the physical and moral strength of nations." When Fridtjof Nansen wrote in his influential *Paa Ski over Grønland* that "ski running is the most national of all Norwegian sports [*Idraetter*], and a marvellous sport [*Idraet*] it is, it deserves to be called the sport of sports [*Idraetternes Idraet*]," he was expressing in Norwegian exactly the difference between *Idraet* and sport, yet the translator had no word for *Idraet* and had to use the English *sport*.[20] "Sport," wrote the Swede Viktor Balck in 1881, "was a foreign word . . . and since we had the word *Idrott* for the physical activities of our active ancestors, I picked that up and the *Tidning för Idrott* (Newspaper for Sports) was born."[21] Åke Svahn, whose ideas inform my analysis, has suggested that before 1920 there were only *Idrott* clubs; after 1920 sports clubs were formed.[22]

Much of the discussion had to do with nation building, an idea of particular importance to Norwegians who were beginning to free themselves from Swedish control. Exercise should implant "the ideals of toughness and purity of mind and body" in the young along with "virtue and pure morality." If "moderation, virtue and skill are the foundation of all states," the reasoning went, it was outdoor exercise that could develop "the physical and moral strength of nations." "One day," the Swedish *Ny Illustrerad Tidning* of 1872 wrote, it might be common that "a knowledgeable man is also an *Idrott*-man." The regeneration of the nation was to be accomplished by the all-round man and woman by making all citizens dignified, courageous, skilled, healthy, and moral.[23]

Scandinavians, and particularly Norwegians, brought these philosophical attitudes with them when they settled in the United States and Canada. The foundation of the skisport was based on these ideas which first surfaced in the individual clubs in the Northwest and then in the national organization.

The National Ski Association was founded in 1905 at Ishpeming, Michigan. Six of the seven founders were Norwegians and they sponsored a yearbook entitled *The Skisport*. The long-time secretary, Norwegian-born Aksel Holter, wrote about the growing popularity of the "greatest, cleanest, healthiest and most exhilarating of all outdoor sports . . . the skisport," and called for a continuation of "our glorious work for the betterment of mankind, letting the world know we are ever ready to enthuse and assist in the building up of humanity by getting more boys and girls to join us, exercising in the open, fresh air, getting away from the overheated fireplaces and getting better acquainted with the beautiful nature of our creator."[24] Here is evidence of the transplanted *Idraet* which formed the foundation of American skisport.

The primary source material for preorganized skiing (except for California skiing) is sparse and scattered. Only one work, the diary of Fred H. Harris, shows any continuous interest. Harris admitted in his diary entry of 27 January 1907 to having "skeeing on the brain evidently." Mentions of skiing by Norwegian immigrants in letters home, a few memoirs, auto-biographies, and occasional articles provide stray references. Most come from the western United States, from men involved in the ministry and mining, with occasional remarks by a winter forester, trapper, and out-doorsman. There is, however, a wealth of material from gold rush California. During the winter the local papers concerned themselves extensively with the trials of the postal service in cases where mail was carried by mailmen on skis, as well as with the carnivallike race meetings.

Beginning in 1857 skiing gained wider publicity in *Hutchings' California Magazine*. In the 1880s it was picked up by other popular magazines, such as *Leslie's, Harper's,* and, for the youngsters, *St. Nicholas.* Around the turn of the century specialist magazines like *Outing* and *Scientific American* pub-licized what they perceived as a new winter activity. *Munsey's, Scribner's,* and *Popular Mechanics* were describing "The Wooden Wings of Norway" and offering instructions for making skis.[25]

When organized skisport began to grow—with the formation of clubs in the 1880s and school and collegiate clubs by 1909—constitutions, minutes of meetings, newspaper coverage, catalogs put out by ski manufac-turers, the National Ski Association's *Skisport,* and America's first full-fledged book on skiing in 1913 all became available. Memory too can be tapped; oral history tapes have been collected from a few who remember what it was like to ski before the First World War.

These sources make it clear that skis were a necessary means of winter communication once the big storms settled in. Those on skis from necessity came to enjoy using them. The early history of American skiing for recre-ation and sport comprised two very different enthusiasms: first, the razz-matazz of gold rush miners and their consorts wanting "to let the world and creation know that they have a man that's on it in the snowshoe line" and are ready to put $100,000 on him to prove it; and second, that of individual men, both those who continued to use skis as they had in their old world homelands and those who discovered skiing as recreation and eventually generated enough enthusiasm to form clubs and lay the foundations of the skisport.

2 / California Gold Rush Snow-Shoeing

EXULTING ON SNOW-SHOES.—Should the snow continue to fall until sufficiently deep to cover stumps, bogs and ditches, and render the surface comparatively smooth, all humanity will be on snow-shoes. Only think of going a mile a minute on snow-shoes, ye foot-pads in the valley mud! Your railroads are at a discount, your horse and buggy going only a mile in four minutes could not be thought of, while the remembrance of your slow steam-boats and horse-cars make me nervous. Get out of the mud! mount up to the hills, where all nature is clothed in spotless white; where we daily tramp glittering diamonds under our feet. Come up in the pure air and dwell nearer Heaven.

—*Sacramento Daily Union*, 16 February 1865

Nineteenth-century California skiing is all of a piece: immigrants arrived, found skis necessary for travel, showed others how to use them, came to enjoy themselves in an autotelic way, and turned skiing into a sport. It was almost as if modern skiing was an instant invention.[1]

Although there was an occasional pantheistic nod to nature, California skiing was thoroughly secular, with no moral connotations. In the race meetings women, children, and Chinese laborers competed in separate events. Race courses were discussed and conditions agreed upon. We know the names and the concoctions of those who made "dope," as wax was always called, and we have some information about the formation of clubs. Quantification was often expressed in terms of cigars or gallons of lager, but it did exist. We also know the length of the race courses, time taken, and, therefore, the speed of the runners; Tommy Todd was clocked at over 87 mph. These elements are all the marks of a modern sport. But it was not modern; it was a period piece.

When the gold in the valley streams ran out, men searched higher for instant wealth. By 1852 camps were established at snow line and above. Communities developed that lasted only as long as the gold and silver could be mined. It was necessary to move about at high altitudes in the deep snow. Snowshoes of the racquet variety did not work well. Skis were chosen for mobility by miners and others whose work took them into high country.

What little communication did take place was often supplied by the mailman on skis, and he played a conspicuous role in the social cohesion of the mining camps. The snowbound miners also enjoyed themselves and clubs were formed that sponsored race meetings. When the gold and silver ran out, skiing activity decreased and finally was carried on by the few individuals who, for one reason or another, stayed on and kept to their skis as a matter of necessity.

California skiing was not the foundation for American skiing. Even when skiing had its heyday in the Sierra, the rest of the United States hardly knew that there was such a winter activity. "It will likely never become a popular sport in California, Texas or Florida," concluded the widely read *Leslie's Monthly* in 1893.[2] Certainly one of the reasons California failed to receive the Winter Olympic Games in 1932, the year the summer festival was held in Los Angeles, was that California was thought to lack ski tradition and expertise.[3] It is a curious hiatus but one explained quite simply. Although Norwegians were probably the first to ski in the Sierra Nevada, California skiing was not rooted in the *Idraet* tradition and developed almost entirely on its own in the hurly-burly of the gold rush. Those who made a sport out of skiing manufactured special skis designed for a type of racing held nowhere else in the world. The various facets that made up gold rush skiing smacked of modernizing tendencies but skiing itself was really "to fill in the time during the long tedious winters when everybody is idle, affording an innocent amusement and health-giving exercise, thereby keeping the muscles in tune for the labors of the summer," as an officer of the Alturas Snow Shoe Club wrote in an article explaining the club's founding in 1867.[4]

Utilitarian Skiing

There is overwhelming evidence that skis were needed for everyday affairs. Men went to enormous efforts to keep tracks open for wagons and foot travelers, but high winds and deep snows often made their task unenviable and sometimes impossible. Since the racquet variety of snowshoe was not efficient in light and deep snows, people who lived and worked in the mountains found skis practical winter equipment.[5]

It is unclear when skis were first introduced. Although no direct evidence has been found for 1852, at the end of January 1853 the *Marysville Herald* mentioned casually that "the miners do all their locomotion on snow shoes."[6] The next year at Onion Valley, the snow lay twelve feet deep and it was reported that "no one attempts to travel without snowshoes."[7] The word *travel* indicates more than just door-to-door visiting and gives the impression that the use of skis was already commonplace. When Charles Hendel wrote a general description of skiing for *The Mining and Scientific Press,* he, too, judged skiing to have started about 1853.[8]

Skis were adopted in the mining camps on a local basis. Charlie Nelson was credited with introducing them in Gibsonville and the surrounding area.[9] In 1861, Anderson and Depew put two pairs of skis in the window of their liquor store "for the inspection of such . . . as have seldom seen these novel means of locomotion."[10] When Weaverville was snowed in, people enjoyed good sleighing and skating.[11] Evidently skis had not reached that community yet. In the severe winter of 1859 Pine Grove had little trouble because skis were common, and it was said that "had these shoes been in vogue in 1852 and 1853, there would not have been so much suffering in the mountains."[12]

Entire communities came to rely on skis. With six feet of snow on the streets of Silver Mountain, "travel on snowshoes is now the order of the day."[13] Downieville invited people to "come up to the pure air and dwell near Heaven" where "all humanity will be on snow-shoes" should "the beautiful" continue to pile up.[14] It was recorded that a "snow shoeist glided over the house and shouted down the stove pipe." People paid calls, checked their claims, and brought a testimonial across the mountains from Carson Valley which wished to be part of California. Hunters tended their traps on skis, railroad repair crews used skis, Union Water Company men checked water levels on skis, trapped miners made makeshift skis from clapboards and escaped. One hundred men went on skis to help the survivors of a mine whose entrance had been covered by an avalanche. Doctors made their rounds on skis when all else failed, clergymen ministered to the outlying mining camps by ski, marriages and funerals also involved ski travel. Some died on their skis as snow and fatigue overcame them.[15]

Skis, as *Hutchings' California Magazine* pointed out, were "particularly adapted to the rugged features of our mountains," although the writer allowed that the racquet snowshoes were sufficient in level country.[16] "Nearly all have Norwegian snowshoes," reported the *Plumas Argus* in 1859. "All" included women and in some communities skis were "so common that the ladies do nearly all their shopping and visiting on them."[17] Up in Grizzly twelve bachelors asked that if there were "any nice young ladies who are on the marry, just tell them to get on their snowshoes and ride into Grizzly."[18] Teacher Mary Condon took to skis and inspired one local lad to claim he would "marry on sight any girl that could tack up one side of those mountains and down the other."[19] At Claire Cuyot's wedding, the bridal party skied into Little Grass Valley. Following the ceremony, bride, groom, and attendants gaily rode their skis to La Porte.[20] Birdie Haun traveled tandem with Jerry Curtis whom she "grasped around the waist [as they] sped swiftly along while he guided or braked with his single pole."[21]

Occasionally there were people other than mailmen who crossed the Sierra ranges on skis. Headlined in the local paper as participants in "The Greatest Feat of the Age," Mrs. Stevens and her daughter came over the range with a party of gentlemen. The local bloods immediately got up a dance in honor of the occasion.[22] Other parties of ladies and gentlemen simply went visiting as they skied from La Porte to taste the hospitality of Brandy City.[23]

Skiing was just as available for women as it was for men if they chose to participate. Men admired a certain toughness in women who were able to manage the snowy Sierra winters. There was a freedom for women hardly found elsewhere; social convention carried little weight in ten or twenty feet of snow. The extraordinary variety of reports of ski-related incidents leaves the reader of the local gold rush press certain about the usefulness of skis in winter; they were vital for those who wished any sort of mobility in the snow.

Mail Service

However necessary skis were, however much ludic divertissement enlivened the winter, however feted winners were on race days, it was the men who brought the mail to the snowbound communities who were most appreciated. Public encomiums of their daring coupled with the novelty of mail delivery on skis have made it difficult to assess the role of these men. They have been given but a passing glance by historians of the gold rush. Only one has received much notice—"Snowshoe" Thompson—"a man who laughs at storms and avalanches and safely walks where others fall and perish," as a contemporary description put it.[24] Thompson first became widely known when he carried the mail on skis in 1856 and 1857. Although he continued to carry the mails on skis from time to time, he spent much of the 1860s running a freighting service and, for a time, he was taken up with keeping the road open across the Sierra for the Overland Mail.[25]

Thompson's reputation was built on his initial service of carrying the mail from Carson Valley to Placerville, ninety miles over the mountains. Important newspapers in Sacramento and San Francisco frequently noted his exploits from 1856 to 1859. *Hutchings' California Magazine* created a wider audience for his deeds and Dan de Quille gave him a superlative write-up in 1876 which set the tone for later stories. Thompson's skis were on public view in 1874 and again in 1939, and they are presently one focus of the Western Skisport Museum where, larger than life, Thompson is

Found among the Hendel papers, this drawing may be the original of John A. "Snowshoe" Thompson from which others such as in *Hutchings' California Magazine* (1857), were copied. (California State Library, Sacramento)

memorialized in bronze outside the museum. He is part of American folklore preserved in song on Columbia records. His grave in Genoa, Nevada, is a ski pilgrim's goal; the Norwegian Olympic team who was at Squaw Valley for the 1960 Games paid a visit and left a plaque.

Heroics aside, the reason for all this appreciation, as the *Placerville American* noted in 1857, was simply that "the only way in which the people of Carson Valley can procure in winter season, such articles as they happen to need is through the agency of Mr. Thompson."[26] It was true. What Thompson had done was join the Great Basin and the Pacific coast for the first time with an efficient service, thereby fulfilling a goal that had been contemplated for some years.

In 1851 a monthly mail route between Salt Lake City and San Francisco was let to George W. Chorpenning. The journey took about sixteen days in summer. The winter trip presented the formidable challenges of feeding animals, housing passengers, and overcoming enormous snow depths. Attempts to use the old Spanish Trail to the south were unsuccessful, and the sixty days it took to go over Beckwourth Pass was considered far too long. The papers were full of statistics. Typical are these taken from the winters of 1852–53 and 1855:[27]

Salt Lake City to San Francisco

Departure	Arrival	Days en Route
1 November 1852	5 January 1853	68
3 January 1855	8 February 1855	37

A few carriers attempted to cross the Sierra on Indian snowshoes but no one was able to provide any regular service.[28] Thompson's mail delivery on skis, which began in 1856 was not the first delivery to be taken across the Sierra in winter, nor was Thompson skiing in unknown territory. Skis were not the only attempt at innovation during this time. In 1857 mail was carried locally by dog sled and, for a number of years, by horses outfitted with wooden snowshoes.[29]

The skiing mailman, however, was the most efficient, and it was Thompson's instant success that made that method so popular. His second trip in January 1856 took 3½ days and compared favorably with the 8-day delivery on snowshoes. By February, Thompson was hailed as "the adventurous and hardy mountain express man," a reputation that was borne out when one of his crossings only took him 2½ days. Later that first season he had other delivery times of 4½ and 10 days.[30]

Early next season Thompson made one of his well-publicized rescues. He saved a man who had survived for twelve days on raw flour. His mail service continued so successfully that he hired an assistant to help carry the more than one hundred pounds of mail and express matter.[31]

After some financial misunderstandings (there would be more of those) at the beginning of the 1858–59 winter, Thompson kept the route open with snowplows, so that his self-built "Alpine Boat," christened the *Sierra Nevada,* could haul the increased amount of freight. The next season he had eight men working for him and a stable of seventeen horses. In reports in the *Sacramento Daily Union* that winter there is no mention of Thompson's making any trips on skis, except for noting what good use he had made of them "in days past."[32] It appears that he devoted himself to his freighting business. The next time his skiing exploits receive attention is in the 1870s when he was somewhat ignominiously defeated in a series of races—but of that later.

Thompson was given to understand from postmasters at both ends of the route that he would be paid, but he received nothing.[33] He had worked for Chorpenning but Chorpenning had gone broke; Thompson never received any money. He also carried the Overland Mail with no contract in hand.[34] After successfully bidding on the postal route from Genoa to Silver Mountain for the four year period 1870–1874, he became convinced that the government owed him money for his previous freighting and postal service.[35] A petition was started in his favor and state officials signed it. His skis were put on view with the idea of raising six thousand dollars. A congressman introduced a special bill for his payment and the *Alpine Chronicle* pressured senators for its passage and urged the states of Nevada and California to step in should the law makers prove niggardly. But the eastern press, if we are to believe the *New York Sun,* felt that Thompson was sitting in San Francisco barrooms telling tall tales, and the seven hundred dollars Congress contemplated appropriating for the man who "was compelled to go on foot over the dreary and solitary mountain range carrying back and forth such mail, express and newspaper matters as the necessities of the day required," never was paid.[36] In 1872 Thompson journeyed to Washington to lobby for himself. Although he did obtain one hearing, he received no money.[37] He returned home an embittered man. Four years later he became ill and died on 15 May 1876.

Thompson was the only man known the length and breadth of the Sierra mountain ranges for expert skiing. Since his mail service affected business in San Francisco and Sacramento positively, he was instantly recognized as an extraordinary asset. The newspapers, capitalizing on the novelty of the use of skis for mail delivery, accounted for his wide recognition. He gained stature from his astonishing rescues, his hefty loads (sixty-five pounds and his assistant, forty-three), and his dependability in fair weather or foul. Thompson never exaggerated his own exploits for personal recognition. The publicity he received was the work of others, and by 1876 he was elevated to hero status by Dan de Quille after a long interview, which took place just before his death.

Many local heroes surfaced as the West was settled, but only those who affected state, regional, and even national development are remembered at all levels. Many are commemorated in poem and song, in book and film. Thompson is honored by the U.S. Postal Service and by skiers—the two worlds he combined. There is no letup in the promotion of him as a hero; we like someone who accomplished his derring-do with flair.[38]

Dozens of mailmen on skis worked in the Sierra mountains in the late nineteenth and early twentieth centuries.[39] Although the Pacific Union Railroad in 1869 joined East with West, mail still had to be carried from the major stations to the mining camps. The men who undertook delivery on skis were as appreciated as Thompson. When the road from Nevada City to Onega was closed for two months it was reported that "our brave expressman never failed and our mail service is regular. Through these intolerable snow conditions he carries our eastern correspondence, our 25 *Tribunes* and our 30 *Ledgers*. Not any of us would take his job. . . . He has the blessings of our town's winter population."[40]

There was an attempt to make mail delivery by skis as efficient and regular as possible. Entrepreneurs advertised departure and arrival times:[41]

Knowles' Snow Shoe Express
Between La Porte, Saw Pit, Nelson Point, Quincy
Leaves La Porte Every Monday Morning
W. H. Knowles, Prop.

Papers also carried news items such as "Benjamin Sawyer is now running a snowshoe express from Downieville to Sierra Valley. He leaves Downieville every Monday morning."[42] One of the most respected carriers was Granville Zacharian, proprietor of Zack's Snowshoe Express, the only expressman known to stamp his letters with a skiing mailman. He was a "snow shoe heeled Mercury, . . . a stunner, a velocipede."[43] As one snowshoe mail service came to its seasonal end in April 1876, the *Alpine Chronicle,* in more prosaic terms, "was pleased to note the fidelity of Thomas Brown . . . who carried the mails during the severest winter known in this county, and at all times, through drifting snows and blinding storms, commendable dispatch has been the rule."[44]

Blinding storms and intolerable conditions were sometimes deadly. Joseph Metcalf "perished in the snow" while on his Forest City to American Hill route in 1863.[45] In 1890, Malcolm McLeod, an experienced skier became "bewildered and traveled in a circle for many hours" and froze to death.[46] Alexander McGee, the Badger Pass mailman, suffered the same fate a week later.[47] Gus Berg was lucky enough to ride out an avalanche. Both his skis were broken, but he managed to borrow another pair and brought the mail into town.[48]

In the mountain mining districts, mail service was appreciated for the personal contact that a letter from home could bring, and for the economic advantage regular mail delivery offered, which was very important to the opening of a territory. But it meant more than that. Settlers seem to have equated the arrival of mail with the arrival of civilization. To bring civilization was comparatively easy in summer, but it required special expertise in winter and depended upon a hardiness of physique and character if cut-off snowbound camps were to keep in touch. "Keeping in touch" are simple words, but in a region where twenty to thirty feet of snow were not uncommon and where communities were isolated for months, it is little wonder those who facilitated the contacts by carrying the mail were so admired.

Recreational Skiing

All these occasions were essentially utilitarian, but there is much evidence that men, women, and children enjoyed skiing for its ludic quality as well. Famed mountaineer and explorer John Muir reveled in the "lusty reviving exercise on snow-shoes that kept our pulses dancing right merrily" as he and some friends performed "giddy rolls and somersaults" along with many "queer capers" before "gathering [the] runaway members together."[49] Effusiveness aside, Muir was patently having some marvelous fun on the hills above Lake Tahoe where he had gone specifically for relaxation.

Snowbound mining communities also took to their skis for recreation and entertainment. By 1861, an evening amusement for Pine Grove, lasting for an hour or two, was to climb up and swoop down Sugarloaf Mountain.[50] When snow came to Dutch Flat before Thanksgiving 1865, a reporter wrote, "we anticipate a jolly time with snowshoeing parties."[51] Young courting couples in Silver Mountain availed themselves of moonlit nights "to go a snowshoeing and, as they rush, hand-in-hand with a tight squeeze, down a six hundred foot declivity, envy not the insipid enjoyment of the skating rinks of San Francisco and Sacramento."[52] Moonlight skiing was so appealing that it was mentioned in Crofutt's 1882 guide and again, as one of Thayer's "Marvels of the New West," ten years later.[53] Perhaps William Thayer should have included an industrial marvel too. In the 1880s locals persuaded the Johnsville mine owners to activate the steam boiler on Sundays. Folks lined up at the stamping mill at the bottom and rode the ore buckets up the mountain—surely the first "lift" in the world![54]

Race Meetings

When snow halted all mining operations, skis not only became the best means of communication, they also provided recreation and sport. There was a very different feeling from the work-a-day trudge through the snows when miners met for carnival high-jinks. Thus we read the challenge from the Alturas Snow Shoe Club: "This is to let the world and the balance of creation . . . know that . . . members of the Alturas Snow Shoe Club do hereby agree and bind themselves to furnish a man to compete with . . . anybody else that's 'on it' in the snowshoe line, for any sum of money from $1000 to $100,000."[55]

The first clubs were formed in January 1861 at Onion Valley and La Porte.[56] Members held Sunday practices and races. It was rare fun, "invigorating, a developer of the wind and better than cod liver oil or hypophosphites of lime and soda."[57] At La Porte the club announced three days of racing "in the regular turf style" for purses of from twenty-five to seventy-five dollars—not inconsiderable sums when three dollars a day was the going wage.[58] Purses were part of the attraction: at Howland Flat the camp intended to raise one thousand dollars.[59] When Onion Valley and Saw Pit camps heard of these prizes, they made special skis and experimented with various dope concoctions to ensure the skis would run as fast as possible. Some men simply challenged others: Andrew Jackson wagered one hundred dollars against Jake Lutz. Pete Reandeau challenged "all the world and the rest of mankind" and put up to five hundred dollars on the outcome. Betting on the side was the norm.[60]

DOPE IS KING.

THIRD ANNUAL MEETING

--OF THE--

ALTURAS
SNOW SHOE CLUB.

LA PORTE, PLUMAS COUNTY. CAL.

FOUR DAYS' RACING

COMMENCING ON MONDAY, FEBRUARY TWENTY-SECOND, 1869.

SIX HUNDRED DOLLARS IN PURSES.

PROGRAMME.

First Day. Club Purse of $100 00. Free for all. Second Race. Purse of $50 00. Free for all but the winner of the first race.

Second Day. Club Purse of $75 00. Free for all. Second Race. Purse of $50 00. Free for all but the winner of the first race of this day.

Third Day. Club purse of $50, free for all. Second Race. Purse of $25, free for all but the winner of the first race of this day.

Fourth Day. Club Purse of $100 00, free for all. $125 00 to the winner, and $25 to the second man in the race. Second Race. Club purse of $100, free for all but winner of first race of this day. $75 to the winner, and $25 to the second man.

Purses for Boys' will be made up during the week. Racing to commence at one o'clk each day. All entries for each days' racing to be made before 11 o'clk each day with the Secretary. Entrance $1. If on Monday, February 22d, the weather should be unfavorable, the races will be postponed from day to day until favorable. By order of the Club.

Alex. H. Crew, Secretary.

JOHN CONLY, President.

Broadside for the 1869 Alturas Snow Shoe Club meeting. John A. "Snowshoe" Thompson, who was roundly defeated, dismissed the La Porte meet as "nothing but dope racing." (Western Skisport Museum, Boreal Ridge, Calif.)

The championship belt was the highest honor. As in boxing, the champion had the right to keep it until he was beaten. The belt became a symbol both for the individual and for the camp. Onion Valley's belt in 1861, valued at twenty-five dollars, was of "beautiful black morocco with the word CHAMPION on the back, in solid silver letters, and a large silver buckle on the end engraved O.V.S.S.C."[61]

The race for the belt was always the high point of the meeting. The editor of the *Marysville Daily Appeal* described the scene in 1861:

> Then the announcement was made that the belt would be run for, when eleven entries were made—the party divided into six and five—judges were chosen—and two poles were set up on the side of the hill about seventy feet apart, a judge standing by each pole. The party of six climbed with their shoes thrown over their shoulders. The crowd got in favorable positions to see; the runners took position on a line about eight feet apart at the top of the hill, and the word was given—"Go!"—when every runner began to descend, pushing himself along with his pole. . . . Again the crowd hurrahs. . . . Robinson shoots through the poles like lightening, with Metcalf close at his heels. Again the word is given—"Go!" Hurrahs. Down they come! Falls—one has to be carried to the house. McDowell ahead and Sweet close behind. Norman who had won the belt two weeks ago, declined to run; so he forfeited the belt, and now it lay between Robinson, Metcalf, McDowell and Sweet; but the shoes being so unmanageable and it being so dangerous on account of the hard crust, the race was adjourned to some more favorable day.[62]

For this particular contest there was no stop watch, "but by counting I think the time was 25 seconds; distance half a mile." The editor learned that the course had been run in 18 and 18½ seconds the previous winter, and Norman was believed to have done it in 16 seconds.

The race for the championship was the most important, but it did not take away from other events during the carnival. When it was known which camp champions had challenged each other, tension mounted as conditions changed throughout the day: William Metcalf, Onion Valley's man, was pitted against Ralph Lee from Whiskey Diggings. As the two took their places at the top of the hill, the crowd hushed.

> Both started handsomely making some half dozen strokes with the snow shoe poles in very quick time, that sent them forward with great velocity. Young Lee seemed to be leading his man in gallant style until they came to the most precipitous part of the track where Metcalf's shoes darted by and led the way to the poles, winning the race by about 15 feet. Time: half a mile in 25 seconds. Many have seen swifter races but none claim to have seen a more handsome one. Both contestants struggled nobly for the prize, both rode their shoes in splendid style and it seemed almost a pity that either should lose the race.[63]

Four abreast at "a mile a minute." Typical gold rush racing in the Sierra ranges. Although speeds of 60 mph were common, the thrill was in the personal competition and mining camp rivalry. (Western Skisport Museum, Boreal Ridge, Calif.)

These reports from the *Downieville Mountain Messenger* reflected that moment when the skisport had all the trappings of modernization, yet still retained the spontaneity of premodern activity. These races were highly orchestrated, with judges and prepared tracks. The Metcalf-Lee race was the match the crowd had come to see; the two champions were well known and the honor of the mining camps was at stake. Although the course was carefully set out and timed, this was a man-to-man race, and the fact that the time was comparatively slow mattered not one whit. The handsome style the racers adopted on their skis and the struggle between the two on the course thrilled the crowd.

There were plenty of less important races during the three days of carnival fun: races among the scrubs for purses of whiskey and cigars; individual challenges; races for boys and for girls. There were women's events, as well as those for Chinese laborers. Camp prestige was part of these races too. When a Gibsonville man carried off the breastpin—hardly a major prize—the local paper at Onion Valley admonished "our snow shoe racers; never should [they] allow a Sierra country chap to carry prizes out of the county—it sounds bad."[64]

Women's events provided added spice to the male-dominated race meetings. Lottie Joy, the "snow-shoe pet of the St. Louis diggings" was cheered handsomely while winning the Ladies Purse of twenty-five dollars at the La Porte meet in 1867. "She dropped low . . . while the others, carrying too much sail . . . came through all standing, but too late to win."[65] Lottie had adopted the Californian men's racing crouch, breaking with the normal skiing style for women who had to take care that their skirts (the "too much sail") did not billow over their heads, as well as with correct female behavior; women were not expected to crouch. Some objected to the "delicate creatures" doing this sort of thing but most would agree that "properly dressed we see no reason why they should not participate in what are termed manly sports."[66]

If women's races were popular, those of Chinese workers provided raucous entertainment. Twenty Asians, representing La Porte, Howland Flat, Poker Flat, and Saw Pit, put on a "truly rich, rare and racy scene" for the spectators who watched them tumble down the hill.[67] The Chinese provided an entr'acte; the vaudeville on snow added to the carnival spirit of the occasion.

These frolics should be set against the seriousness with which the tracks were prepared, the care with which the skis and dope were made, and the effort expended to ensure as fair a competition as possible. These concerns coupled with the club activity and the accompanying officials and record keeping that the race meetings required have all the marks of modernization. Yet, if we look at each one of these facets, we find that they were only of local and temporary importance.

Each camp tended its race hill and if conditions were not suitable on one, the meeting was transferred to another. The tracks were cleared of obstacles, were usually between one and two thousand feet in length and down a hill of 15° to 25°. The width varied according to the terrain, so squads of four, six, or eight men running abreast raced against each other.[68] At the bottom there was room for the hundreds of spectators who "gambled all night and snowshoed all day," as one old-timer remembered the race meetings.[69]

The skis themselves merited much attention, as can be seen in this account: "From each camp came one to a dozen riders packing on their shoulders a pair of polished, trim and favorite 'racers.' Some of the shoes were beauties, each town seemed to have a shoe different from the others . . . all was much criticized and commented on. Some were as limber as whale-bone, others thick; some had narrow grooves, others wide ones."[70] These racing shoes were long, 10½ to 14 feet, sometimes tapering toward the back. The grooves on the underside of the skis were about three-eighths of an inch deep.[71] Many made their own skis, and some towns had men who were renowned ski makers. On view at the museum in Quincy is a twelve-foot pair weighing some twenty pounds, made by John Williams for Joe Bustillos.

Skis themselves became known as winners.[72] Like race horses, their value depended on the number of races won. The race horse metaphor provided journalistic color: "Young America's Thoroughbred Snow-Shoe Racers" met for competition on their "wooden war steeds," promising "greater speeds than the fastest race-horses," as they raced in the "regular turf style."[73]

The "sine qua non of snow-shoe racing is dope," judged Charles Hendel. "Every racer has at least half a dozen recipes for compounding the dope."[74] All hoped their own "greased lightening" would win the day. Concocting dope was a matter of experimentation. Farmers used buttermilk, others rubbed on furniture polish, floor wax, soap. Papally blessed candles "guaranteed to keep the Devil off one's heels," turpentine, glycerine, and costly drugs mixed in secret brews gave rise to "Skedaddle," "Catch 'em Quick," and "Breakneck."[75] When the indefatigable Snowshoe Thompson came to race the La Porte boys in 1869, he lost handily. He had expected what he called scientific snow-shoeing, "but it was nothing but dope racing."[76] Frank Steward and Johnnie Williams were recognized dope specialists. One of the few known recipes is Steward's Old Black Dope:

> 2 oz. spermecetti
> ¼ oz. pitch-pine pitch
> ⅛ oz. camphor
> 1 tablespoon balsam fir
> 1 tablespoon oil of spruce

We may know the ingredients but the cooking time remains a secret.[77] Generally, mixtures contained varying quantities of "Spermecetti, Burgundy Pitch, Canada Pitch, Balsam of Fir, Venice Turpentine, Oil of Cedar, Glycerine, Camphor and Castor Oil"; so great had the science become "that friction is now counted nearly nothing."[78]

There was consistent effort to ensure fairness and equality in the conditions of competition, one of the characteristics of modern sport. During race week in 1867, all agreed that Tuesday and Wednesday were too cold. Thursday was frigid too, but the organizers let the younger boys race. A vote was taken on Friday after the track was inspected and, in spite of the icy condition, the race was held. Although the Gibsonville contingent had voted against racing, they won the money that day.[79]

Justice in a mining camp milieu might be found outside a court if someone broke the rules. Bob Oliver was murdered because it was believed that he started in the La Porte races of 1868 before the tap of the drum. He had no right to the championship belt; Robert Francis threatened "to shut

Earliest drawing of a race scene, 1874. The track is cleared for six racers. Doping goes on, bottom right. Drinking and gambling were part of the race scene. (Western Skisport Museum, Boreal Ridge, Calif.)

his wind off." Retrieving the honor of the championship was what mattered and Francis recovered it with a bullet.[80]

The great attraction of the races was speed, yet the actual rate of descent hardly mattered. Even so, races were clocked, and many knew the time it had taken to cover the tracks: La Porte's 1,400 feet was done in twenty-one seconds, its 1,200 feet, in fifteen, and another one of 1,230 feet, in fourteen seconds. At Port Wine, the track was 1,030 feet and the winning run took twelve seconds; at Howland Flat the track of 1,135 feet had been run in twenty seconds.[81]

The enormous variety of tracks precluded anything in the nature of a modern record, which supposes that an event may be repeated exactly. In the Sierra, it was the idea of beating every other man, of being champion, that was all important. Sometimes race results were listed by time and feet. Jake Gould, for example, won a race in twenty-four seconds by 20 feet, Robert Oliver in twenty-six seconds by 5 feet and so on. Races were won by as little as 1½ feet and as much as 80 feet on a course taking about twenty seconds.[82]

Early Californian skiing passed unnoticed because no western adventure writers included the razzle-dazzle of the skiing miners and their companions in their tales. Indeed, when James F. Mullen wrote to the National Ski

Association in 1905 about sending a California contingent from Plumas and Sierra counties to compete at the national championship, no one at Ishpeming, Michigan, bothered to reply. It is more significant that officers of the NSA, imbued as they were with Norwegian *Idraet,* felt the miners' "services will not be needed"; they had men enough in the Northwest to make a good tournament.[83] There was, then, virtually no recognition for what skiers in California might provide by way of competition.

In nearly every respect California "snow-shoeing" differed from what Norwegian immigrants believed about skiing. The early Sierra Nevada owed only its traveling skiing—not its racing—to the Norwegian influence. When the search for ores drove miners up into the higher ranges, skis became a necessity. When the snows stopped all mining operations, California gold rush communities passionately embraced skiing as a carnival sport.

California skiing did not have a muscular Christian quality about it, a concern for health in God's great outdoors, which made up the *Idraet* ideal that was apparent in the Northwest; it was an entirely secular pursuit wherein one could even be killed for cheating in the championship. The conditions of competition were laid out with a roughness that was good enough for the mining camp squads. If a race was to be "from the top to the bottom of the heaviest timbered mountain" that could be found, then those chancy conditions were equal for all.[84]

There were specialists in Sierra skiing. The various race officials, including starters, judges, drum tappers, and timers, were vital. Most essential of all were the dope makers; "Dope is King" headlined the broadsheets for the races. The favored racers were marked men.

In spite of the statistics available, the quantification and the quest for records remained the least developed side of skiing. Little thought was given to repeating the conditions, hence the modern idea of records and record breaking did not obtain. What mattered to each miner was that someone from his own camp held the championship belt.

Once the ore veins had yielded their silver, the miners moved on and many of the camps became ghost towns. Snowshoeing remained the only way to move about in the deep Sierra snows, for the few who stayed: to California skiers of the 1930s, they were men from a bygone age.

3 / Utilitarian Skiing and Ludic Enthusiasms

All travel, except from cabin to cabin right in Camp was necessarily on snow shoes. Skis were imperative and we were all busy making them. Fortunately there was an endless supply of fire killed spruce which is the best timber in the world for these shoes. Our first shoes for the soft snow were large, twelve foot long. Later in the winter after the trails were packed the shoes were as short as seven or eight feet. At first we were all clumsy but it was not long before we could travel on the regular ski trails between Ruby and Crested Butte and we thought nothing of skiing down to Teachouts ranch (twenty miles) for a couple of square meals with fresh meat and potatoes and Mrs. Teachout's biscuit and syrup.

—George Cornwall, Colorado, 1880s

In colonial and early republican America, people trampled the snow for as long into the winter season as they could in order to keep paths open for foot, horse, and sleigh travel. The Indian snowshoe was used by native and settler alike. When the Scandinavians arrived, however, they introduced the ski, finding it far superior to the native snowshoe. The influx from Norway, Sweden, and Finland reached a peak in 1882 when over one hundred thousand immigrants arrived. They often joined relatives and old neighbors in the established communities, and they brought their winter culture with them.[1] Once settled in the snow areas of the Northwest—today's Iowa, Wisconsin, Michigan, and Minnesota—and New England, they used their skis in their new environment just as they had at home. To begin with, at least for two generations, the traditional patterns continued on this side of the Atlantic. Skis had provided for winter mobility among the villages in the valleys of Norway and Sweden and skis were used in day-to-day matters in the immigrant settlements; folk in Telemark and Morgedal had enjoyed fun and games on skis for centuries and skis were used as a recreational outlet for the snowbound in this country too. This ludic activity was entirely spontaneous and required no organization; it was merely a matter of individual amusement. This traditional enjoyment of skiing was a major factor in creating the skisport in the 1880s. This chapter

This illustrates the journals of Major John Owen. It is one version of an 1865 painting by Peter Tofft, a Danish immigrant. From time to time Native Americans took to skis, but most remained faithful to their snowshoes. (New England Ski Museum, Franconia, N.H.)

details the utilitarian and recreational use of skis in the immigrants' normal winter life, before any club organization.

The earliest record, noted twenty-eight years after the event, of a skier in the United States is from 1841. Gullik Laugen from Numedal, Norway, and a friend skied from Rock Prairie to Beloit in Wisconsin to buy flour. Others may have fashioned boards before but they were not mentioned because skiing was so common among Scandinavians that it went unremarked. But Laugen's ski tracks caused speculation from Americans unacquainted with skis who wondered what sort of animal or backwood monster had left the curious marks in the snow.[2] Awesome beginnings of ski history in the United States!

Hunting

Immigrants traditionally used skis to procure their winter meat supply. Two thousand years of Scandinavian winter culture were bound up with hunting. From the folk memory of the Samer (as Lapps now wish to be known) Johan Turi retold of the reindeer hunt: "In winter when the snow was thick in the forest they began to follow them on their skis and took

When the snow lay "four ponies deep" in Colorado, hunting on skis was sometimes the only way to obtain fresh meat. *Harper's Weekly,* 1883. (New England Ski Museum, Franconia, N.H.)

them when they tired."[3] Hunting on skis is a major motif beginning with pictographs from the pre-Christian era and continuing through drawings in the late nineteenth century.

Immigrants hunted in the United States just as they had at home over the centuries. From the Waupaca parsonage in the winter of 1857 came the claim that "over a hundred deer have been killed by the Norwegians here." The method was the same as in the homeland; the deer "cannot escape the hunters on skis. The men tire the deer out, and several times they have been able to walk right up to one and plunge a hunting knife into it."[4]

In Scandinavia there are drawings of wolf hunts and descriptions of hunters on skis killing wolves. The earliest extant Canadian ski was used in successful wolf hunts in the 1870s.[5] Later, around 1900, when Americans were beginning to expect organized collections, skiers hunted elk for zoos. Five men swept down upon a panicked herd, singled out the one they wanted, and "threw their lariats over the branching horns and literally 'drove' before them the elk steeds they had taken." This looked like an early form of skijoring. Bear and wolves were taken in the same way.[6]

But hunting was not the only activity in which skis were used. If we look

All dressed up and only skis could get you to town! Probably in Crested Butte, Colorado, area, 1902. (E. R. Warren Collection, University of Colorado Museum, Boulder)

at examples geographically spread from east to west, it becomes obvious that men, women, and children found countless everyday occasions for skis.

New England

The earliest documented use of skis in the Northeast comes from an all-Swedish immigrant group brought over to help populate northern Maine in 1870. A school had been built and children came "slipping over the snow on *skidor,* Swedish snow-shoes" from five miles away, as the Maine legislature was informed.[7] What was good for *Gamla Sverige* was good for New Sweden.

Other immigrants in Maine also took to skis: forest warden Frederick Jorgensen had no difficulty in catching snowshoed poachers, as he was able to cover up to fifty miles a day on his skis. The skis became, as he said, his everlasting trademark.[8] Given the obvious advantage of the ski, the continuing respect paid to the traditional snowshoe is surprising.

In neighboring New Hampshire, John Perry's diary reveals how the teenager constructed his own skis in the 1880s after reading an account of how Norwegians made them. "We did not make them as he described but merely took 2 smooth barrel staves and put loop straps for the toes to step into them, and ran about on the snow that way. Last winter we made 2 staves into one ski by joining them with a piece of board. This winter C and I have some better still. He made his according to Mr. Boyesen. About 6 feet long before steaming and bending the tips. I made mine out of three barrell staves each. . . . The skis should be carefully polished and greased. . . . C made his last skees of white wood—fir and hard pine are very good." In 1888 he went to school "almost entirely on skees," and once he slid off to the dentist to have three teeth pulled.[9]

We have no certain knowledge of how many people were skiing, but there were certainly not many. Individuals started skiing, got their friends interested, and either kept it up or let it drop according to temperament, opportunity, or necessity. In the Hanover area—later famous because Dartmouth College played a pivotal role in American skiing—"skiis did not begin to come into use until the end of the eighties," wrote astronomer Edwin Frost in his autobiography. "I inherited a pair of skiis [which] were so long that a pair of shoes had been attached to the rear for a second passenger. The situation got very painful for the man riding behind when the leader began to toe in and the skiis spread in the rear."[10] This may sound fantastic, but skiing double appears in Scandinavian print and woodcut, and there is an occasional reference to it in the United States as well.[11] Frost used the word *passenger;* evidently skis were considered primarily in terms of travel.

In nearby Stowe, Vermont, now well known as a ski resort, skiing began in 1902 with a couple of fellows making a track behind the Burt sawmill. But that thrill did not catch on immediately. It was not until three Swedish families started to farm in the valley in 1912 that skiing was noted again.[12]

In those parts of New England where Scandinavians settled, there is scattered mention of people using skis: a farmer near Damariscotta, Maine (1896); some Finns near Newport, New Hampshire (1895); and a Norwegian around Concord, Massachusetts (1876). To complete the geographic coverage, the earliest extant skis from Connecticut are a pair from the Hartland area, home-made by a Norwegian around 1900.[13]

The Northwest

The majority of Scandinavians entering the United States settled in the Northwest. They used skis for travel and for necessary domestic tasks.

There are only a few references to skiing in letters, some of which have been published, and in diaries and memoirs; there is an occasional photograph, as well as some accounts in the northwestern press. The lack of information, which in itself seems remarkable given the numbers of immigrants, is because using skis was an everyday occurrence and was simply not newsworthy.

The earliest reference to travel on skis in Minnesota is from 1853, when "one of those snow-skaters" turned up in St. Paul having skied all the way from Lake Superior.[14] Halvor Simon made a sixty-five-mile trip from Glenwood to St. Cloud to obtain provisions in winter.[15] Religious men, such as the minister in 1857 who found his path blocked as he made his way to the Norwegian communities in northern Iowa, took to skis. That same year—a heavy snow year—A. V. Hiscock also went to see his parishioners on skis.[16] An enterprising tax collector took to skis and as a result the Fergus Falls, Minnesota, budget was balanced in 1881. A county sheriff and his deputy made the rounds on skis summoning jurors for the local court in the winter of 1893.[17]

There was also an occasional mailman on skis, Grandpa Hewitt in Iowa, for example, and in the Rochester, Minnesota, area, another skiing mail carrier was mentioned, more because he was seventy years old than because he used skis.[18] Given the success of the skiing mailmen in California and the Rockies (and in Norway and Sweden, too), it is surprising that virtually no one used skis to deliver mail in the Northwest.

In a long article on the history of Scandinavian immigration in 1888, the *Minneapolis Tribune* regretted the passing of the pioneer quality of life. Civilized amenities were encroaching on many areas of the Northwest.[19] As immigrant communities became part of the achieving society of the United States, they turned what had been a matter of necessity into a recreation and sport.

The Rocky Mountains

Skis in the workaday world of the mining regions of the Rocky Mountains—as they were in the Sierra Nevada of California—were "one of the necessities of life."[20] Beginning in the 1850s, skis were used increasingly in the high altitudes where silver was mined. All sorts of mountain people took to skis: ministers, miners, mailmen, hunters, trappers, doctors, editors, shopkeepers, homesteaders, farmers, women, and children.

In Ute City, now Aspen, two Swedes introduced skis to the community.[21] An illustrated article on prospecting in the San Juan mountains drew attention to the use of skis there.[22] When Dr. Charles Gardiner arrived in the Elkhorn range in 1887, he immediately learned to ski, and in Gunnison County another doctor saw to his patients on skis.[23]

One of the first to use skis in Colorado—"snowshoes of Norway style"—was a Methodist minister, the Reverend John L. Dyer, who is enough of a folkloric figure to be enshrined in stained glass. He spent the winter of 1864–65 on his Norwegian shoes, working out of Mosquito about four times a week to bring the gospel, along with the mail, to isolated communities. His nine- to eleven-foot skis ran well when conditions were right. In spring, when the snow softened, it stuck to the underside of his skis, so he took to traveling by night when the snow had crusted. During the day, now in the sun, "I had to wear a veil to keep from getting snow-blind, the dazzling light be so intense." This is the earliest reference to this problem. Other skiers used smoked glasses or smeared their faces with burnt cork, charred wood, or damp gun powder; some put on black suits.[24]

As they had elsewhere, skis provided mobility. "Occasionally someone crossed the mountains to Silverton," wrote a young lawyer from Del Norte. Another man proposed to act as messenger using "pieces of pine board from seven to eleven feet long, turned up at the ends by steaming."[25] This naive description reveals an inexperience that was not uncommon among new arrivals in the mountains.[26]

North of Colorado, in the Orofino Creek area of Idaho territory, miners with gold in their pokes used skis in April 1861 to bring out their haul, along with the news of the strikes. The next winter skis were in general use: "All winter long, men were daily leaving Oro Fino on snowshoes with heavy packs on their backs." These were miners, trappers, gamblers, and an entrepreneurial saloon keeper carrying chemicals to spice his brew.[27] Most made their own primitive skis. "All through the Idaho mountains one could see lying on the ground near the roads or the trails rough snowshoes made of split tamarack or pine logs. . . . A man could make a pair in a very short time and invariably drop them at the spot on the road where he had no further use of them. The next man that came along was entitled to their use as well."[28]

In Montana miners and hunters were reported on skis in the 1860s and 1870s. The *Nordiske Folkeblad,* a Norwegian-language newspaper, carried the story of Sven Pettersen's death on skis in 1868. A Helena paper commented on the use of skis by Norse immigrants of the area in 1871. This was about the same time that A. Bart Henderson took a Christmas trip from his ranch near Bozeman into the Yellowstone area on fifteen-foot boards.[29]

The mining community in Alta, Utah, used what were commonly called "Flip Flops" in the 1860s and 1870s. These were any broad piece of board

STAKING CLAIMS.

By summer, ten thousand miners would be trying "to woo the giddy goddess." These two used skis to get ahead of the crowd in the San Juan Mountains of Colorado. *Harper's Weekly,* 1883. (New England Ski Museum, Franconia, N.H.)

to which a leather thong was fixed to secure a boot. In the 1890s, an official of the Grizzly mine showed one of his admirers his real snowshoes of 14½ feet and "pointing to the precipitous mountain wall opposite, he astonished us by saying he had ridden down it on his skees." Here, too, Scandinavian immigrants were the early skiers. One recollection particularly mentions Finns. Few others used skis; in 1916 only two pairs were in the Alta camp, and it seemed advisable to send away to Minnesota for some more.[30]

Washington and Oregon

There are so few references to skiing in these areas that it seems likely that skis were used only occasionally. Two boys, by no means good skiers, in the early 1880s were able to rope a couple of wild horses for themselves from skis.[31] In Oregon's gold country of the Blue Mountains it was reported that "the inhabitants, when they wish to renew their supply of bacon and flour at the stores of the little mining camps, put on their skees and skim over the drifts." Readers of *Harper's Weekly* enjoyed a story on skiing in Oregon and a front cover picturing a skiing mother and son on a shopping trip.[32]

It is not clear why skis were not used; Scandinavians were among the settlers and miners often migrated from one "rush" to another. Oregon skiing was featured and even pictured in *Harper's*, so it seems likely that there was more skiing than the record shows.

In the spring of 1890 a four-man expedition of Norwegian immigrants with skis was chosen by the *Washington Post* to leave Seattle for Alaska. No travel details have been found and what the paper expected from its sponsorship is unknown, but it does reveal how necessary skis were for traveling into difficult back country. Norwegian immigrants had the know-how to attempt it.[33]

Mail Service

Skis were used by a variety of people as they performed a number of tasks, but their use by skiing mailmen is the best documented. Although there are only occasional references from the nineteenth century to mail delivery by skis in Minnesota and Iowa, the Rocky Mountain newspapers, like the gold rush press in California, provide a wealth of detail on winter mail delivery.

In Colorado the Reverend Mr. Dyer mentioned earlier carried the mail with his Methodism on a thirty-seven-mile route. He augmented his low pay—eighteen dollars a trip—by carrying miners' express matter.[34] Pay for all mail carriers in winter was poor. "There is no class of laborers," the *Colorado Sun* told its readers in 1892, who were "so poorly paid as . . . the mountain mail carriers," and went on to explain that the men who contracted the mail year round took it during the summer when it was a "soft snap," and then subcontracted it when the snow came. Many an out-of-work miner would accept the low wages.[35]

Newspaper reporting tended to dwell on the difficulties and deaths. The tale of Swan Nilson who failed to show up with the Christmas mail from Ophir in 1883 made excellent copy when his body was discovered with the mail bag still strapped to his back in August 1885. This story became standard fare. The writer of the *Colorado Sun* article that commented on the low wages knew at least half a dozen skiing mailmen who had lost "some portion of the body."[36]

Occasionally the mailmen themselves told a little of their lives: Will Ferrill recounted how it was usual for a small group to be on hand at the post office to wish him well. He and others like him took as good care of themselves as they could afford; Ferrill maintained that however rough and cheap his outer garments might be, he wore silk next to his skin.[37] As in California, local communities appreciated "the faithfulness to duty, the hardihood and dash of daring these men show, when in the midst of a terrific mountain storm they strap the mail bag on their shoulders and start

An Idaho mailman with his dog team, c. 1900. In the deep of winter, mail delivery on skis was often the only link with isolated mining communities in the mountains. (Idaho State Historical Society, Boise)

out, vanishing in the whirling, blinding snow; or come staggering in at night after a day's battle with the storm, beard and hair a mass of frozen snow and ice, [which] compels admiration, and the mail carrier is usually one of the most popular men in the camps."[38] These Colorado mailmen were even mentioned in Europe in one of the earliest books on skiing, which is both a recognition of their worth and another indication of how little attention was paid to Californian skiing.[39]

In Idaho mail was delivered on skis under the same conditions as in Colorado and California. Here, too, local papers dwelt on excitement and tragedies; stories of wolves, avalanches, and, of course, deaths made good reading. In 1886 George McKenney froze to death with the Christmas mail on his back. One of the best known Idaho skiing mailmen was Moses Kemper. He ran the thirty-mile route from Idaho City to Banner, and he was appreciated enough to become part of Idaho's folklore:

> The Banner mail carrier
> (Moses Kemper is his name,
> And he "snowshoes" for scads and fame)
> Stops for no barrier
> Great or small
> Skims over 'em all
> And is known farther and wider

This handsome snowshoe glider
Than any other slider
Round about "these here diggins."
Right through drifts of snow heaped hugely high
He'd go, in times gone by,
And come gracefully flying in on time.[40]

We should not wince at frontier rhyming; Moses Kemper's skiing ability was as admired as the regularity of his mail delivery. The versification is a nice mix of pathos, embracing many of the ideals of nineteenth-century manhood.

U.S. Military

Winter mail was also carried to troops in Yellowstone Park who patrolled against poachers. Company M of the First U.S. Cavalry was equipped with skis in 1886–87. This novel winter duty attracted little attention at first even though the patrols made an occasional arrest. Captain Moses Harris was not sanguine about the use of skis and added in the official report that "the difficulties of snow-shoe (ski) travel in the Park are such . . . that it is not to be recommended as a diversion."[41]

The soldiers, however, thought otherwise; they found their skis afforded their families "the only chance for enjoyment during the winter months," and one visiting correspondent predicted that hotel interests would soon encourage winter travel.[42]

Famed Arctic explorer Lt. Frederick Schwatka, on the lookout for further publicity, mounted an expedition into Yellowstone which included a photographer. Schwatka mismanaged equipment and entourage, became ill, and abandoned the project. The photographer, Frank Jay Haynes, took off with three companions and, on skis, completed a 175-mile circuit of the park. He returned with a marvelous display of "Mid-Winter Views of Wonderland." Some of the photos also depicted patrols and scouts. It was the first time the public saw the U.S. Army on skis. Elwood Hofer and Emerson Hough also drew attention to the military's use of skis with an account of their adventures in the 1890s.[43] Serious military consideration was voiced in the *Proceedings of the Association of Military Surgeons* in 1900 which concluded that "the ski in Yellowstone Park . . . [is] indispensable to United States troops." All this military activity was important enough to be noted in the foreign military journals.[44]

The repute of the soldiers on skis was assured when Frederic Remington painted them. They had become part of the frontier lore of the West.

Antipoaching patrols of the U.S. Cavalry on skis in Yellowstone Park in 1886. One of Frederic Remington's drawings of ski activity. *Harper's Weekly,* 1898.(Robert J. A. Irwin Collection)

Skis as Artifacts

Much of the evidence about the actual skis presented so far has come from written sources. The artifacts themselves, skis and poles for the most part, provide other clues. Many are housed in the four major ski museums in the United States: in California, Colorado, Michigan, and New Hampshire.

In most cases, skis were made from woods available locally. Ash, pine, and birch were the most popular, but fir and spruce were common and even oak was used. Hickory, ubiquitous later, was seldom seen until 1900.

The length and width of these early skis varied considerably. People used skis to travel across deep, untracked snow, and the more primitive boards were up to six inches wide in order to prevent skiers and their loads from sinking in. The more carefully wrought skis, anywhere from seven to fourteen feet in length, also kept the skier riding on top. When the snow settled or regular paths were beaten, some skiers then used the shorter skis. The length of the skis was a matter of personal choice, and standardization was not a concern. In fact, quite the opposite was true; anyone making skis wanted them to have a character all their own. Lars Stadig's skis were as well known in New Sweden, Maine, as Haagen Asgaard's in Ishpeming, Michigan.

Skis that have survived from the nineteenth century can only be dated in a most general fashion. The nucleus of the Western Skisport Museum's collection was accumulated by Bill Berry whose interest in ski history began in the 1920s and has been a passion ever since. He was not careful in his record keeping, but it would have been difficult to date the skis correctly, even as he collected them. Berry, a journalist with a flair for enthusiastic involvement, was also the historian for the National Ski Hall of Fame in Ishpeming. That institution collected skis in a random manner, through advertising and word of mouth.[45] The skis on exhibit are poorly documented, and the archives provide little further evidence. This situation exists at the Colorado Ski Museum's collection as well. A few of the New England Ski Museum's skis are the remains of a collection begun at Dartmouth College in the 1930s, and there is virtually no documentation for any of them. All the museums receive skis from attics and barns of donors who themselves often have no idea of how the equipment came to be there.

No study of the material artifacts has been attempted in the United States, but in Scandinavia, because *Ski-Idraet* was so important, anthropologists have published a range of monographs that provide a thorough study of skis, their functions, and how they were made, from 2500 B.C. to the present.[46] The Russians are presently claiming a find from around 4000 B.C.[47] The Scandinavian studies show that different types of skis were made in different regions. Within a region, too, there were minor variations. In the nineteenth century, certain men became known as ski makers, and some of their skis can be identified.

There is no such corpus of knowledge for early American skis. However, the Scandinavian studies do help in identifying American-made artifacts. Skis have turned up in the New England Ski Museum, for example, which either were brought over from Morgedal (very unlikely) or were made by an immigrant from that valley. Frequently those who came from one village or valley in Norway settled with their kin in the United States. There were fifty Telemarkians in Muskego, Wisconsin.[48] Since there are many skis from Telemark in Oslo's Holmenkollen Museum, it is easy to identify the Telemark ski when it shows up over here.

A variety of typical turn-of-the-century skis. Second from left is a finely crafted ski, probably the work of a Finnish immigrant. Third from left shows the popular leather-encased bamboo foothold. Third from right is Zdarsky's Lilienfeld ski, one of the few in the United States. Its metal binding has a spring-loaded hinge. (New England Ski Museum, Franconia, N.H.)

Decoration on the ski is another indicator of the origin, value, and purpose of the ski. There were basically two decorative elements: patterns of lines grooved in front and back of the foot plate, and the crafting of the ski tip. Most of the skis on view in the two major Scandinavian repositories in Oslo, Norway, and Umeå, Sweden, have remarkable lined patterns often with intricately carved drawings, hunting scenes particularly. The care with which the skis were made and the delicacy of the illustrations indicate they played a special role in the culture of survival.

I have not seen any skis in the United States decorated with sophisticated carvings, although I found one report mentioning animal heads on a pair in 1895.[49] There are a few geometric designs but these are simple if compared to some of the Norwegian and Swedish skis.

The tips of skis were given much consideration in Scandinavia. In the Eddas skis were likened to "ships of the snow." As the Viking prow cut its swath through the waves, so the ski carved its track through the snow. Finland's national epic, the *Kalevala,* makes it clear that skis were made with care and given special attributes. Here is Lylikki, ski maker, master artist who

> Whittled in the fall his snow-shoes,
> Smoothed them in the winter evenings,
> One day working on the runners,
> All the next day making stick rings,
> Till at last the shoes were finished.
>
> . . . .
> Then he fastened well the shoe-straps,
> Smooth as adder's skin the woodwork,
> Soft as fox fur were the stick rings,
> Oiled he well his wondrous snow-shoes,
> With the tallow of the reindeer.[50]

Most of the skis exhibited in museums in the United States are carefully crafted, albeit lacking the decorative embellishments found in the Scandinavian exhibits. Alas, rarely on view are the simple and crude utilitarian skis. They were used in great numbers and are more representative of the early era than the fancy ones displayed for our admiration. In the 1880s a Coloradan reported, "these skates are of not enough value to be kept from one season to another . . . and you constantly come upon them thrown away by the side of the trail, where the snow goes out toward spring."[51] An old-timer recalled "pictures in books of beautiful bent wood. . . . Experience is a sad teacher! I never saw anything in the snowshoe line in Idaho fancier than those."[52]

Skiers usually carried a single strong staff from five to six feet long.

Tipped with iron, it was used for pushing along the flat or for going uphill. On the downhill glide it acted as a balance pole. When skiers needed to turn or slow down, they leaned on it. Some straddled it in witchlike fashion when they found themselves on a steep descent.

The single pole is a vestige of Norse hunting, where it doubled as a weapon. Two poles were probably first used by the Finns, but the single pole remained standard equipment into the twentieth century. As late as 1933, when skiing had become a social sport and recreation, the use of a single pole still showed up in the popular literature. For the Basque herdsmen in Idaho, its continued use went unquestioned in the years before the Second World War.[53]

No special boots were used for skiing; normal winter footgear was held to the ski by a leather toe thong nailed to the sides of the ski or slipped through a mortise. Popular in the mountain West but also found elsewhere, a laced leather toe pouch could be adjusted to the width of the boot. Various methods kept the foot from sliding out of the toe hold. A small wooden block was tacked under the instep or behind the heel on primitive skis. Leather-encased bamboo or even makeshift iron "riggings," as bindings were frequently called, served the same purpose but most used the loose leather heel strap which was common for decades.

For going uphill, deer or elk skin was tied to the underside of the ski; the pelt prevented sliding backward but allowed the forward glide. A burlap sleeve slipped over the back of the ski or criss-crossing rope served the same purpose of providing traction while climbing.

It was individual ingenuity that accounted for efficient skis. This experimental attitude born of necessity was more usual among those for whom skiing was new rather than a traditional heritage. Once the younger generations had learned from the immigrants what to do, they added their own refinements whether they were in Connecticut, California, or anywhere in between.

Recreational Enthusiasms

For centuries skis provided Scandinavians with recreation. An eighteenth-century print shows two boys on skis playing a game of picking up hats dropped randomly in the snow.[54] Folk customs from the old country often associated with holidays provided occasions for fun and games. When the immigrants had leisure time, they used skis in spontaneous games as they had in their home valleys.

Americans were quick to pick up the pleasures of skiing, whether they were schoolboys like John Perry who had "abt. two hours genuine good time" with his friends in 1885 or Dartmouth students jumping over each other on skis ten years later. John Ash, with western experience, showed his roommate how to make skis out of old fencing. "We had a lot of fun around there [Dartmouth]," he recalled, "but only a few of the boys got into the act; most preferred to stay in their warm rooms."[55]

Across the river in Vermont, skiing in the ruts of the St. Johnsbury toboggan chute was a popular pastime until 1914.[56] It seemed to have every advantage; with good balance and a little luck, speed—always a great attraction for those on skis—required little effort.

A natural hill called for skill in controlling the skis and in turning and stopping. The time to experiment and practice was only available to the well-to-do unless the skier had been brought up on skis. The most complete record of what it was like to learn to ski and become involved as a recreational skier in the years before organized skisport can be found in the diaries of a Brattleboro, Vermont, high school student, Fred Harris. The entries are complete from 1904 to 1911 with seldom a day's activity unrecorded, and they show what it was like for one who had "skeeing on the brain evidently" at a time when there were few to enjoy what he found so marvelous. He made his own skis, remarking when he obtained good bends; he fixed "dandy brass tips" on the front of the skis. He experimented with woods; made poles of spruce, hard pine, hickory, ironwood, and oak; told of cross-country trips and of the successes and failures on his "slides," as he termed going down hill. He built jumps, broke skis, hurt his back, and once even confided to his diary that he had been "overdoing lately and decided to lay off for one day."[57] Although he had occasional companions, his was a lonely pleasure in these early days.

Harris worked hard at his newfound recreation. His joys were the joys of an experimental mind, one that was determined to master the technical difficulties as well as those brought on by failure of technique or bad weather conditions.

What a difference between Harris's attitude and that of John Muir, whose capers above Lake Tahoe were recounted earlier, in Chapter 2. This committed environmentalist enjoyed skiing as recreation and as play. He spoke of a friend who, with no skiing experience and heedless of advice, launched himself in "wild abandon, bouncing and diving, his limbs and shoes in chaotic entanglement, now in the snow, now in the air whirling over and over in giddy rolls and somersaults that would shame the most extravagant performances of a circus acrobat!" He quietly gathered himself, picked the snow from his neck and ears, and judged his performance "the very poetry of motion." Muir himself talked of the "lusty reviving exercise on snow-shoes that kept our pulses dancing right merrily."[58]

In the Aspen area, miners "must be a jolly sort of fellows, sliding, skating, leaping, shooting chutes and jumping chasms," the *Denver Times* guessed in 1901. At Grand Lake, skiing replaced dancing as the most popular winter activity, and many photographs show people engaging in fun and games on skis.[59]

Although there were ski races among the mining camp communities in Colorado, the sport never became part of the total culture in the way it had in California.[60] Instead—if we may believe photographs from around the turn of the century—skiing became a social matter. Pictures in the Colorado Historical Society in Denver, show a group of women at Breckenridge in 1889, members of the Crystal Club, and an outing near Mt. Sneffels in the San Juan range. This early recreational interest became a major reason for organizing the skisport in the Rockies, but it contrasts with the cause of its development in the Norse-centered Northwest.

The one area where no reports of recreational skiing have surfaced is in the Washington and Oregon mountains where there was only a slight interest in the use of skis anyway. The *Spokane Falls Review* commented on other winter sports from time to time along with mining news and avalanches but no ski activity was mentioned until Olaus Jeldness, a man with Norwegian, Michigan, Colorado and Canadian experience, promoted a jumping carnival in 1913.[61] Still, it is hard to believe that no fun and frolicking went on. Even when whaling ships were in Arctic winter quarters, skiing vied with snow-soccer and snow-baseball for recreation among the crews.[62]

As immigrant communities turned into American towns, the settlers became part of the materialistic America that was emerging in the late nineteenth century. The immigrants used their winter leisure hours to organize both pleasure and competitive skiing in the hope of bringing renown to their club and their town, as well as recognition to their native country with its *Idraet* heritage. These economic, social, and cultural factors provide the foundations of the skisport.

Foundation of the Skisport

> The visitors at the meeting agreed that Ishpeming is entitled to the National organization's headquarters. They all said that they doubted very much if any of the other cities represented by clubs could handle a tournament as well as the one conducted here this week. . . . It is understood that the one big event of the year will take place in Ishpeming. . . . All national tourneys will be held under auspices of the association, and association rules shall govern the national as well as the minor tournaments. The rules drafted will be similar in many respects to the rules in force here Wednesday.
>
> —*Mining Journal*, Marquette, Michigan, 1905

In the thirty years from about 1880 to 1910 which coincide with the peak years of Scandinavian immigration, local clubs promoted the skisport and laid the foundation for modern skiing.[1] There was only an occasional attempt to "pull off"—to use the expression of the times—a cross-country race. The ethnic exclusiveness of *Ski-Idraet* was the underlying force behind the clubs. Just how this transplanted winter culture fared in its American setting makes an interesting study: tradition transforms and is itself transformed in the modernizing process of the skisport.

One of the marks of a modern sport is the equality of both the competitors and the conditions of the competition.[2] Early skisport's inequalities were natural and often written into club constitutions to ensure what was perceived as the purity of *Ski-Idraet*. Fridtjof Nansen, the explorer, provides an excellent guide to the many different ways in which *Idraet* influenced the American skisport: through the language of skiing, through the formation, the organization, and the discrimination of the clubs, and in the style of competitive jumping. The National Ski Association (NSA) was founded in 1905 in Ishpeming, Michigan, to regulate club activities and so produce equality in competitions.

Nansen and Idraet Influences

When Norwegians, joined by few others, founded clubs to promote skiing, they turned it, often unwittingly, from an unstructured pursuit to a cult that had nationalistic overtones. This should come as no great surprise; the latter nineteenth century, after all, was rampant with nationalism. That the nationalism of skiing should be Norwegian in its thrust can be explained partly because there were few immigrants from the other countries where skiing was prevalent (skiing in the Alpine regions of Europe only started in the 1880s). Swedes tended to be assimilated easily into American society, as were Norwegians who settled in large cities.[3] Those who ended up in smaller communities in the Northwest—Minnesota, Wisconsin, and Michigan—saw skiing as an occasion for socializing as well as a sport that retained features of their native way of life. The involvement of Scandinavia with skiing was epitomized in the person and exploits of Fridtjof Nansen who crossed Greenland on skis in 1888 and whose book *Paa Ski over Grønland* was available in English in 1890.[4]

Nansen was "something of a soloist," remembered a friend, "steadfast towards those to whom he attaches himself; but there are not many."[5] He was not the first into Greenland on skis, but he captured the public's sporting imagination. *The Times* of London caught his appeal exactly: "Nansen was not only a naturalist but a first class sportsman as skater and snow-shoe runner, and a crack shot. Before he was sixteen he had taken all the medals and premiums obtainable for so young a man, and at the concourse in Christiania he became champion ski runner. Last winter he made a kind of dress rehearsal by running on snow-shoes through some of the highest mountains in Norway, drawing his fully laden sledge along with him."[6]

Here was a muscular Christian in action, the equivalent of the rugged American individualist whose virility was proved by conquering yet another piece of the globe. Nansen added to his own and to skiing's mystique:

> I know of no form of sport which so evenly develops the muscles, which renders the body so strong and elastic, which teaches so well the qualities of dexterity and resource, which in an equal degree calls for decision and resolution, and which gives the same vigour and exhilaration to mind and body alike. Where can one find a healthier and purer delight than when on a brilliant winter's day one binds one's ski to one's feet and takes one's way out into the forest? . . . Civilization is, as it were, washed clean from the mind and left behind with the city atmosphere and city life; one's whole being is, so to say, wrapped in one's ski and the surrounding nature. There is something in the whole which develops soul and not body alone, and the sport is perhaps of far greater national importance than is generally supposed.[7]

There can be no exact measurement of Nansen's influence on outdoorsmen and ski runners in Europe although many attested to it.[8] In this country, the *Skiklubben* at Berlin, New Hampshire, eventually became the Nansen Club, and when the great man made a stop at Berlin on his lecture tour in 1929, a local commentator wrote: "For a quarter of a century his countrymen have been telling us of him. We feared to see him lest his actual presence should dim the lustre of his fame."[9]

Nansen used the word *Idraet* which, as shown earlier, was translated as sport but meant much more. Nansen's analysis took in the Classical and later Renaissance notion of *mens sana in corpore sano*—a healthy mind in a healthy body—which educated Victorians romanticized into an orthodoxy. It valorized the urge to go to the ends of the earth, the character building that was assumed when going against impossible odds, the drive of discipline, the acquiring of skill, the overcoming of fear. All these were accomplished by Nansen, and so his hero status was understandable. Nansen's exploits and his description of just what skiing does for the individual fitted the perception of American rugged individualism. For classless America there was also an added charm. Nansen had selected a team for the Greenland crossing: Lt. O. C. Dietrichson, Otto Sverdrup, Kristian Trana, and two Samer, Samuel Balto and Ole Ravna. There was no kow-towing to class pressures; these were simply the best men.[10]

The very venue had a romantic pull. Greenland was more than "outdoors," the antithesis of indoors, more even than "the great outdoors"; it was just about as far from the foulness and malaise of achieving, urban society as one could travel. The extremes of distance and climate gave a mix of danger and adventure that could only be imagined.

How was all this transfused into American skiing? To begin with, the language of the skisport in the United States was Norwegian. Clubs had full-fledged Norwegian names like *Den Norske Turn og Skiforening* of Minneapolis or the *Holmenkollen* of Colfax, Wisconsin. There were two Fridtjof Nansen ski clubs. Constitutions and minutes of club meetings were often in Norwegian. Banquet speeches and toasts after meets were frequently in the immigrants' mother tongue.[11] The NSA's annual publication, *The Skisport*—incorporating *Ski-Idraet* in its title—gave prominence to many aspects of skiing in Norway; a regular column "Fra Kristiania" ("From Christiania"—as Oslo was called) kept the immigrants informed of home country activities. When a problem about jumping came up, *The Skisport* editor simply published verbatim and in Norwegian the rules for disqualification, and added in English that these rules should be immediately adopted by the NSA.[12] At meets Norwegian flags decked the jumping hills, and the Norse language was spoken so ubiquitously that one reporter called it the "official language."[13] One non-Norwegian remembered how teams were chosen as late as the 1920s. "Before the big meets, the meeting [of the club] was well attended. You'd go, hoping to be picked. Half the time the meeting would be conducted in Norwegian. Sometimes if you hadn't close ties to Norwegians, then you wouldn't be chosen."[14]

When immigrants first formed clubs they naturally used their native language at meetings. Many then wrote ethnic exclusiveness into their constitutions. The Skiklubben of Berlin, New Hampshire, was typical: "The business meeting shall be in Norwegian, and the colors of the club shall be the colors of the Norwegian and American flags. Any Scandinavian of good reputation can be a member (but not under fifteen) living in Coos [County, in northern New Hampshire]. Any member who attends a regular meeting in an intoxicant frame of mind can be refused to take part in the business of the meeting. If a member speaks ill of the club . . . he shall be stricken out of the club."[15]

The flags, which tied the old world to the new, and uniforms gave a social cohesiveness which was assured by limiting its membership to male Scandinavians. After some years, however, the *Skiklubben* changed its name to the Berlin Mills Ski Club, attesting to the economic importance of the area's logging industry and to the inevitable Americanization. Then the name changed to the Fridtjof Nansen Ski Club and, in 1912, was simplified to just the Nansen Club, both to retain part of the Norwegian heritage and to appeal to non-Scandinavian speakers; French Canadians dominated the work force in the mills.[16]

The early ethnic exclusiveness was typical in the Northwest too. In 1886, for example, the constitution of the Aurora Club of Red Wing, Minnesota, called for the officers to be "Scandinavians or of Scandinavian descent." In La Crosse, Wisconsin, Scandinavian officers invited young men of all nationalities to join them; however, non-Scandinavians remained apart and were known as the "American faction."[17]

These early ski clubs were often matters of the moment, formed from existing snowshoe clubs or for a single carnival. Ishpeming's Norden Ski Club began when a half-dozen men were enjoying themselves on a hillside. The local saloon keeper appreciated the sport and supplied a nip after each run down. "I don't believe it would have happened then," recalled Ole Sundlie, if it had not been for the "riding for a swig."[18] There is an opportunistic naivete here which in the individual case makes nonsense of sociological terminology such as "rationalization," one of Allen Guttmann's indicators explaining the modernization of a sport.[19]

In the 1890s, interest languished, then mounted again so that in 1901 a reborn Ishpeming Ski Club invited "men of all nationalities of good character" to become members. As a matter of policy now the meetings and all the minutes were in English.[20] When Carl Tellefsen, president of the club,

The Norden Club of Ishpeming, Michigan, was founded in 1887. Members pose with their "peculiar ten feet 'skees,'" navigated only by Scandinavians." Their "longed for suits" provided warmth on outings and social cohesion among the immigrant mix in the upper peninsula of Michigan. (National Ski Hall of Fame, Ishpeming, Mich.)

addressed members three years later he reminded them that "we are all Americans, not Englishmen, Swedes or Norwegians, and . . . there is no discrimination shown, no favors, the best man gets there. I mention this because . . . some Busy-Body, outside the Club, thought that the different nationalities ought to be represented. I will earnestly ask you not to bring the nationality question or any other question foreign to the sport into the club."[21]

This serious effort to rid the Ishpeming and other clubs of ethnic biases testified to the Americanization of the skisport which was to receive official sanction, as it were, with the founding of the NSA in Ishpeming in 1905. Under Tellefsen's leadership and with the unflagging promotion by club secretary Aksel Holter, Ishpeming had held a splendid tournament which drew ten thousand spectators the year before.[22] The club determined to capitalize on this success and on Washington's Birthday in 1905 pulled off—as the expression of the times had it—another grand competition. Although President Theodore Roosevelt had to decline the invitation to attend, the fact of his possible presence helped give the day a national outlook.[23] After the meet, the National Ski Association was founded with a board of directors heavily oriented toward Ishpeming and its *Idraet* tradi-

=== SECOND NATIONAL ===
SKI TOURNAMENT!

Greatest Exhibition of Skiing Ever Witnessed in America.

Many Foreign Riders will Participate.

America's Best Clubs All to Send Representatives.

Railroads Will make low rates.

Send for Reserved Seats....

to H. S. THOMPSON, Ishpeming, Mich.

Price $1.00 Including Admission.

ISHPEMING, FEBRUARY 22, 1906.

The National Ski Association had its headquarters at Ishpeming, Michigan, and used well-tried promotional techniques to "pull off the Greatest Exhibition of Skiing Ever Witnessed in America." Jumping remained the most important part of the meet until the Alpine disciplines dominated competition in the 1930s. (New England Ski Museum, Franconia, N.H.)

tion. The major object was to obtain uniform rules which would cover local tournaments as well as the annual meet.[24]

Through the NSA's *Skisport,* Aksel Holter promoted policies of Americanization while trying to maintain the *Idraet* ideal. For example, he publicized the lone American who promoted skiing at Escanaba, Michigan, and "even Italians" joined the Norwegian Ski Club of Stillwater. When "Irish Mick" Barney Riley, gained the three hundred dollar Nor Trophy, Holter editorialized that "true lovers of the sport were greatly pleased" because "one from a different nationality from the Norwegian, with whom skiing is a national sport, will stimulate and encourage all nationalities, Irish, German and French and others to take up the sport which the National Association wants to make the National winter sport of America."[25] It seemed to prove, once and for all, that non-Scandinavians would not be discriminated against, but in fact non-Scandinavian Americans continued to feel disadvantaged from time to time.

Part of the nationalistic ethos was bound up with strictly regulated socializing in which club dress played a cohesive role. Uniforms were remarkably important. Discussions of outfits occurred almost immediately after a club was founded. Ishpeming came out in favor of tight fitting suits in November 1901. In December, caps and leggings were discussed, and the "long-wished for suits" were first used in a parade in March. Colors were also important. Aurora's "red cap, white blouse, blue knee breeches, red stockings and blue belt" reflected the red, white, and blue of the old and new homelands.[26] Clubs gained social cohesion as well as exclusiveness by wearing uniforms. As late as 1925 the *New York Times* told its readers that "it is not in the best form that any but the ablest ski runners . . . adopt the Norwegian dress."[27]

Uniforms—emulating the military—also provided the right background for medals. The militaristic tone of many sports was a response to the perceived degeneration brought on by urban living. The style of American ski organizations, the emphasis on order and discipline, the flag waving, and the uniforms all attested to a military ideal where a right mind could only exist in a disciplined body. Among the Aurora Club officers were a captain and a lieutenant whose duty it was to "call members together for drill and practice in ski running." On the less serious side, when Karl Hovelsen was hired to ski leap in Barnum and Bailey's circus in Madison Square Garden in 1907, he was touted as "Captain" and dressed up in pseudo-military garb.[28] His uniform and title glamorized the spectacle.

If there were successful efforts to bring non-Scandinavian men into the skisport, attempts that were made to attract women's participation were not so effective. Women were rarely mentioned as skiers in the nineteenth century; in club activities they were decorative and useful adjuncts. Some clubs admitted women to membership to give a club a social aspect, others to swell the uniformed ranks on public display on competition day. There was one all-women's club, but after an initial flurry of commentary about the costumes in the local paper in 1903, nothing more was heard from the "Nora."[29]

Club tramps at Ashland, Wisconsin, often included women who enjoyed torchlight skiing. In St. Paul, on the other hand, the men would "swarm pell, mell to wind up the happiest bunch on earth at our destination, where we were greeted by our lady members who had taken the train to Red Rock earlier in the day."[30]

There were those who protested against women's skiing. *The North*, a Minneapolis paper, took the trouble to translate Mrs. Nansen's rebuttal which had appeared first in a Norwegian paper. In speaking of her own experiences on skis she used phrases such as "the purest beauty of life," "ennobling influence," and "all the health . . . conferred on body and mind." How could anyone seriously believe, she inquired, that women became demoralized by skiing "even though they be in the company of gentlemen."[31] What was most interesting about the University of Wisconsin's ski club was that "it admits women to full membership." In fact in 1914, forty-six of the eighty members were women.[32]

The NSA's Holter was a constant publicist for the benefits to women. His annual reports tended to stress two themes when analyzing the role of skiing for women: their active participation and the benefits to their health. Skiing "will give pale cheeks a healthy color . . . , will make your nervousness disappear, will make of you . . . a better woman. . . . [Skiing] gives the young lady, shut up in an office or store all day new vigor and energy."[33]

Although social outings on skis provided healthy companionship, competition for women was considered unnatural. Men, however, were expected to compete; that was the American way.

Problems of Idraet: *Cross-Country*

Cross-country racing in Scandinavia was designed specifically to test a skier's all-round ability on open ground, through woods, across hills, and over fences. When transplanted to the American Northwest it found little support as a form of competition. However popular club cross-country tramps became, and however much effort clubs made to include cross-country races in meets, little enthusiasm was generated. In the *Idraet* tradition, club constitutions called for "at least one meeting with a ski distance run" (Nansen), or for the promotion of the skisport "by annual tournaments such as long distance races" (Ishpeming). As early as the 1890s *The North* suggested, "the ski boys must go to work and show what they can do by way of a distance run"—meaning fifteen to twenty miles, the norm in Scandinavia—if the skisport was to be the grandest and most healthy sport on earth, but there was little response.[34]

In 1901 a real cross-country race was held, although the distance was cut to eleven miles because the organizers believed it was "not thought best to follow the old custom here." Eight men started and only five finished. The rules permitted each competitor to choose which streets he took out of town before following a flagged course. No skier could carry his skis up hill; only one staff was permitted. Matt Johnson, just over from Norway, won with his collar "not even damp" while most of the "other riders were almost done up."[35] Johnson's lack of sweat was noted because that was a major indication of his fitness; that was what *Idraet* stood for. The race though was hardly a success; "the boys would rather jump than participate in long distance contests."[36]

A group of Finns took up the sponsorship of cross-country racing again in 1902 with a twelve-mile run, but that was not a success either. Four years later another effort was made by the Finns of Ishpeming. No cash prizes were offered, only medals of gold and silver, and nine runners took part. The NSA secretary took note and suggested that endurance races be more prominent in tournaments and that a long-distance race be included at the up-coming national meet.[37]

At Ashland, Wisconsin, on 7 February 1907, the first United States National Cross-Country Championship was run over a nine-mile course of "somewhat broken territory, up, down, through ravines covered with heavy underbrush, over level fields with fences to be climbed" and ended with a five-mile run across a snow-covered lake.[38] Norwegian cross-country rules were strictly adhered to. The course was posted by red, white, and blue streamers and watched by members of the Nor Ski Club of Chicago. A Finn, Asarja Autio, came home the winner by two minutes and immediately called himself Champion of the World and challenged anybody for one hundred dollars.[39] But the race was not popular with runners. "How are we to develop skiers to compete with the European champions," complained the secretary, "when we cannot induce our sturdy boys to partake in cross-country runs?"[40] In 1912 the distance was down to 3½ miles. By 1916 a professional class was instituted, but it was not well supported. For the national event at St. Paul in 1917, no entries were received at all.[41]

Problems of Idraet: *Jumping*

In industrializing societies the workplace has become increasingly specialized; there is little room for the Jack-of-all-trades. The skisport in America has paralleled this change. In nineteenth-century Norway, where skiing was part of the folk culture, most people simply skied in winter. Naturally some could ski faster than others, jump farther, or look more graceful.[42] When skiing across the countryside and jumping from hillocks were factored into competition, cross-country and jumping specialists emerged.

Mikkel Hemmets-
veit and his two
brothers (Torger
is shown here)
from Norway set
the style for jump-
ing by which all
others were mea-
sured. Mikkel
dominated the
early organized
American ski-
jumping competi-
tions. Skiing "is
one of our foreign
imports which is
absolutely unob-
jectionable," com-
mented *Leslie's
Weekly* in 1893.
(New England Ski Mu-
seum, Franconia, N.H.)

In America those involved in early skisport organization looked to the
Idraet ideal hoping it would produce a moral person in an all-round skier.
Yet America recognized the specialist achiever and measured perfection not
by morality but by money. Economic motives promoted ski jumping over
cross-country and a class of professionals was fostered whose main concern
was fairness in competition where the jumping style was open to objective
judgment.[43]

In the early ski clubs of the Northwest the *Idraet* tradition remained
influential; jumps were referred to as "courses" and "races" because in
Norway jumps were a part of a race down a track (*Laam*). This *Hoplaam*
had become formalized with the construction of jumps. There were few
natural hills in the Northwest where a competitor might start at the top, lift
off a bump on the way down, and finish his run at the bottom. Jumps,
therefore, were very contrived structures yet the elements of the *Laam*

remained part of the culturally important all-round expertise. This mix of traditional and new can be found in reports of early competitions where, for example, one competitor "showed up comparatively poor in the regular race, and only when the long distance contest was started did he come into form."[44] This is an account of jumping, not cross-country, and shows the immediate interest in the length of the leap; distance assumed priority in spite of the traditions from the home country.

Immigrant communities made local rules for managing the jumping contests and these were generally agreed upon. There was no standardization for the height of jumps, for the length of in-run or out-run, nor of style. The Aurora Club constructed a special jump with a movable take-off platform: two feet for the beginners, four feet for the better riders, and six feet for the experts. Visiting skiers did not object.[45] For the club's 1890 meet, five hundred copies of its rules for competition were distributed. But when the competitors found the take-off poorly situated, the club simply changed it to suit the jumpers.[46]

Rules not only addressed the length of jump, but also the style. Mikkel Hemmetsveit provided the standard for style. His "gracefulness [and] elegance [was] something beyond imitation almost." He had sped down the hill, and "at the jump he gathered himself for the leap, and with a mighty bound sailed into the air. Twice he gathered himself together and leaped while in mid-air, raising himself apparently as a bird would raise."[47] This way of ski jumping came to be recognized as the "Red Wing style" all over the Northwest. Style was associated with excellence, and that excellence was graded on a scale of 1 to 10. The aesthetics of one particular style came to dominate, and other competitors were measured by Hemmetsveit's expertise. A special technique was emerging along with sets of rules like those the Aurora Club drew up for its 1890 tournament:

1. The character for standing run from 6 to 10.

2. The character 5 is reserved for the man who falls and raises himself again within a distance of 75 feet from the jump.

3. The character for a falling run 1 to 4.

4. Touching the ground with the hand is to be judged as a fall.

5. In summing up the standing of the competitors the number of feet jumped for every jump and the character given are added up together.

6. For the first fall a deduction of 15 pts. is made from the total sum. For a second fall 25 pts. are so deducted. Any character below 6 would indicate a fall.[48]

The Aurora gave much more weight to the length of jump than to the form of the skier in its point system. Results were given in this fashion: Thompson 57 feet, character 9.[49]

Immediately after its founding, the NSA published its own rules:

1. 1 to 20 pts. given for character.

2. Character given in all cases, and to be taken from beginning to finish of run.

3. One point given for each foot jumped.

4. 30 pts. deducted for fall.

5. Touching with both hands is a fall.

6. Touching with one hand, 15 pts. deducted.

7. Length of jump to be measured from a point three feet back of face of bump, to point where feet of skier strike.[50]

To this the NSA added "The Form of Skier to Be Considered in Giving Character." The start had to be straight with body slightly bent, skis close together with one leading the other slightly. The leap position was described, the flight in the air had to be with "body straightened to its full length, still somewhat bent forward, easy movements with the arms to keep the balance, the skis parallel with the hill, always close together and on the same plane." The landing was to be "strong, with a composed, limber body," one foot well before the other and skis close together. The finish was to be accompanied by either a turn on the outer or the inner ski, which later became officially described as the Telemark or Kristiania turn. Character points were assigned to each part of the jump.[51]

It is interesting to compare the club's regulations to those of the NSA. By doubling the points given for character, the NSA stood firmly in the Norwegian *Idraet* tradition where the aesthetics of style were of greater importance than actual distance. Crowds should have come to see one jumper out-perform, not out-distance another. The influence of the *Hoplaam* continued in the points assigned "from beginning to finish of run." The NSA's stricter rule on falling was also to ensure that competitors stressed the perfection of form. Performance was a matter of judging aesthetics, and to ensure fair judgment, the skiers themselves presented a list of judges.

The seventh rule required exact measurement, and the men in charge were scrutinized, for it was said when Mikkel Hemmetsveit had made his great leap of seventy-eight feet that "the markers were a little partial . . . and stretched their tape a few feet." The NSA did not want any of that sort of malarkey.[52] The NSA regulations were debated, but over the years they changed comparatively little.[53]

The Decline of Idraet: Professionalism

The interest that competitors, towns, and the NSA took in the skisport was not merely concern for a fair competition. Communities jealously guarded their jumping success because good jumping brought renown and money to a town. When Mikkel Hemmetsveit showed his Holmenkollen winning form in a St. Paul tournament, citizens tried to persuade him to move there. But he was not going to forsake Norman County whose ski club had been specifically founded so that when he won the one hundred dollar prize "Ada and Norman County [would] get a share of the honor." The local paper imagined all the neighboring sleepy towns green with envy. A suggestion was even made to send him to the senate "as he appears to be the only man in the Red River Valley that can attract the attention of that august body." The next year he moved to St. Croix Falls, even though Stillwater, "a city of push and enterprise" thought of him as "our champion." When he again won the prize at the St. Paul carnival, "in its greed for glory" St. Paul claimed him as its own, as did Stillwater, much to the disgust of the residents of St. Croix Falls. When Mikkel moved to Red Wing later, the Aurora Club immediately elected him a member before the season began.[54]

The local town provided the bulk of the audience for a local meet, but as towns increased the competition for recognition, advertising over a wide area brought in thousands of spectators. Excursion rates on railroads, specially built grandstands, and promotions by hotels and restaurants acted as incentives to bring thousands into town on competition day. When large cash prizes attracted the best riders, even more people came and then clubs competed for which could put up the most prize money. By 1901 there was already a classification of "experts," invited jumpers from out of town who had all expenses paid and a shot at the seventy-five-dollar first prize.[55] As the leaps lengthened, "Knights of the Spruce Blades" and "Cloud Hurdlers" were advertised with promises of breaking the one-hundred-foot barrier. This class of professionals provided what was often termed "the real riding." A special event for length only was given due billing too: tumble-jumping, the desperate stretch for length, became an anticipated attraction of many meets.

Prize money caused much soul searching among those who believed that jumping competitions should be simon-pure. Although money had been

Ole Feiring doing some "real riding" for Duluth. Norwegian and Swedish flags are a reminder of the Scandinavian presence, still very strong in 1907. (New England Ski Museum, Franconia, N.H.)

awarded to winners in Norwegian tournaments, the outright bid for cash never had the materialistic attraction in Scandinavia that it did for the immigrants in America.[56] When formal jumping competitions began in the 1880s, the prizes were medals of known worth; Ishpeming's gold medal for first place was valued at twenty-six dollars. By the time Mikkel Hemmetsveit made his mark, thirty-five dollars in gold was being given for first place, along with shaving sets, mugs, scarves, and other wares secured from local businesses.[57] In 1901 Ishpeming promised seventy-five dollars for the winner of the expert class. For the amateurs, the top prize was fifteen dollars.[58]

Money was the attraction, and the amounts increased almost annually as local tournament organizers offered "extra inducements to good riders" besides the chance for the one-hundred-dollar first prize. In 1908 the North Star Ski Club distributed $220, the Cameron put up $69, the Red Wing, $175, the Itasca, $240, and the Superior, $200.[59] These prizes for a successful jumper represented a lot of money at a time when two to three dollars a day was the going wage for a miner in the copper belt of the upper

JOHN RUDD, of Duluth, Turning a Complete Somersault on Skies.

The beginnings of the ski show: this somersault was spectacular enough to warrant a postcard in 1913. (New England Ski Museum, Franconia, N.H.)

peninsula of Michigan. Ole Feiring's winnings one season comprised: thirty-five dollars at one tournament, a first, second, and third at three other tournaments where cash prizes of unknown amounts were awarded, one sixty-dollar prize and two others of fifty dollars each.[60]

There is very little indication that these men trained; they all held other jobs. Towns promised employment to well-known jumpers and some of the men actively sought work in skiing communities.[61] They were expected to instruct the boys with the hope of providing a continual supply of excellent jumpers, thereby bringing to themselves and the town honor, glory, and money.

The mounting cash prizes, the strenuous efforts to lure "name" jumpers to town, and the increasing attention paid to winnings rather than winners roused the NSA to try to protect the *Idraet* ideal by abolishing all cash prizes. The result was that the jumpers decided to boycott the meet. The Ishpeming hosts, fearing their tournament in jeopardy, guaranteed "every wish of the riders" and immediately put up an extra two hundred dollars to ensure the meet.[62] Tellefsen and Holter were incensed and particularly sad that some of their own Ishpeming boys were involved. The association officers were caught in a bind: they admired the best jumpers, but in order to secure them for competition, the prize money had to be higher. They sometimes endorsed the "'All-American' ski bunch of eighty professionals," but more usually stressed the need to promote amateur qualities.

When foreigners criticized the emphasis given to money prizes, Aksel Holter justified it by replying that Americans were "amateurs of heart—professionals of necessity."[63] These arguments among the clubs at home as well as on the international level lasted well into the 1920s.

If the professional jumpers provided the "real riding," the daring feat of a double jump, hand-in-hand by Mikkel and Torger Hemmetsveit, had been performed off the Aurora jump as early as 1893 to an ecstatic crowd. The two Oles from Coleraine, Westgaard and Mangseth, performed at Duluth; there were jumps by women; a clown took to the air at Fergus Falls; and, marvel of all marvels, John Rudd did somersaults. "Where did anyone ever hear of tricks done on skis?" asked Holter in *The Skisport*. "Acrobatic performances do not belong to the skisport and should not be encouraged. . . . A club saves money and reputation by keeping fool tricks out of their tournaments."[64] It was said that the public "does not cater to foolish performances where they do not belong," but, in fact, the public loved them, and even Holter himself could not deny that Axel Hendrickson's somersault at a speed of 55 mph was "the real thriller of the day" at Norge's annual tourney at Cary, Indiana, in 1911.[65] Was the acrobat replacing the sportsman? The answer was no, yet for the increasing spectatorship, ever expecting superlatives, the skisport was becoming the ski show.

Jumping captured the crowd's imagination and gave dramatic proof of achievement. It was not only graceful and heroic but it also became big business for competitor and town, and spectators did not object to paying for a stunt or two to vary the program. The NSA, ever protective of *Idraet*, struggled against the materialistic emphasis on display. It tried to promote cross-country races, but that was work and sweat, as unheroic to perform as it was unspectacular to watch. The cross-country skier's all-round ability and the fitness implied were less adaptable to the American ethos than the jump, and only a few regretted cross-country's passing.

5 / Controlling the Skisport

A rough calculation of the rider's speed . . . can be made with the aid of the never-should-be-forgotten formula $V^2 = 2\,a\,s$. In this case s [is] 110 feet and the speed is found to be 55.5 miles per hour.

—"Skiing, the Engineer's Sport," *The Ski Annual* (1920–21)

Send us your age and height, and whether or not you are a new beginner, and we will tell you just what is suitable for you. We do a mail order business exclusively. We can serve you better this way than through agents and middlemen and thus guarantee perfect satisfaction in every instance, whether the order is for a pair of Dollar Pine Skis or for some larger order for Expert Hickory Skis. We handle besides our own manufacture, Imported Norwegian Ash Skis and the Strand Ski. Skis in Pine, Ash, Oak, Birch, Hickory. Ski Poles, Ski Shoes, Ski Bindings, Ski Socks, Ski Mitts. Everything of the best quality and at right prices. Address Aksel H. Holter, Ashland, Wisconsin

—Advertisement, *The Skisport* (1908–09)

In order to organize the skisport, it became necessary to set up a bureaucracy to standardize procedures and quantify statistics and to establish a process for making and keeping records to ensure historical accuracy and guarantee consistency. These facets of the modernizing process became increasingly apparent, then vital, for the control of the skisport. However, they were all comparatively unsophisticated and so comixed that an analysis of one aspect does some injustice to another.

Different specialist skills developed in spite of the continuing Scandinavian ideal of the all-round skier. As more people engaged in the sport, the production of equipment also became specialized. Manufacture began on a local level as an after-hours industry, but by the early years of the twentieth century a few factories were turning out thousands of pairs of skis annually. Through this period, the National Ski Association struggled to stay true to the tenets of its Norse-based philosophy, which ran counter to the new pressures of Americanization.

Efforts to Control the Skisport

Standardization could only be accomplished if a single bureaucratic organization had jurisdiction over the individual clubs. This need was addressed with the creation of the NSA in 1905. The five founding members, two clubs each from Minnesota and Michigan and one from Wisconsin, though geographically apart, were homogeneously ethnic, all from the Norse immigrant matrix. Members of one club often had a hand in founding another.[1]

By 1907, the NSA comprised twenty-four clubs, with one, "The First Kingdom of the Ski," as far away as Utica, New York.[2] This New York club was a group of twenty amateurs whose whole attitude hardly had a Norse quality about it. The motto of the club was "Soc et Tuum," and its skiing was an unsophisticated and entirely social affair. One member, C. H. Blair, obtained factory-made skis from the Northwest but discarded them "because they [were] not suited to the more rough work we were used to" and he favored his own home-made variety.[3] Furthermore, as more and more middle-class skiers took up the sport (the First Kingdom's membership included owners of second homes, a dentist, a retired textile executive, a lawyer, a furrier, physicians, and a state safety commissioner), the NSA, which still considered jumping to be the major attraction of skiing, seemed increasingly irrelevant to those for whom skiing was a sociable pastime. The First Kingdom's members could quite happily admit that "hardly one of us could make a jump of twenty feet."[4]

The most important publication of the NSA was its journal, *The Skisport*. The first report listed the charter clubs and the elected officers along with giving news of committee work on the constitution and by-laws. There were twenty-two clubs with a total of 756 members ready for the 1906 season. This was an indication of the strength of the organization which, from time to time, had problems with disgruntled clubs (five formed an International Ski Association in 1912) and with the professionals.[5]

Reporting on the second convention in 1906, *The Skisport* gave notice that prize money might be abolished. Rules were being drawn up "to govern all tournaments in the future." The membership was assured that Ashland's (Wisconsin) plans for the national tournament were well in hand and the secretary stated that the success of the tournament would mean "a great deal for the future of this the best of all winter sports."[6]

The Skisport increased from nine pages in 1905–06 to seventy-nine in 1911–12. That issue gave details of the year's events, numbers of contestants and spectators, names of prize winners with the length of their jumps and, often, the money they won. The NSA's constitution appeared regularly, as did rules governing ski contests and desired style in ski jumping. Newsworthy items such as the details of a new trestle for jumping were included along with the secretary's goal of showing "oh how glorious it is" to be on skis: poems, a story of rabbit hunting, how it was in the Old Country "where all love the sport," photographs (one of sunbathing in the nude—"it happens sometimes"), and homilies on the clean, amateur sport that would regenerate America.[7] In all these ways, *Skisport* served the NSA's leadership in controlling the direction skiing was taking as seen from the Northwest's *Idraet* base.

The ski jump, the most important aspect of any meet, received continuous attention from the NSA. One effort to control the sport was an attempt to standardize the actual construction of jumps: no club should build a trestle higher than eighty feet above the take-off. The NSA recommended that one construction firm, W. S. Wetherall, become the sole builder of all jumps throughout the Northwest.[8]

Standardization, however, did not follow. Towns continued to construct ever-higher jumps, off which increasing distances were attained as jumpers, spectators, and economic interests turned to the business of record making.

The Lure of Record Breaking

When Ishpeming brought in Red Wing "experts" to promote its tournament in 1901, the organizers added a new event to the regular jumping program, "the long jump." This proved immensely popular.[9] Casting all form aside, casting *Idraet* aside, the desperate reach for achieving length began. At other meets the lure of length even made for intentional mismarking: one 112-foot jump was criticized as being "measured by saloon keepers with rope with rags on." Ishpeming believed that Red Wing measurers had used "pumpkin vines . . . with all crooks and turns" to measure a jump.[10]

Ishpeming tried to capitalize on the appeal to both jumper and spectator of record making and breaking. "It is expected," the local paper announced on the eve of a competition, "that some new records will be made."[11] The promise of a new record was based on the elongation of a jump. Intertown skisport rivalry, which grew unabated in the first decade of the twentieth century, spawned the building of larger hills with higher take-off bumps, the advertising of the previous week's achievements, and the proffering of a gold medal for any jumper who reached over 100 feet. In 1904 Ole Westgaard was the winner at 96 feet—tantalizingly near the magical 100. When the American record stood at 106 feet, from the Red Wing jump,

Ishpeming built a new slide; there was "no better . . . anywhere in the United States, or in Norway for that matter," and located the grandstand on the 100-foot line. On Munising's new jump, "it will be an easy matter . . . to break the American record." There were even some who felt the "world's record will be crowded" the following year. Bovey promised records, and Ashland's hill could "easily produce jumps of record breaking nature," but there were none in 1907 because the snow was sticky.[12] Ashland, Munising, Red Wing, Ishpeming were all striving to have the record broken on their jumps, and if it could be done by a local, even more honor and economic advantage would accrue to the hometown.

The 1908 skiing season was not good because there was not much snow, yet it was "exceptionally interesting," as Aksel Holter noted in his report to the NSA, "in as much as the American record was broken again and again on the different improved hills and a new world's record came very nearly to being established on this side of the Ocean."[13]

The city of Duluth had entered the lists by capturing the record in January 1907 with 112 feet, although it lost it three days later when a jump of 114 feet was recorded at Red Wing. The record returned to Duluth on 13 January 1908, and was increased three days later to 117 feet. But in February, a leap of 122 feet was made at Ishpeming. Then

> Duluth made changes on the Take-off and conducted a tournament on 15 March but the object of the tournament was not accomplished. Ole Feiring cleared 124 feet but fell in the attempt. Not yet satisfied Duluth announced another tournament for 22 March, being intent on beating the record. Nearly every contestant almost equaled the American record, and John Evenson beat it by 9 feet, clearing 131 feet in good form. Feiring sailed a distance of 134 feet, but fell in his attempt. . . . Arnold Olson of Duluth established an amateur record of 119 feet.

Evenson and Olson were the heroes. "Duluth thus established what it had been looking for, two American Records by two Duluth Skiers on a Duluth hill."[14]

This excerpt shows precisely how the particular profile of the jump changed the nature of record making. Evenson and Feiring no doubt made impressive jumps, but the fact that a number of competitors could jump to the American mark when the take-off was adjusted says more about the profile of the hill and its take-off than it does about jumping expertise. Too, the report makes it absolutely clear that this was a Duluth effort. The civic minded had "won" the national meet of 1908 and they were determined to profit from the success. Fortuitously the old trestle had collapsed in a storm the previous summer and the city had built a higher one. Some of the local business leaders had invested in the land for the hill. The report was correct in crediting Duluth; it really was the city itself that owned these records. When the record passed to Chippewa Falls the next season, Duluth skiers made several attempts to beat champion Oscar Gunderson's 138 feet, but failed by a mere 4 feet.[15]

Oscar Gunderson's 138 feet was noted in the *New York Times* as the first world record achieved in the United States.[16] There had been earlier claimants but differences between hills and the ambiguity of whether a record could count if a jumper fell made true comparison with Norwegian claims impossible. Norwegians and other foreign observers—as well as the NSA—began to wonder about the ever-increasing length of jumps. The Germans were told erroneously that the NSA's slogan was "New hills and higher scaffolds" and as a result they castigated American skiers for their professional orientation.[17]

The NSA which had tried to limit the height of jumps was never clear where it stood on the matter of jumping records. Aksel Holter sensed the excitement of record breaking in ever-enlarged outdoor ski jumping theaters. "The American people are eager for results," he wrote, "they are not content with good form alone in a ski jumping contest, they want something more, they want long daring leaps and the establishing of records. The nature of our people is such that it demands first place in all athletic events, and they will support anything in which there is a question of new records being established, while they would soon tire of a performance where only good form would be a predominating feature."[18]

Here Holter was speaking to the interests of American skiers at a time when the Norwegians were turning their rules into international rules. Holter let the Norwegians and others know how those in the United States felt about the ski jump. However much the United States might be criticized for "cultivating length," to use the words of C. Egger, a Swiss critic, spectator crowds in Germany, Switzerland, and Italy were also much taken with record-breaking leaps. Stung by the Swiss criticisms especially, Holter suggested sending to Europe half a dozen experts. "We refuse to be in the back seat and if records are what will bring us to the front we are going after them and we will get them by the horns. Sure!"[19] Holter might dare his remarks to the Swiss, but, when the secretary of the Norwegian Ski Association denounced the American record mania, Holter became philosophically torn between the old world and the new.

"RECORDS, RECORDS, Always Records," the Norwegian secretary's letter had begun. Holter, loyal to the cultural tradition and sensing the endlessness of record breaking, remarked that "Norway could send scores of experts to the ski hill in Brummundalen . . . where records could be established every day." But, of course, the Norwegians were not interested in doing that; it was no part of the *Idraet* ideal (Norwegians had held or believed they held every world record up to 1909, but that was considered coincidental). "To establish a record," he went on, "the hills should be of the same proportions, both as to approach and landing." If a skier could simply slide off the jump and glide because the lower run fell steeply away, distance would not be difficult to attain. But Holter also understood that Americans "wish to be where we belong—IN THE FRONT—consequently it is a hard matter to get away from the idea that a new record ought to be made at any and all tournaments. . . . We now build one approach long and steeper than the other," he went on, "in order to beat some other hill and by trying to establish a record, thrill the vast multitudes that venture out to witness this spectacular attempt, the hope of seeing a record jump being foremost in the minds of the majority at all times. This can not go on forever."[20]

Holter was speaking literally, but the record breaking went unabated. Ragnar Omtvedt, in the United States for less than a year, broke the world record as a professional with a leap of 169 feet in 1913. When Steamboat Springs, Colorado, announced its carnival "it was easy to prevail upon Ragnar Omtvedt to come" because of the special jump that promised world record possibilities. In fact Omtvedt failed, but with further improvements the next year, he made 192 feet 9 inches and it was predicted that he would go over 200 or 210 at the next carnival. By 1917 the record stood at 203 feet and by 1919 at 214. On 9 February 1921 Henry Hall flew 229 feet at Revelstoke, British Columbia.[21]

The Norwegians' antagonism toward the infatuation with record attempts was a measure of their concern for *Idraet* and, more practically, of the challenge it presented to their international control of the sport. The Holmenkollen competition was their own "Olympic Games of the North" and, naturally, was run under Norwegian rules.[22] These were formalized into unofficial international rules when ten foreign representatives met in Oslo in 1910.[23] The supremacy of Scandinavians in all events almost precluded anyone else from questioning how things were done, and Scandinavians continued to maintain their control by holding all the major offices. Although only eight nations were represented at the 1922 meeting in Stockholm (the United States was not included), international rules were officially adopted.[24] When the international games held in Chamonix, France, in 1924 proved successful (Swedes constructed the jump and Norwegians won the first three places), they were retrospectively called the First Winter Olympic Games, although these international meets had always been thought of as the Winter Olympics.[25]

By 1924 the United States' NSA was affiliated with a variety of home, foreign, and international sport associations, and the United States was one of sixteen member nations at the founding of the Fédération Internationale de Ski (FIS) which, in spite of its French title, was Norwegian dominated. Five of the six purposes of the FIS concerned the regulations governing skiing. The three that most directly affected standardization were:

> To create precise Rules for Ski Competitions and for hills and courses approved by the FIS.
> To approve only those international Ski Competitions which are organized according to the FIS rules and to see to it that the rules are observed during these competitions.
> To serve as last court of appeal for protests concerning International Ski Competitions.[26]

Norwegian rules went virtually unquestioned in the 1920s until those promoting the Alpine disciplines of downhill and slalom, especially the British in Mürren and Wengen, were strong enough to demand FIS recognition.[27] Even so, at the 1932 Olympic Games at Lake Placid, the Norwegians, dissatisfied with the take-off position of the jump, simply changed it. When American Dr. Godfrey Dewey, in his position as president of the "Head Committee" objected, the Norwegians paid no attention whatsoever![28]

One of the FIS goals was to create precise guides for the construction of jumping hills. When it became possible to judge jumpers on hills with the same contours whether they were in Sweden or Switzerland, it also became possible to understand why one man could jump farther than another. The enormous interest generated by air flight gave a boost to the aerodynamics of ski jumping. In 1926 a Swiss, Dr. Reinhard Straumann, published the results of his findings. These were available in English two years later.[29] The FIS rules and new aerodynamic jumping technique should have had the effect of standardizing the sport on an international level. But American jumpers and their sponsoring towns wanted nothing of it.

In America there were some general guidelines. Most of the knowledgeable would agree with Fred Harris, who in 1924 stated that jumps should not be south facing in the direct sun and should have as much protection from trees as possible. If a good jump was "an engineering problem" then an expert should be called in.[30] In America where spiky iron pilings of varying heights and contours rose into the sky as early as 1909, any good jumper was an expert. The jumps were ubiquitous. Looking at the early photographs one wonders how so many survived as long as they did. The Norries slide at Ironwood, 110 feet high, was constructed in 1922 and had a hill record of 182 feet until it was brought down by wind in 1930.[31]

In spite of all the NSA's efforts and in spite of the United States member-

The U.S. Olympic team for St. Moritz, 1928: Anders Haugen, Charley Proctor, and LaMoine Batson. Manager Godfrey Dewey was really there to secure the next Olympics for Lake Placid. On the right is Augustus T. Kirby of the American Olympic Committee. (New England Ski Museum, Franconia, N.H.)

ship in the FIS, there was no standardization of the size or contours of the hills. Even though regulations governing the actual jumping style and the characters assigned to various parts of the jump became more uniform on a national and international level, there was still plenty of leeway for subjective judgment throughout the 1920s.

Ski Manufacturing

Most of the nineteenth-century skis held in museum collections were made by men who, like a gentleman in Minneapolis in 1885, decided to start "a manufacturing establishment in the city . . . to make a desirable pattern of shoes [skis] in sufficient quantity to supply any future demand.[32] However, nothing is known of these early attempts to create a ski business until Mikkel Hemmetsveit moved to St. Croix Falls, Wisconsin, to form the Excelsior Ski Company—owned by the Hetting family. Skis were "all the go" by January 1888, and after that first successful season "50 A No. 1 Skis" were ready before the snow came the next winter. There was enough business to contract out the making of skis to Elmquist and Weinhardt who later set up on their own. When Mikkel Hemmetsveit was enticed to Red Wing, the Excelsior Company appears to have gone out of business.[33]

There were a number of other men who manufactured skis. In 1900 Aksel Holter obtained seven pairs of hickory skis from the Hagen factory in Norway and began producing similar models as "the celebrated Ashland ski, none better," the price ranging from fifty cents to seven dollars a pair. This was a small business, and the skis were sold locally in Ashland, Wisconsin, at Danson's, known for its books, candies, and nuts. Dopp and Watson's also carried Holter's line along with crumb trays, embroidery scissors, and pearl-handled knives. There was no such thing as a ski store in those days. Holter reached a wider clientele by advertising in *The Skisport* but after disagreements over the management of his factory, he "gave his business" to Martin Strand.[34]

Strand was the most successful of the early ski manufacturers because he catered to the vast majority of skiers who did not wish specialized and expensive equipment. He started his business in 1896 in a shack behind his house in Minneapolis, and he moved to New Richmond, Wisconsin, in 1911. That city enticed him with an offer of five years of rent-free buildings and free heat and light. Strand put up a fifteen-hundred-dollar bond and promised to employ twenty-five locals. The first batch of skis were bent by mid-summer and none too soon, as fifteen hundred pairs were on order.[35]

Most of the skis were made of Norway pine brought by railroad from South Bend, Indiana. The reporter from the local paper gave a run-down of the manufacturing process during the first week of operation. "Having shaped the raw lumber, the pieces are soaked and then steamed and bent, then placed in frames and racks and transferred to the drying room." After being sanded by machine, they were mortised and trimmed by hand. "Next the skis go to the varnish room where they are striped, given the first coat of shellac, and dipped in varnish, which is the last coat." A rubber footrest was put in place before the skis were stacked in the store room. They took up so much room after the straps were attached that these were put on just before shipping.[36]

The *New Richmond News* and the Industrial Club felt that the "well established business . . . with an exceedingly bright future . . . is going to do much . . . to advertise the city throughout the length and breadth of the land."[37] It was true. Strand was in business until the Second World War.

The history of the Strand factory cannot be followed in detail because the records have disappeared. However, the method of construction hardly changed in the first decade. In 1923, Lyman Johnson joined his uncle who had worked for Strand since 1914. Johnson worked in all areas of the manufacturing process. He recalled one job "matching jumpers for weight

One of four rare views of early ski manufacturing, taken in 1923 in Martin Strand's New Richmond, Wisconsin, plant. Skis are stored without bindings for ease of stacking. (Lyman Johnson, New Richmond, Wisc.)

and grain"; the two skis had to be within three ounces of each other. All sorts of wood were used: "edge-grain pine" from Georgia; hickory from Louisiana and Mississippi; maple from nearby Spring Valley, and, when that ran out (about 1930), maple and ash from Vermont. Louisiana magnolia was used to make cheaper skis. "It had a beautiful, greenish coat, like walnut 'sap stain.'" The cost of shipping the wood was sometimes greater than the cost of the lumber itself.

Johnson remembered that Strand went into the actual work areas infrequently, for the most part only when there was a special order from a name jumper or a request for a really fast pair of skis. Then Strand would look the wood over—straighter grain meant faster skis—and have four or five pairs specially made. He picked the best pairs to complete the order.[38]

Martin Strand employed one salesman, a Mr. Stoddard, who went all over the country. Stoddard was popular with the workers; he was interested in how the skis were made and offered suggestions, such as higher gloss finishes, that helped to sell the skis.[39]

The Strand factory had competition; Christian Lund, another Norwegian immigrant, founded the Northland Ski Company in St. Paul in

1911. But there was enough business for all. Jobbers like Marshall Wells of Duluth and others in the cities ordered as many as four thousand pairs of skis a season.[40]

In the east, the Theo. Johnsen Company of Portland, Maine, sensed the possibilities of a wealthy clientele and produced its finely made Tajco products, which it advertised in America's first ski sales catalog in 1905. Half of the catalog was devoted to instructing readers in "The Winter Sport of Skeeing." Top-of-the-line ten-foot skis sold for eighteen dollars, and skiers were advised to have three pairs to ensure good sport in all sorts of snow conditions. The company proved unprofitable and only marketed its skis for a season or two.[41] Martin Strand commented on the excellent quality of the Johnsen skis but knew why he was more successful than the Maine company. "The average young American is a sort of hot house plant," he wrote to a customer, "who does not wish to spend very much time out of doors." The majority spent their money on show houses and pool rooms rather than on good skis, he went on a little bitterly. He was successful because he had opted "to make skis in this country that the people will buy"—cheap skis.[42]

Early bindings had been simple pieces of leather tacked to the sides of the ski, but Strand cut a mortise in the wood for the leather strap to be slipped through before going over the boot. The more sophisticated binding, often imported from Norway, included a heel strap with assorted buckles and clips which held the foot on the ski while allowing the heel to be raised. There were many local variations.[43] This simple and cheap binding was common into the 1920s.

The ski pole shows various cultural influences. Partly because Norwegians used either no poles at all or, more usually, one strong staff, in America a single pole was used only as a balance or braking device, although many felt even this "pole riding should be tabooed" because of its gracelessness.[44] Of course, beginners might use the pole "as a third leg to stand on" but it was thought better to avoid using it as much as possible.[45]

The use of two poles appears to have originated in Finland.[46] The stigma attached by the Norwegians to needing two poles caused one Dartmouth undergraduate in 1912 to try out his new pair at dusk so no one would see him.[47] But even in the early 1920s, Dartmouth's first ski coach approved the use of one pole and encouraged the use of two.[48] It was one of the important issues for college skiers in the 1920s, Betty Whitney remembered from her Smith College days.[49] Drawings and advertisements in popular magazines continued to show the use of one pole until 1934.[50]

Until about 1910 most skiers used their normal winter footwear as a ski boot. The knowledgeable immigrant skier, however, was concerned about special boots. The Aurora Club debated whether to use "high or low overshoes." Both were a moccasin type of oiled shoes that offered extra play in the ankles to accommodate the thick socks that were essential.[51] The Johnsen Company sold a special Norwegian-made boot for twelve dollars.[52] American manufacturers competed for a lower scale market with "shoe-pacs . . . of oiled cowhide." Chippewa took out a full page advertisement in the 1909–10 *Skisport* for a $5.50 pair of ski boots, but there was little to distinguish them from work boots. Bass began marketing ski boots in 1912.[53]

Socks and stockings were important for warmth and also as a way of displaying club colors. Leggins—thick toeless stockings of a loden material—were popular with some groups. Toques—hats—were available in different wools and worsteds.[54]

This emerging equipment industry was run by immigrants who saw possibilities of diversification from their established line of manufacture or found enough of a market to warrant continued production of skis; Wold's, a piano maker, supplied skis to U.S. troops patrolling Yellowstone, and Strand switched to paddle and oar manufacturing for summer business.[55] Only the Theo. Johnsen Company made an effort to expand the base of its clientele, and their success was short-lived.[56] The problem was keeping up with the demand from recreational enthusiasts. As jumping became increasingly a sport for experts, most skiers left it to the star performers. All manufacturers made jumping skis and advertised the successes a particular performer had obtained on their model. However, most skis were sold for recreational use and, as Martin Strand wrote, he made skis to public demand, rather than trying to market high-quality models.

Although the NSA was the organizing and controlling body of American skisport, it found itself increasingly unable to enforce its view—rooted in the Norse tradition of *Idraet*—of the way skiing was meant to be. As immigrant communities became more American, and as more people took up skiing who were not steeped in the *Idraet* ideal, the NSA was plagued by the ethos of achievement measured in terms of length of jump and amount of prize money. Moreover, it was faced with the difficulty of enforcing regulations nationally. It would be wealthy easterners who would give a new direction to American skiing as a social sport.

6 / *The New Enthusiasts*

If you love the great out-of-doors, and if you like to live,
really live, in the clean, wide distant sweep of a limitless
horizon, breathe an untainted air, boundless as the heavens
themselves and enjoy a freedom that can be found in no
other way, a keen, stimulating, exhilarating pleasure that
thrills you through the very center of your being, you will
understand what motives led to the organization of the
Dartmouth Outing Club.

—*The Skisport* (1911–12)

I am quite convinced in my own mind of the desirability of
getting the Williams men more out in the mountains and of
having them participate more largely in such healthful outdoor activities. The only question is how to bring this
about. If your experiences in the White Mountains and
among the Dartmouth students would throw any light on
this question, I should very much appreciate your writing
me on the conclusions which you reached.

—Ford B. Sayre, assistant to the president, Williams
College, Williamstown, Mass., to J. S. Apperson
of Schenectady, N.Y., 1914

W hile the National Ski Association was having its trials controlling the
skisport, people who used skis solely for recreation were giving a major new
thrust to skiing. These were men whose social milieu was the almost totally
non-Norse environment of the well-to-do club and college. The Norwegian winter culture of skiing was the guide, it is true, simply because
there was no other. These wealthy skiers were looking for sociable yet
manly recreation. New York and New England furnished the physical
playground where the change first took place. California and the Rockies
held promise for the future.

The Educated Sportsmen

Dartmouth College is usually given the credit for founding America's first
outing club, in 1909. This is not strictly true, but although other colleges
had established something similar before this date—St. Olaf's in Minnesota in 1888, the Michigan School of Mines in 1904, and Plymouth

Normal School in New Hampshire in 1907—it was Dartmouth that provided the collegiate leadership for other colleges to follow.[1]

Fred H. Harris acted upon the recommendations of an energetic master at Vermont Academy, a nearby preparatory school, whose scheme "to get the boys going" included short ski races, ski jumps, a cross-country event, and a winter expedition.[2] These were exactly what Harris incorporated into his suggestions for the Dartmouth Outing Club. In December 1909 he proposed to the college community that a ski and snowshoe club be formed.

1. To stimulate interest in out of door winter sports.

2. To have short cross-country runs weekly and one long excursion each session, say to Mooselac [a Dartmouth-owned mountain].

3. To build a ski jump and hold ski jumping contests.

4. To hold a meet on a field day during February at which a program of events similar to the following may be contested: 100 yard dash on snowshoes, cross-country run on snowshoes, obstacle race on snowshoes, 100 yard dash on skis, cross-country run on skis, ski jumping contest and other events that may be suggested. . . . Dartmouth might well become the originator of a branch of college organized sport hitherto undeveloped by American colleges.[3]

Harris had been impressed by the Montreal winter carnival; he knew of the "big ski jump contests" in the Northwest and had contemplated some sort of club for Dartmouth for over a year. Although there was some initial interest in December 1909, there was also much scoffing at the suggestion, and Harris can hardly have been encouraged by the skiing expertise of those who by 1911 had begun to show some interest. A note in his scrapbook reveals ten names, and by each is a comment: "good nerve," "an old snowshoer," "just took it up," "thinks he would like it." With some there was more hope: "jumps well," "makes good telemarks."[4] That winter there was enough intramural competition to hold a carnival.

Dartmouth College, located in northern New England on the Connecticut River, bordered by rolling farmland yet hard by the forested granite mountains of New Hampshire, provided just that outdoor setting that appealed to the educated youth of the post–1890 generation. Here the first collegiate endeavor was launched to put the skisport into an organized framework; Harris even used the term "organized sport" in his proposal. He combined the virility of the college men with the spaciousness of New

Frank Merriwell, the up-and-coming Yalie, in yet-another desperate adventure, this time on skis. Dartmouth, not Yale, was the focus of collegiate skiing from 1910 on. (New England Ski Museum, Franconia, N.H.)

England woods and mountains when he invited the Dartmouth community "to take the splendid opportunities afforded by our college." Those opportunities may be best followed in his diary. In December 1910, for example, Harris and his friends took a train to Pompanoosuc, a half-dozen miles north of Hanover. They returned to the college by ski and snowshoe. "Found 3 good slides. Stopped by the side of a pond and cooked some coffee and bacon with doughnuts. Got in before the snowshoe men even though we took several slides twice."[5]

The next weekend Harris made "a dandy trip. Cooked quantities of beefsteak for supper. Dandy skiing by moonlight. Slept in a farm house." And then he had the adventure of climbing on Mount Washington, the highest peak in the eastern United States: "Started up the mountain about 10. Got to the Half Way House a half hour ahead of the snowshoe men. Went on up the mountain. Had to take skiis off in places. Men that had my bag of food turned back. I slipped once and only a bush saved me from death. Watts came along with picaroon and helped me. Finally got so hungry we decided to turn around. Had feed at Half Way House. Made 4 mile slide down mountain in 14 minutes without stopping."[6]

This had the derring-do that romantic tales are made of; here was civilization washed clear away; here was moral fiber proved by physical effort; it is as if virility and character went hand-in-hand as man met nature in the great outdoors, and like-minded souls communed over the day's adventure.

Harris's 1920 article about the Dartmouth Outing Club in *National Geographic* was illustrated and aptly captioned. "Coming through the woods without caps or shirts" showed a half-dozen students on a trail. "Not only has the Outing Club improved the physical well being of Dartmouth's student body, but faculty statistics show that scholarship has profited by the weekend excursions of skiing parties." *Mens sana in corpore sano.* The trail was portrayed as "a skyway leading through grandeurs of winter scenery wholly unknown to those who nestle beside steam radiators." It meandered "to seek solitude in the solemnity of Nature's cathedral trees." Freshmen applications for admission rose over 300 percent from 824 to 2,625.[7]

The Dartmouth Winter Carnival, the "Mardi Gras of the North," whose crowning event was the ski-jumping contest ("what the chariot race of the Olympic games was to the ancients"), provided one-third of the illustrations for the article.[8] The ski jump had always held a fascination for Harris, and he chose a drawing of a ski jumper in action for the frontispiece of one of the earliest books on American skiing, which he edited in 1913.[9]

At Dartmouth the jump received annual attention. Outing Club members increased the height and constructed a permanent scaffold, learning their technique from hints picked up from *The Skisport* but mostly by experiment. In 1916 Gustav Paulsen, Nansen Club member from neighboring Berlin, New Hampshire, was secured as the major carnival attraction.[10] The somersault, accorded a two-page photographic spread in Harris's article, supplied "the thousands of spectators [with] a topic of conversation for months." Even though Paulsen was not a polished technician, he taught John Carleton, who was later to be on the 1924 Olympic team, the new dare-devil trick. Carleton, "Ace of the Carnival," thrilled the crowd, who marveled at his looping the loop with his body as the machine in the air.[11]

Dartmouth men had a captive audience for the jump at carnival time, but the jump appealed to others in the East and brought spectators out in the thousands: three thousand in Brattleboro, Vermont, in 1922, and six thousand at Tarrytown, New York, in 1924. The Nansen Club attracted similarly large crowds after it built its new jump in 1921.[12] Some of the spectators came to see the big names who were advertised along with "ski artists" from Montreal and "Four Clever Ski Jumpers" from Chicago. Spills could be expected, the more heroic the better. Dartmouth "ace" John Carleton broke his arm in practice the day before a meet, but still managed to place second in the competition.[13] At Briarcliff, New York, Johannes Anderson fell and was knocked unconscious for ten minutes. His head was bandaged, but he made three more leaps and on the last one lost several teeth in another fall.[14] This cavalier disregard for safety was thought to prove the moral quality of the man as well as provide the usual voyeuristic titillations of all dangerous sports. Safety had not been an issue in the Nordic world because there were no accidents in cross-country running. "Descendants of Vikings" who indulged in "sky jumping" accepted the risks willingly.

These spectacular performances were publicized locally and nationally, and Dartmouth's outing club idea flourished in the liberal arts colleges of New England: Williams, Middlebury, Harvard (which already had a mountaineering club), and Yale. The state universities of Vermont and New Hampshire were quick to take up the idea. There is little record of skiing at women's colleges (Smith, Vassar, Wellesley, and the like) before the 1920s. The immediate interest skiing created in the men's colleges made skiing in the East a middle-class organized leisure activity. The inequalities in the ethnic-centered *Idraet* were replaced by inequalities associated with wealth. College students spent their leisure time learning how to ski. In a society in which time was money, skiing for pleasure in the East became an activity for only the well-to-do.

ENJOY WINTER—
BUT PROTECT YOUR SKIN

With a little precaution the keen exhilaration and joy from the winter outdoors need not be lessened by chapped face, lips or hands.

First, avoid the use of harsh, caustic soaps. They dry the skin and promote roughness and chapping. RESINOL SOAP contains only the purest, soothing ingredients which protect the skin while cleansing it. The rich lather works right into the pores keeping the skin soft and healthy, and helping it to retain its natural radiance.

The next step in safeguarding the complexion is to rinse off the lather thoroughly, then dry the face with care as nothing is more conducive to red, chapped skin than to leave it damp.

When used as directed Resinol Soap rarely fails to bring the complexion unharmed through winter's cold. Ask for it at your druggist's or favorite toilet goods dealer's today. They both sell it. A 25c. cake will last long enough to show you the value of your investment.

Trial on request. Dept. 1-E,
Resinol, Baltimore, Md.

Resinol Soap

In the post–World War I years, advertisers began using women to portray the social attractions and health benefits that could be derived from skiing and their product (1921). (New England Ski Museum, Franconia, N.H.)

The Clubs

Wealthy sports enthusiasts were not necessarily all in college. Many graduates were already involved in outdoor clubs. Three of the most prestigious organizations were among the first to indicate an interest in recreational skiing. Two of them—Boston's Appalachian Mountain Club (AMC) and San Francisco's Sierra Club—had a mountaineering-hiking orientation. The third was something quite different. Discriminatory and geared to wealth, the Lake Placid Club in the Adirondacks of upstate New York was a resort.

The AMC had already included a "skeeist" or two in expeditions in the 1880s and 1890s, and members began taking winter trips to the White and Green mountains of New England, staying at some of the few hotels that remained open in the winter.[15] At the Eagle Mountain House in Jackson, New Hampshire, they found a hostelry with "a decidedly Norwegian flavor and a pair of skees which gave the front snowbank a superior look." Some members decided to try the "skees."

> We did not have the leisure to master these foreign shoes, nor was there anyone hardly familiar with their use, to instruct us; but we did experiment enough to learn that there is a great deal of fun to be had with them, while they afford ample opportunity to study the principles of mathematics and physics. When the skees mark out for themselves divergent tracks, and are permitted to follow their divided purposes, the resultant force is always in the vertical and downward. When this fact has been proven experimentally, the skees, freed from their limiting tendencies, skim like birds over the snow to the lowest possible level each after its own fancy, forming in a twinkling an isosceles with the late passenger at the apex. What to do under these circumstances is a problem. At Jackson there was usually the choice of waddling in the deep snow, rolling on the light crust, going around by a road or having someone on snowshoes assemble the separated elements. The latter course is not easy for the skee-er; and one afternoon I performed missionary work . . . in getting the skeeman and the skees together after their periods of dissipation, so to speak.
>
> On rises there are places where the shoes barely hold, where to move forward is to invite a slip backward, to the point of beginning, and to turn is not easy.
>
> At Jackson the feat of feats was to skee down the toboggan slide. Our skeeman tackled the chute early in the trip, and after three or four trials had mastered it. To him afterwards the toboggan seemed a tame affair.[16]

Lack of expertise mattered not one whit for this AMC party; what did count was the camaraderie of intellectual outdoorsmen, together in the snows of northern New England.

Delineator (1927). (New England Ski Museum, Franconia, N.H.)

Sensing winter business, hotels like the Woodstock Inn, in Woodstock, Vermont, supplied skis for guests but snowshoeing was more popular until a visiting Englishman showed guests how much enjoyment was to be had on skis.[17] Peckett's on Sugar Hill, New Hampshire, was as busy in February 1911 as it was in any August with parties from Providence and Boston bringing their winter gear, including skis, to enjoy "one long gladsome period," as the local paper thrilled to the economic prospects created by winter tourism.[18]

The Lake Placid Club, tucked away in the Adirondacks of New York, combined the exclusiveness of gentile wealth with the fun and frolics of social skiing. The club remained open in winter for the first time in 1904 for ten members who had a choice of forty skis and poles which had been ordered from Norway. Two years later the club had winter space for fourteen hundred members. Melvil Dewey, known for his three enthusiasms—his library decimal system, his simplified speech, and his antisemitism—ran the club autocratically. The club's winter success says much about wealthy America. The Lake Placid Club pioneered the winter sports center, and Dewey liked to believe that he emancipated "thousands from the radiator"—patrician thousands perhaps.[19]

Three thousand miles away in California, the Sierra Club made its interest in skiing known by reprinting John Muir's account of his enjoyments above Lake Tahoe.[20] In 1915 the club's *Bulletin* ran two articles. One gave an impressionistic description of skiing and followed it up with a full-fledged account of Lake Tahoe in winter, "an ideal resort for the red blooded; for the Viking and near Viking." Sierra Club members were attracted to skiing because it tested physical ability and mental agility, and it provided fun. Carnival time in the area included sleighing and skating, but ski racing and jumping were promised to be the most exciting.[21]

Tahoe became a favored place because it was on a railline. It offered skiers marvelous vistas, crisp air, and exciting opportunities—just the right attractions for middle-class vacationers who spent their lives in San Francisco offices. They encountered trappers and railroad workers on the traditional "California snow-shoes" of the mining era. Postal carriers, too, skied their mail routes to out-of-the-way communities on the old long boards of nine and ten feet.[22] These hardy local folk may have ridiculed the fancy outfits and short skis of the recreationists, but the new skier who came to the mountains for sport was the harbinger of the future.

So, too, in Colorado. In the Rocky Mountain gold-and-silver era, men had taken to racing in much the same way as they had in California. There was even an incipient race circuit, but that aspect of the sport never engendered the enthusiasm it had inspired among the Sierra mining camps.[23] What seems to have taken its place was an emphasis on recreation on skis.

Norwegians inspired this leisure activity. Karl Hovelsen, whom we last met as a captain thrilling the circus crowds in Madison Square Garden, moved to Hot Sulphur Springs and began to draw enthusiasts to his sport. Between 1912 and 1920, the year Denver obtained the national tournament, ski clubs were formed in many parts of Colorado. Although Scandinavian immigrants gave most of the clubs their impetus, less attention was paid to old-world *Idraet* than was the case in the Northwest because the numbers of Norwegians and others brought up in that tradition were small.[24]

Members of clubs looked to skiing for companionship and enjoyment. "An overland skiing party was made up in town [Hot Sulphur Springs] on Wednesday morning: C. Hovelsen, A. Schmidt, John Peyer, Mrs. H. B. Fuller and Miss Pansy Perry. The tour included a distance of 10 or 12 miles among the timbered hills southwest of town. A delightful time was had."[25]

George Cramer, pioneer in the development of Denver's city parks, watched Hovelsen ski and then tried it himself before joining the Colorado Mountain Club on its 1917 expedition to Fern Lake in Estes Park. Some members were on snowshoes, others on skis, including Herman Buhl whose speed was admired but whose ability to turn was "an unheard of feat."[26] Near Leadville, a group of engineers and their wives, led by one of Thomas Edison's assistants who had spent two years in Norway, formed the Silver Plume Ski Club in 1914. Members enjoyed skiing and put on their own little tournament.[27]

Essentially social in nature, this club skiing provided ludic enjoyment for middle-class people. Colorado had all the ingredients needed to furnish recreational skiers with a virtual paradise, but it was record-breaking jumping that brought the state notoriety. A Hovelsen-built jump at Steamboat Springs brought record-seeking jumpers from the Northwest. Thirty thousand turned out to see the first jumping competition on the Genesee slide just outside Denver. Over in Dillon, a lone Norwegian, Peter Prestrud, founded the Summit County Winter Sports Association and built a jump to rival the one at Steamboat.[28]

These jumps and the annual arrival of skiers such as Ragnar Omtvedt and Lars Haugen forced the National Ski Association to recognize that jumping was important in other places than the Northwest. When Anders Haugen and Henry Hall were flying over two hundred feet on these Colorado jumps, the NSA had to admit that Denver might be the spot to hold the national championships in 1920, the first time it was ever held outside the Northwest. That year President G. C. Torguson acknowledged that "the Rockies will become the center of skiing in the United States."[29] It was quite an admission.

As more Americans took to skiing and to watching ski jumping, as clubs promoted the sport for honor and money, as the NSA struggled to inspire and control the sport, the *Idraet* ideal upon which the whole sport was founded was undermined by forces available in the nontraditional society of industrial America. While *Idraet* lost much of its goodliness and godliness in the Northwest, it remained the basis for the sport in California, Colorado, and New England. Particularly in the Northeast, however, the processes of modernization were combined with factors unusual and unknown in the Northwest: new clientele, new technique, new ambience. In New England, with wealthy Bostonians playing a major role, skiing was to change from a premodern sport exhibiting many facets of modernization, to one dominated by technology, technique, and speed.

THE MECHANIZATION OF SKIING, 1920–1940

7 / Post–World War I: Prelude to Skiing

At the National meeting in Chicago on 4 December 1932 Downhill and Slalom racing was first adopted as a competitive phase of the sport. Even then it was not thought of as of equal importance to the classic events of skiing—jumping and cross-country.

—Roger Langley, NSA secretary

After the Great War, many in the United States enjoyed a decade of relaxation. Much of the increased money available was spent by the urban population on leisure activity out-of-doors, whether watching baseball or enjoying the beach. Automobiles and trains enabled people to go quickly from city to countryside. The war had brought an intensity to the lives of the soldiers who went abroad in the great adventure. People who remained behind enjoyed the excitement vicariously through letters, papers, magazines, and films. In winter this vitality seems to have drawn great numbers of the wealthier sectors of society to the "hair-shirt sport" of skiing.

For a time the skisport was perceived in its *Idraet* ideal, but in the mid-1920s there were notable changes at all levels. The skisport's governing body, the NSA, which had set standards and been in charge for twenty years, was pressured into a divisional structure by the increasingly strong United States Eastern Amateur Ski Association, always known as Eastern. At the same time the NSA—with all its midwestern traditions—was the only recreational body speaking on behalf of winter recreation to a blue-ribbon government conference on the outdoors. The NSA thought in terms of club tramps, but urban skiers from Boston, New York, and San Francisco thought in terms of trail development. Later these city dwellers would become addicted to speed.

The NSA also sponsored a team at the 1924 Olympic Games which easterners had much to complain about. The greatest challenges, although not immediately seen as such, were the new ways of skiing that were being imported from the European Alps. Called "Downhill" and "Slalom" they were first attempted at Dartmouth College, already a force in Eastern.

Clubs in New England initiated ski instruction, widened hiking trails for ski trips, and organized trains for ski excursions. These developments were responsible for the major changes in the following decade, and the locus of activity shifted from the Midwest to New England and New York.

Challenges to the Skisport

Oscar Oyass, president of the NSA, had much to be proud of when he assessed the 1924 and 1925 seasons: his organization had joined the American Athletic Union and the Fédération Internationale de Ski (FIS), thus raising its status at home and abroad. The NSA sent a team to the 1924 Olympic Games in Chamonix, France, thanks in some measure to the Minneapolis Ski Club which hoped that by fielding a team it would thereby become the American venue for a future Olympics.[1] Oyass appeared particularly pleased that the 1924 national championships had been held in Vermont, for it signified the nationwide interest in the skisport. (Fifteen hundred people attended the ball that concluded the event!) Gustave Lindboe represented the NSA at the National Congress of Outdoor Recreation. "It will thus be seen," Oyass concluded, that the NSA "has become an acknowledged organization . . . not only on this continent but in the entire world."[2]

In reality, the NSA was in trouble. During the Great War, membership in the NSA declined, but by 1921 it was up again to twenty-three clubs, geographically spread from New England in the east to Colorado in the west. The problems of managing a larger number of clubs, increasingly dispersed, created the need for regional associations. New England was the first to found one, in 1922, the Rockies followed in 1923, northern Minnesota in 1925, the Midwest in 1927, and California and the Northwest in 1930.[3] The United States Eastern Amateur Ski Association was founded with seven clubs in 1922 and had twenty-eight two years later.[4] Demanding a divisional structure, Eastern formed the most powerful region and secured control of the NSA with the election of Fred Harris as treasurer in 1929 and Dr. R. S. Elmer as president in 1930.[5]

The analysis of *The Skisport* in Part 1 shows clearly that the journal had played an important role in controlling the sport. The NSA published it for the last time in 1925. In 1928 and again in 1929 Eastern published it alone. When Elmer became president, the journal was still billed as a national yearbook but by then Eastern dominated it. Of seventeen major articles, eleven concerned Eastern matters, three were on California, and only two were about the Midwest. Significantly, there was also an article by Arnold Lunn, an Englishman who was totally unknown in the Midwest but was already a mentor to a number of eastern skiers.

By 1930 the control of organized skiing had passed from the Midwest to New England, both nationally and internationally at the Olympic Games. Staging Winter Olympics had been discussed as early as 1908 and had actually been planned for 1916, but World War I interfered.[6] Holland, where the 1920 Games were staged, was too flat for skiing, so it was not until 1924 at Chamonix in the Haute Savoie region of France that the first winter festival took place, retrospectively called the First Winter Olympic Games.[7]

The NSA had great difficulty in choosing a team, partially because the best prospects had become professionals and, although they had "returned" to amateur status, they had not done so within the stipulated time.[8] It was feared that the eligibility of most of the jumpers would be questioned, but those who knew themselves to be the best were simply determined to go to France no matter what. One-time professional Hans Hansen left Minneapolis to catch the boat for Europe and Anders Haugen, the best jumper, persuaded himself and presumably the NSA that once the International Olympic Committee (IOC) saw his record, they would permit him to compete. With one exception, John Carleton, all members of the United States team were Scandinavian immigrants. Carleton—a well-known Dartmouth College star—appears to have been chosen because he was at Oxford University as a Rhodes scholar and was already in training at Chamonix. He was also appointed coach of the team.

Although forming a team in this manner runs counter to our modern sense of order and fairness, it hardly raised an eyebrow at the time. Besides, the U.S. team presented no challenge in the cross-country events. None of the members was entered in the marathon, and Norwegians won the first four places as expected.[9] The jumping, however, was a different affair, and "affair" is the right word.

Anders Haugen led the field with a 50 meter jump. Following him were two Norwegians, Thams and Bonna, with 49 meters each, and Thorleif Haug, another Norwegian, with 44½ meters. But distance was not the only consideration; the point system reflected style as well. Thams won with 18.96 points. Bonna had 18.68, and Haug, 18.00. In spite of Haugen's distance, he was judged extremely harshly, which, along with some dubious mathematics, brought his total points to 17.91. The so-called manager of the U.S. team lodged no protest because he was told by the Czech judge (the other two were Norwegian and French) that Haugen's style and form were much inferior to the three Norwegians ahead of him. Even reporters could tell that "he threw all style aside and bent all efforts only on distance." A disinterested Englishman observed that "the American . . . jumped with fierce determination that was admirable, but his style was atrocious."[10] Patently the Norwegian ideals still guarded the purity of the sport.

There is a twist to this story. Almost immediately it was suspected that Haugen had not been merely misjudged, but that the calculations were incorrect. "Skiers and critics have come to the conclusion," editorialized *The Skisport* that "Anders should have been awarded 2nd place according to official score cards," but nothing was done. At the Winter Olympics' fiftieth anniversary celebration in Oslo in 1974, the scoring had been recomputed to show that Haugen had in fact gained third place. In a nice gesture, the eighty-six-year-old Haugen received the bronze medal that Haug had been awarded in 1924—rightfully his by 0.095 of a point. At the First Winter Olympics, the spirit of *Idraet* damned atrocious style. Fifty years later figures proved one man better by less than one-one hundredth of a point![11]

When the U.S. team returned home, a number of jumpers competed at Brattleboro, Vermont. Haugen failed to place, and other team members jumped only to seventh and twelfth places.[12] It seemed that something was very wrong, and when the leadership of Eastern discovered that the manager of the team had seen his men only four times while they were in Europe and had scarcely visited Ragnar Omtvedt after he had broken his leg, they determined to have more of a say in future American participation in international competitions.[13]

After their earlier failure, the NSA showed little interest in organizing a team for the next Olympics in St. Moritz, Switzerland. Eastern's executives received no reply from the NSA about assembling a team or about funds to support Olympic participation. Godfrey Dewey, son of the Lake Placid autocrat, arranged to act as manager of America's team when one was chosen. His real purpose, though, was to go to Europe to gauge whether the Lake Placid Club could stage the Games in 1932.[14]

It is not clear how the American team was actually selected. Henry I. Baldwin, one member of the selection committee, has no recollection of it at all.[15] Charley Proctor remembers that "they hunted around and found some people who were available and asked me to go." Training, such as it was, took place on the boat going over. The team had been given cloth for its outfits which were made up by a St. Moritz tailor after they arrived.[16] The Lake Placid Club simply chose Rolf Monson, its own favorite, and as a bow to the Midwest and a recognition of his past experience, Anders Haugen was named to the team.[17]

When Dewey arrived in Switzerland, he paid two years worth of back dues to the IOC so that the team could compete.[18] The Games were hardly a success and they were made difficult by appalling weather. The U.S. team had no entries for the marathon and finished in the last three places in the eighteen-kilometer event. In the jump, Monson's sixth and Proctor's fourteenth were impressive placings. The veteran Haugen leaped to eighteenth.

There were many difficulties at St. Moritz: the Norwegians almost refused to attend, partially on account of the expense, but also probably because they believed the Swiss to be incapable of running such a ski gathering properly. Their jumpers only competed after the judges had changed the positioning of the take-off to suit their wishes. The English complained that their downhill and slalom races were given scant consideration. Many found the expense too high.[19] As a result of all this discontent, the future of the Winter Games seemed in doubt.

The pessimists underestimated the determination of Godfrey Dewey to bring the Games to the Lake Placid Club. He reported to the interested local and national public—using the phonetic spelling advocated by his father—that "if the establisht precedent brings the Olympic winter games to the United States in 1932, they can be held here in a manner fully equaling or surpassing the high standards which have been set abroad." He lauded Lake Placid's excellent terrain and winter climate, the availability of a jump, skating rinks, cross-country courses, and the club's experience in organizing big meets. "We need offer no apologies to the best European resorts." The only thing missing was a bob-sled run, and there was money available for construction.[20]

Charley Proctor, a competitor, saw it all in a different light. "I don't see how either country [U.S. or Canada]," he wrote home, "can expect to get the Olympic winter sports. . . . It is absolutely impractical. The countries over here have all they can do to finance teams only going a few miles. And then again as a Swiss . . . told me yesterday, it is impossible from the standpoint of time. He says they can't leave their jobs for the length of time for training in the United States without automatically losing them. . . . They all would love to come and think it would be fine for the sport but they just say, 'Impossible, how can we?'"[21]

The groundwork laid by Godfrey Dewey in 1928 was responsible for securing the Winter Games for Lake Placid, or more exactly put—and a point of contention—for the Lake Placid Club. The Californians had expected to act as host to the Winter Games; they had, after all, been granted the summer festival and they had charts to show that snow conditions could not be better. But the skisport had languished in the Sierra; there was not even a basic ski organization in the state whose publicity had promoted only its sunshine image.[22] The Lake Placid Club, however, could boast of continuous ski activity since 1905, a tradition of jumping meets since 1917, and of cross-country racing since 1920. Its collegiate week drew international competition. With financial support on local and state levels, the IOC awarded the Games to the club.

Only sixteen countries sent teams to the Adirondacks, which had so little

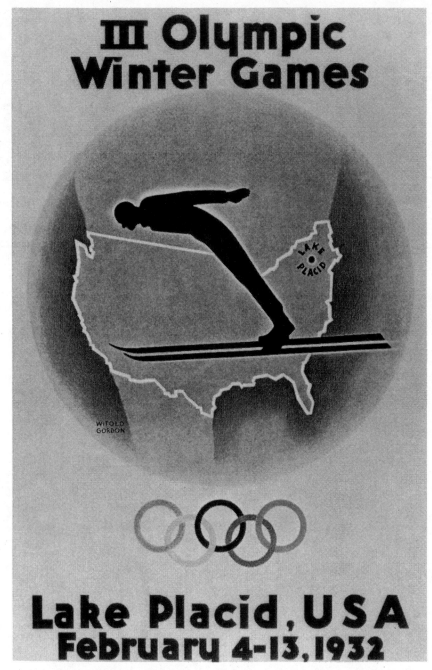

The Olympic Games of 1932 were the end of an era. They were the last to have only Nordic events and the last in which there were no women's ski competitions. Contrary to popular belief, the Olympics did not spark the 1930s skiing boom. (New England Ski Museum, Franconia, N.H.)

snow for training that the Swedes went to the Laurentians and the Norwegians to Chicago, much to the annoyance of the Lake Placid organizers. Once the Games did get under way, there were requests to have them moved entirely. The Lake Placid Club was not responsible for the weather, and members tried to make the sports a success, which meant hauling snow onto a twenty-five-kilometer track which the skiers circled twice in order to cover the appropriate marathon distance. When the take-off of the jump did not suit the Norwegians, they simply changed it. Dewey protested vigorously but the technical committee—Norwegian dominated—allowed the change because it would permit safe and spectacular leaps. There were arguments over having a professional in charge of tramping the snow in the outrun; over the height from which contestants should start their jump; where spectators were permitted, and so on.[23]

The FIS published a stinging censure. While admitting that the weather added to the difficulties, chairman of the Technical Committee, Norwegian Ingvald Smith-Kielland (who chaired the Grand Jury and held a seat on the Jury of Appeal) concluded that "too big burdens were undoubtedly laid on a few men's shoulders and these did not manage to perform all that was up to them. They also lacked skilled helpers possessing knowledge and initiative. . . . The arrangements of the skiing contest . . . must be termed unsatisfactory. This is in the first place due to the fact that management was not entrusted to skiing experts, but placed in the hands of people who also had to make arrangements for contests in other branches of sport."[24]

If some believed that Lake Placid and its club gained some benefits from the 1932 Olympics, most did not see beyond the costs. New York state taxpayers were assessed for about $600,000, the town of Elba contributed $230,000. Expenses totaled over $1 million and gate receipts only brought in $93,415. About eighty thousand spectators had watched 364 competitors.[25]

From a skier's point of view the Games were simply not very exciting and made less so by the lack of snow. Only two of America's 103 points came from Caspar Oimen's fifth place in the jump. Skiers did not write much about the Games; there was no ski annual between 1931 and 1934. Men who recall the 1932 Olympics tend to dismiss them as ineffective in the promotion of the skisport. If the *New York Times* is a guide, the number of articles on skiing actually decreased during the Olympic year. Although the Games failed to promote skiing, one could not tell this from listening to the interested parties or by reading the popular press. But in spite of radio coverage, the presence of numerous journalists, the use of posters, and the issue of fifty million commemorative stamps, skiers seemed uninspired. Comments that American athletes "perfecting their performance year by year . . . turned back the challenge in winter competitions" were simply not true where skiing was concerned.[26]

There were other matters: this international festival of the skisport was managed by a private club headed by a librarian! In spite of all the effort, the club was not up to it. Money, a fast pace, a questioning of the traditional skiing technique, and even a new ski language threatened Norwegian dominion of the ski world. The 1932 Games were the last to hold only Nordic events. They were the last in which women were excluded from skiing events. In the Adirondacks of New York, it was becoming difficult to find the *Idraet* of the skisport. .

The Challenge of Skiing to the Skisport

Those with leisure time and the inclination to spend winter out of doors created a new social form of *Ski-Idraet*. As long as the Norse quality of ski enjoyment prevailed, the educated and professional urban groups happily entertained the notion of athletic health and play in the winter snows.

In the postwar period, however, a new skiing technique found favor in the Alps of Europe. It appealed to those wealthy enough to travel to Switzerland and Austria to experience the heady lure of the thrill of speed. The worldwide acceptance of "downhill" and "slalom," as Alpine skiing was called, was largely the work of Hannes Schneider of Austria and Arnold Lunn of Great Britain. To understand their prevailing influence on American ski development, a brief analysis of their contributions is necessary.

Hannes Schneider began skiing just at the time when controversies about ski techniques received notice in the European ski press. Norwegian telemarks were being replaced by "stem turns" in parts of the Alps. Schneider learned the stem in 1904. By 1907 he was hired as a ski instructor for a hotel in St. Anton am Arlberg. Three years later he had so many students that he divided them into three groups of different abilities and hired assistants to help with the instruction. He had convinced himself and others that a radically different method of controlling skis was more suitable for the steeper terrain of the Alps than the upright Norwegian telemark. The Arlberg crouch symbolized the new style of skiing. But because of Schneider's discipline in teaching and his dividing students into classes, the Arlberg—as it came to be called—also constituted a method of teaching. When the Austrian Kaiserjägers took to skis in the First World War, some did so under Schneider's guidance. When the war was over, Schneider used the principles of his ski technique and those of his teaching method with the wealthy skiers who came in increasing numbers to St. Anton to learn from the master himself.[27] By 1921 there were already

The Arlberg crouch arrived in America around 1930. British artist Adrian Allison, well known in Mürren circles, captured the flavor of Arlberg speed for Americans on this 1934 cover of the United States Eastern Amateur Association *Annual*.
(New England Ski Museum, Franconia, N.H.)

voices raised against "the canonization of Hannes Schneider"—a reaction to the awe in which he was held.[28] Perhaps the worldwide decline of the telemark turn began with Schneider's most popular film and book, *Wunder des Schneeschuhs*. Other films, *The Ski Chase* and *Ski Rhythm* only added to his mystique, a mystique that worked annually on three thousand students, including royalty and some titled heads of Europe.

It is hard to believe that Arlberg instruction was very pleasant. If one lifted a leg on a stem turn the instructor "will dash after you and beat you on the lifted leg with his stick."[29] There was no getting out of line either. One interested spectator remarked on the "admirable organization of the scheme of instruction" as "groups numbered from 7 upwards 'parade' by their instructors daily at 10 a.m. and 2 p.m. At noon and 4 p.m. they return, teacher leading the way, to the place of assembly. One almost expects to hear a bugle call." Then the groups were subdivided and those who had progressed sufficiently were rewarded with a promotion to a higher group.[30]

Students kept coming and the Arlberg method spread, first to other ski centers in the Alps, then to North America, and then to Japan where Schneider lectured through an interpreter and received a sword, a kimono, and ten thousand yen![31]

When Nathaniel Goodrich, Dartmouth's librarian, spent a ski vacation with the British in Mürren, Switzerland, in 1928, he could not resist a trip to St. Anton where he "had a glimpse of Hannes Schneider." AMC member Wilhelmine Wright was a wealthy vacationer who spent two months in Kitzbühl where the Arlberg was in full force. "Anyone caught doing a telemark is considered a criminal," she reported. Her article in *Appalachia* described the instructional regimen: first year—stem turn; second year— Christiania turn started. After five years, she was told, she might ski reasonably well.[32] One did not advance to the next stage until the previous one was fully mastered. In this zeal for perfection Arlberg dogma was defended with a devotion bordering on religious fanaticism.

Wealthy skiers from the eastern seaboard also traveled to Europe and became devotees of the Alpine, not Norwegian, skiing in which speed and devil-may-care attitudes replaced the *Idraet* ideal. It was not that health and morality were forsaken. In many cases the joys and difficulties associated with downhill and slalom, with professional instruction, with just about any institutionalizing aspect of skiing which they found in Europe, were explained in terms of the tried ideals.

It was always slightly mystifying to Europeans that Arnold Lunn, an Englishman, should have such influence on skiing in the interwar years. From his winter belvedere of Mürren he was "King of the Ski World." When he died in 1974, Boston's White Mountain Ski Runners were reminded "of the debt all Alpine skiers owe to his enthusiastic involvement in the development, popularization and organization of the sport." "He opened up a new epoch [in skiing]," wrote the Swiss Walter Amstutz, "and it bore his personal stamp."[33] American skiing is particularly indebted to Lunn for three related influences. He was skiing's most forthright publicist and he waged a running battle, not always friendly and often impatient, with the Norwegians as he strove to reduce their influence. He took over the editorship of the British Ski Club's *Year Book* in 1920 and remained in that position until he died fifty-four years later. The *Year Book* was the bible of English-reading skiers the world over.[34] Second, he invented modern downhill and slalom racing and was tireless in obtaining recognition for these Alpine disciplines in world competition. Third, he held administrative positions on many international committees.

Lunn went to Chamonix in 1898 with the first organized ski party of his father's travel agency. His first love was mountaineering but in the years before the Great War, the Alps became a regular winter home, and he eventually made the Palace Hotel in Mürren an outpost of the British Empire where he held sway with regnant authority from 1911. In January 1922 he staged the first slalom and the D.H.O. (Downhill Only) Club, founded in 1924 at neighboring Wengen, symbolized the arrival of what we now know as Alpine skiing. When Lunn proposed downhill and slalom races he was "inspired by the naive concern," as he wrote thirty years later, "that downhill racing would help to develop the kind of technique suitable for ski mountaineering." Downhill running put a premium on running a course in as straight a line as possible. Indeed, for some years the "downhill" was called the "straight race." The Alps above Mürren and Wengen were open slopes and, therefore, caused no problems. But if skiers wanted to descend from Mürren to the Lauterbrunnen valley floor, they had to be expert at what was called tree running. Lunn "invented the modern 'gate' slalom as a substitute for racing through trees." In 1922 he was already convinced that "the only satisfactory method of testing the power of moving among obstacles is a slalom race; i.e. a race down a course defined by *artificial* obstacles, such as flags." Style was unimportant and not to be considered.[35]

Early slalom competitors skied from one set of flags to the next, fell down, got up and went on to the next obstacle. When much of skiing's attraction—whether in Norway or the Alps—was perceived to be in its aesthetic quality, this sliding and falling was most ungraceful. Various penalty points were included for stopping or falling down. Slalom courses became tracked and icy. Lunn, therefore, insisted on two courses: tight turns on hard snow and a second run on soft snow. Downhill fared no better; runs became as icy as the Cresta bobsled track. Before these problems became obvious, Lunn campaigned vigorously for recognition of these events in international contests. The Norwegians did not want anything to do with this "circussport," this "acrobaticsport," this "hotelsport"; it was not going to taint "real" skiing! One Norwegian judgment was that Lunn was the "worst enemy of the ski sport in the Alps."[36]

When Americans made their pilgrimage to Lunn's Mürren, it was not just downhill and slalom that they learned. They came away with a set of attitudes as well. Skiing in the Alps after the war was associated with upper-class British values. This is not as curious as it may first appear. Since the British were undisputed originators of organized sport, what they said and did was treated with deference. More particularly, the British had extolled the joys of mountain climbing, so it was not unnatural that this joy should be extended to climbing mountains on skis. When it came to descending from the conquered peak, "technique" and "form" were not nearly so important as "dash."

The British love of "taking it straight," redolent of the fox hunt, and the appeal of speed (Schneider observed that "it is speed that is the lure") combined to inspire a new form of skiing. Perhaps the charm and mania for speed on skis were simply because there was still so much of the natural world with which to contend. In a period when speed records fell to the industrial marvels of boat (the Blue Riband), train (the Flying Scotsman), and plane (the Schneider Trophy), skiing was autochthonous and therein lay its attraction. Skiers had to know how to manage their equipment, and Schneider and Lunn were the world's two masters in this new era of downhill speed. When Americans returned from their rite of passage, they re-created their Alpine experiences in the mountains of New England.

The two Americans quoted earlier, Nathaniel Goodrich and Wilhelmine Wright, came from Dartmouth College and Boston's AMC, eastern institutions that set in place certain foundations of modern American skiing. Dartmouth, with its firmly established Outing Club, its white Anglo-Saxon heritage, its wealthy student body, and its not-quite-so-serious-as-Harvard sense first took to these new ways of skiing in the latter half of the 1920s and spread its enthusiasm all over New England.

In 1925 in Hanover, New Hampshire, eight pine branches were stuck in the snow on a gentle hill dropping all of one hundred feet: the slalom race had arrived in the United States. That year Eastern devoted one page of its annual report to *The Slalom,* suggesting that "whenever possible a new event, called the Slalom race, be added to your competitions. This is a down-hill race, the competitors having to follow a course marked by flags. This necessitates proficiency in making Telemarks and Christiania swings and brings out the all-around ability of the ski-runner."[37]

This innovative and interesting advice to member clubs shows clearly that they had to be told that the race was to be down a hill. Skiing to most people in 1925 still meant the Norwegian way across field and meadow. The word *proficiency* to describe making the two turns—the telemark from the Norwegian tradition, the Christiania from the Arlberg, in spite of its name (Christiania was the capital of Norway until 1925 when it was changed to Oslo)—was not chosen randomly. Much of British skiing—the formation of clubs, the downhill and slalom races, and the taking of third-, second-, and, for a few, first-class tests (all actually called proficiency tests)—was designed to produce a proficient ski runner, an all-around one, precisely as Eastern indicated.

When others saw slalom racing for the first time they did not quite know what to make of it; some even found it a bit sissy. Newspaper reporters described the event as a "British test in ski proficiency . . . gauged by four flags at 75 to 90 degrees right and left down the steep hill."[38] Much more detailed instructions were published in Eastern's annual of 1929 by the man who brought slalom and downhill to Dartmouth, physics professor Charles A. Proctor. Proctor had corresponded with Arnold Lunn soon after the Great War. In 1925 he persuaded Dartmouth to try an experimental slalom according to Lunn's rules. Two years later he had the race accepted by the Intercollegiate Winter Sports Union, an organization regulating all winter sports among member colleges until 1934, when it became the Intercollegiate Ski Union, the name change the result of the enormous growth of interest in Alpine events. "My inspiration for this," he wrote, "came from the British Ski Year Book" which he had read for years. He was made an honorary member of the Ski Club of Great Britain in 1927.[39]

Following the St. Moritz Olympic Games, Charley Proctor, Charles A. Proctor's son, was invited by Lunn to Mürren, where he was told that he had been elected an honorary member of the Kandahar Club—a racing fraternity. Lunn pressured him to enter a race that same afternoon. The race had a "Geschmozzel" start (a mass start) and Proctor elected to follow an excellent runner wearing a bright red shirt. The next year at Woodstock, Vermont, Proctor experimented with a Geschmozzel start, a direct result of his Mürren experience.[40]

Downhill was also initiated at Dartmouth College. As early as 1914 there had been an impromptu race among a Dartmouth party of faculty and students—led by Professor Proctor—from the top of Mt. Moosilauke. Dartmouth's coach, Anton Diettrich, first suggested organized racing down a hill. By 1925 rules for intercollegiate competition stipulated that the race "shall be from one to two miles in length, entirely downhill, or nearly so, over a course which shall furnish a test of all around skiing ability, including wherever possible a variety of turns at good speed, and some wood running." As in the early description of slalom race courses, this downhill instruction exhibited the transitional nature from Nordic to Alpine skiing. Unlike cross-country skiing, in Alpine skiing "obstacles which cannot be passed or surmounted at fair speed should be avoided." It was suggested that wire fences be opened or protected with boards.[41]

The 1927 downhill race—parts of the course actually went up hill—was won by Charley Proctor in about twenty-one minutes. This race became an annual occurrence. The Moosilauke Down Mountain Race on the old Carriage Road was described in 1931 as "very steep and twisty . . . for the most part through heavy woods." The race was controlled by nature "almost to rate as a long slalom"; it dropped twenty-five hundred feet in two and three-quarter miles. "I was in that race," recalled Al Sise a half-century later. He fell on top of another competitor in the trees. "So we disentangled ourselves and he reached into his pocket and pulled out a flask and said, 'How about a nip?'" Both finished in the middle of the pack.[42]

The English love for high country peaks in winter brought about the development of ski mountaineering; skis offered the easiest means of ascent and the fastest means of descent. As we have seen, the downhill and slalom were not developed for skiers initially but for ski mountaineers. The crossing of a col or the reach for a peak in the nineteenth century, and indeed up until the Second World War, carried with it a mix of adventure and challenge for an all-rounder on skis. It was also very social, bringing with it the camaraderie of nights in a hut on col or alp. When the British, whose mountaineering conquests were as many and varied as their military ones, set the tone for skiing, those from New England understandably followed suit, just as Germans, Austrians, and Swiss had done. However, climbing mountains on skis in the eastern United States was very different from ascending the open slopes of pasture and alp. There was no high country open terrain with a peak or two to attempt in New England. Here climbing on skis meant an ascent and a descent through dense woods, something that might test body and soul, but lacked the companionship of the ski mountain tour of Europe. Winter ascents of American mountains were therefore few in number and accomplished by a handful of men. We know very little about these early efforts even though such well-known men as Fridtjof Nansen and Nobel physicist Irving Langmuir made first attempts on Adirondack peaks. Their efforts were hardly noted.[43]

The AMC initiated another aspect of modern skiing: organized club instruction. In 1911 Emile Cochand was hired directly from Switzerland to teach in the Laurentians, north of Montreal, Canada; in 1922 Dartmouth hired an "expert skee man" as instructor and coach; in the 1920s the Lake Placid Club hired a succession of foreign ski teachers: all taught the telemark turn and modified the ideals of *Ski-Idraet* according to their own particular position.[44] It was also not uncommon for inns to have resident ski instructors available for guests. At the Lake Placid Club there was a charge per lesson, but at most inns the instruction was free. So, for example, Strand Mikkelsen began service with the Hotel Weldon in Greenfield, Massachusetts, in 1928; John Knudsen, another "Norwegian expert" resided at the Shattuck Inn, Jaffrey, New Hampshire.[45]

When the AMC started club instruction in Boston to get ready for the 1928 season, there was an entirely different result. What in the previous season had been a ten-minute indoor chat on how to ski was expanded to four weekly talks on the new Arlberg technique. In December, Otto Schniebs, the club's instructor, gave three sessions on the "crouch technique" which was followed by an anticlimactic explanation of waxing.[46] In 1930, besides talks and practice sessions on grass, there were regular exercise classes in the gymnasium when the weather turned bad. This new Arlberg knowledge was not confined to the club; Schniebs both wrote and was written about in the Boston papers, thus the Arlberg reached a wide audience. Once winter set in, the AMC felt all the practice really paid off and members enjoyed "Lunging, Crouching, Jumping and Hip Swinging." The "diagonal lunge" was practiced for up-hill work—we would call it the herring bone today—and the "Telemark Incognito" was only permitted—just—when all the Christiania swings had been mastered.[47]

Here, for the first time, organized club schooling was offered to recreational skiers "drawn chiefly from clerical and professional groups who . . . were neither athletically developed nor in proper physical condition," a group very different from the college and down-mountain racing crowd. Skiing was popular; by 1931 the number of AMC members who skied had risen from twenty-five to over three hundred.[48]

The AMC realized, too, that these recreational skiers were looking farther afield than the snow-covered greens of the local golf club to try out their newfound skills. Under the direction of Park Carpenter, members surveyed trails in Massachusetts and New Hampshire that in the summer were used for hiking. They gave particular attention to trails that joined two mountain tops. A cross-country ski guide was contemplated as early as 1927, and this idea was then presented to the New England Trail Conference. That fall a crew readied a skiing path bridging the Massachusetts and New Hampshire border. The trail itself was straightened here and there, brush was cleared from abandoned pastures so the slopes of untracked powder could tempt the skiers. The Wapack Trail became the most used because of its ease of access and its proximity to Boston.

AMC day trips for a slide and glide to the Wapack and week excursions to the Laurentian ski fields in Canada retained much of the Norse heritage. The aura of the healthy outdoors and camaraderie were maintained by those with the money and leisure to enjoy the challenge of winter. But the new-to-skiing, office workers also had money to spend, although they might have only a day or a weekend to enjoy what it could buy. These new groups found variety in their skiing pleasures which they coupled with a sense of quest as they ventured on paths opened by the AMC. With the increasing use of automobile and railroad these urbanites spread social skiing all over New England.

8 / The Mechanization of Skiing

> "A whole Coney Island of people skiing where you wanted to ski."
>
> —Former captain of Dartmouth ski team, on ski trains

> "Sounds mighty like another sport gone softy."
>
> —*The Ski Bulletin* (1933), on tows

> On straightaway, minimum width should be at least ten feet, widening to fifteen feet where steep. In a great many cases we leave the bumps; this proves to the runner how important the Arlberg crouch is. He generally comes home saying, "What fun the bumps on such-and-such a trail were."
>
> —*The Ski Bulletin* (1933), on trails

While his AMC friends traveled to the Laurentian hills in 1928, John Holden was among the skiing crowd leaving Munich's *Hauptbahnhof* for the Bavarian mountains. His reports to Eastern and to the AMC stirred the leadership to persuade the Boston and Maine (B&M) Railroad to try a ski-train season.[1]

Ski Trains

The B&M sent out a little pamphlet to a few clubs announcing a trip "to some winter sports center whose skiing, snowshoeing, and other forms of winter activity are at their best." The final choice of venue depended on snow depth and weather reports and was decided three days before departure. Warner, New Hampshire, in the lee of Mt. Kearsarge was chosen for the first trip on 11 January 1931. Of 197 who were on the train, 115 were AMC members, and most of the others were from the Dartmouth Outing Club of Boston and the Harvard Mountaineering Club. The excursionists had a marvelous time. Most practiced on the pastures while the experts attempted an ascent of Kearsarge. The train was used as a "club house [for] naps between exhilarating and strenuous exercise," as another brochure

you'll have a glorious "Sun-day"

Sundays and
Week-Ends
from the
North Station

·LES STOUT·

The SNOW TRAIN
BOSTON AND MAINE

The Boston and Maine assured the urban white-collar skiers both a sun tan and a stem turn if they went north for sociable skiing in the 1930s. (New England Ski Museum, Franconia, N.H.)

described the outing. "All were jubilant over its success."[2] All, that is, except the natives who did not think much of the invading city folk tramping through orchard and field.[3]

Special trips were organized "for experienced runners only" whereas others stressed "real instruction and practise away from the confusion of the crowd" for beginners. If the Warner residents were a little put out on 11 January, a month later Epsom, New Hampshire, was prepared for the deluge, 605 this time, and met the ski train with "smiles, conveyances, and directions."[4] Twelve trains took 8,371 of the winter-minded out of Boston's North Station during that first season, 1,762 to Wilton on Washington's Birthday alone. At the end of the winter, the AMC took stock of what it had wrought and concluded that it had "opened up a new era in New England skiing."[5]

Indeed, it had: the snow trains captured the imagination of younger desk-bound office workers. Regular announcements of planned trips were followed by exciting reports of a day out of the city in the purity of the clean and white hilly wonderland. Within a month of the first snow train in 1931, the excursions began to appeal to those who would not dream of joining the AMC and who were excluded from college and alumni outing and mountaineering clubs. On the 15 February day trip, for example, eighty employees of Harris Forbes, a Boston bank, made up a party for an outing in Greenfield. One Warner woman particularly remembered the employees of the Gillette Safety Razor Company.[6] New Hampshire and Massachusetts towns realized that here was winter income. Lincoln, New Hampshire, had a dozen trucks waiting to take skiers to nearby spots and the Ladies' Aid Society organized a sugar-on-the-snow party to benefit their organization. Newport, New Hampshire, prepared a welcome that included its American Legion band, dressed up in scarlet uniforms, with Boy Scouts ready to act as guides; Laconia, New Hampshire, exhibited its sled-dog teams.[7]

Skiing was not the only attraction of the ski train. "A great many people came up to raise hell. To put it plainly some of them did a marvelous job at it," recalled a shopkeeper. Some came to watch; they were fascinated "by us boys skiing down and making turns. In some cases they'd ask if we minded if they stood on the back of our skis so they could ride a ways," recalled a Franconia man.[8] Some old-timers wished that the AMC had never suggested snow trains; the hoi polloi were spoiling their muscular activities. "It was sort of a disaster, a mess," a former Dartmouth ski team captain recalled, "they'd just engulf you."[9]

Early snow trains took the new enthusiasts to try a slide or two on a sloping pasture or to head up a logging road. For these newcomers, skiing still had about it a pioneering, healthy quality which appealed to Olive Anson on her first snow-train trip: "It was truly a gathering of red blooded, clean, wholesome lovers of winter sports." She contrasted the "tanned faces, clear eyes, frank smiles and genuine laughter" with the urban, jazz-loving wild youth. Young America should choose "clean, healthy sport." Indeed, one Boston physician recommended the "Health Train."[10] Anson was expressing one continuing, strong cultural trend from the late nineteenth century: the connection between health and morality which had imbued many young people. She was also expressing the social prestige associated with a bronzed face, especially in winter.[11] Later the B&M even started "Sun Tan Snow Trains."[12] The difference between a tanned skiing office worker and a pasty-faced colleague separated the two just as it bound together those who knew the camaraderie of a Sunday on the snows. Anson's romantic prose foresaw this ideal as a way to improve the middle class.

But young America did not choose what was so obviously good for it. As trains brought thousands to the hills, skiing as a recreation and a sport became a social occasion. Not only that, but the invention of the rope-tow, which lessened the toughness needed to struggle up a hill and diluted the glamour of a true mountain adventure, attracted ever more crowds. When the up-hill transportation devices provided an easy way to the top of the mountain, the *Idraet* ideal remained only in places where there were no snow trains, no city clientele, and no tows, that is, in the West. But the era of the 1930s belonged to New England. With its large and nearby population centers, with an efficient rail and road network, with a knowledge of Alpine techniques, the area attracted more and more who enjoyed the Germanic *Schuss* more than the Norwegian *Idraet*. The first snow trains stopped for lowland pasture skiing, but by 1933 they deposited the "ski larks" for down-mountain skiing. It was comparatively easy to manage a pair of skis across field and meadow, but to control a rush down a mountainside required some skill. The B&M hired well-known instructors to travel on its snow trains. With special coaches where skis could be rented and waxed (by 1940 an entire ski outfit could be rented on the train!), with assured instruction, good fellowship, and the promise of a sunny *Schuss,* the train provided easy sociability.

There were shops on the train, but some city stores had entire "Snow Train" departments:

> Many a girl who looks well on the ski train
> Proves herself to be quite without ski brain.
> Bonwits and staid Abercrombie and Fitches
> Daily outfit lots of ignorant ladies.[13]

How the old guard loved it—published in *The Ski Bulletin,* of course! Those name stores were in New York City, and the New York, New Haven and Hartford Railroad, thanks to the prodding of the patrician Amateur Ski Club of New York, inaugurated ski trains from New York City to Connecticut, to the Berkshires in western Massachusetts, and to Vermont. Among the passengers who in 1935 took the first train out of Grand Central to Norfolk, Connecticut, were "many who had learned their skiing in the Alps, or at New England colleges." Besides the Amateur Ski Club, local AMC chapter members and the Dartmouth Alumni Outing Club were represented too.[14] In New York, as had been the case in Boston, the organizations who originally sponsored the snow trains had obvious ties to wealth and society. And again, skiing's appeal extended from its original core to an urban white-collar middle-class group. The Norfolk hills and the Berkshires were not as prepared for this new brand of skiers as the state of New Hampshire. The railroad authorities decided to limit the number of seats on their trains according to the number of skiers able to be "accommodated on the available ski slope." When one excursion bound for Bear Town Reservation did not stop there but went on to Pittsfield, Massachusetts, because of better snow conditions, no one seemed to mind.[15]

These early snow trains were something of an experiment, with railroad management and a few skiers making the decisions. Indeed, twenty-four railroad officials were among various interested parties who discussed plans for ski trails on Mt. Mansfield a half-dozen miles out of the village of Stowe, Vermont.[16] The snow train business was of some import; in 1935, for example, trains carried 3,658 to the Berkshires; the next year the total was up to 11,945. By that time several other railroads, the Central, the Delaware and Hudson, and the Lackawanna were competing to take skiers to new destinations. In the first three months of 1936, almost 70,000 skiers left New York City.[17]

When skiers from Washington, D.C., arrived at Glencoe, Pennsylvania, for the first time, the local crowd "gave them quite a hand as they emerged from the train in gayly colored sweaters, mufflers and ski pants, with their paraphernalia swung over their shoulders." The folks of Glencoe had never seen theater like this, but they quickly became used to it as sixteen hundred skiers came to the Poconos on four successive Sundays. In 1940, part of Grand Central was roped off because New York's "newest spectator sport is to watch the ski trains depart."[18] Skiing had become glamorous and set its participants off from the public. In the 1920s Charley Proctor could argue that skiers were a sort of fraternity, different from other college people. In the 1930s that same sort of specialness and pride appeared among a less affluent, less fashionable sector: fur-coated Margaret Emerson McKim Vanderbilt Baker Amory was photographed in a chaise lounge at Sun Valley, America's instant St. Moritz and Amy Smith grinned from the pages of the *Worcester Telegram*.

Taking note of the success of snow train activity in New England, the Chicago and Northwest ran ski specials to Wisconsin and Michigan, as did the Chicago, Milwaukee and St. Paul Railroad. The Burlington had trains bound for the "Mississippi Alps," favored by a rope tow at LaCrosse, Wisconsin. Two Dartmouth alumni were hired as ski coaches for a trip to Sheridan, Wyoming. Trains left Minneapolis for Taylors Falls, and the

Northern Pacific appealed to Helena, Montana, skiers to make up parties for the Blossburg Ski Slide. In the early 1930s the regular train from Denver had to slow down as it approached Winter Park "so we'd throw the skis out and then jump," Frank Ashley remembered. Soon the *Denver Rocky Mountain News,* sensing economic opportunity, sponsored a train to the tournament at Hot Sulphur Springs and, much to its surprise, sold over two thousand tickets. Then came overnight specials to Steamboat, and Safeway stores, the *Denver Post,* and Montgomery Ward all backed ski trains for carnival and sporting events. In the Far West, beginning in 1932 the Snowball Express from San Francisco deposited skiers at Truckee. The University Book Store in Seattle sponsored a regular Sunday train to Stampede in the Cascades in 1935 while Northwest Airlines contemplated "ski-planes similar to snow trains."[19]

All across snow country in the mid-1930s, trains took growing numbers of new skiers to a winter's day away from office and bench. The snow trains that went to slopes outfitted with rope tows became increasingly popular. Train trips to resorts with rope tows first occurred in New England and gave a significant boost to Alpine skiing.

Ski Tows

Although there were haul-back tows in Europe as early as 1908, the first rope tow for skiing was patented in Switzerland in 1931.[20] Whether Alex Foster, a former intercollegiate Canadian jumper, knew of this is unclear, but at Shawbridge, Quebec, he rigged up two thousand feet of rope onto the axle of a Dodge. Any skier with the price, meaning the strength, could grab on anywhere he liked. ("He" is correct; tickets were for gents only.) The tow started operation on 2 January 1933 at $-15°$ and was affectionately dubbed Foster's Folly.[21]

In the United States various up-hill contraptions had hauled skiers to their joys for years before these milestones. As early as the Californian snow-shoeing days, the Eureka mine was fired up on Sundays to give people a lift in the ore buckets up to the minehead so they could have a splendid rush down the mountainside.[22] A tow to haul toboggans was ready for the Truckee carnival in 1910 and then was used later by skiers following the formation of the Truckee Ski Club in 1913.[23] A more sophisticated version that tobogganists and skiers could hook themselves onto was ready in 1928. When Californians did copy the Shawbridge rope, it was with the idea of getting jumpers back to the top more quickly, so that they could make more jumps in an afternoon.[24] That is, this newfangled mechanization was used to aid the Norse sport of jumping (in fact, it had

Early rope tows required strength and dexterity. Hollis Phillips, winner of the first Inferno is hanging on for 2½ minutes to this twisting rope. Rope-tow grippers soon came on the market. (New England Ski Museum, Franconia, N.H.)

been proposed as early as 1915 at Dartmouth College)[25] but it certainly ran counter to the *Idraet* tradition.

The Woodstock, Vermont, "Ski Way" originated the rope-tow era in the United States on 28 January 1934. Foster's Folly plans were obtained in 1933 after three New Yorkers reported on the excellence of downhill running in Kitzbühl, Austria, due in part to the available "funicularity." They were having a last spring fling back home at Woodstock. "Thoroughly fed up after one long hard day in which [they] only got in a few runs," they persuaded their landlady to do something about it. David Dodd was hired to put together "an endless rope which runs over pulley wheels attached to a timber horse guyed to a tree at the top of the hill." A Model T powered four or five skiers up about nine hundred feet at 5 to 10 mph. The trip took a minute, which compared favorably with the fifteen-minute slog on foot.[26]

It was significant that about seventy members of the Ski Club Hochgebirge were on hand in Woodstock, just as they had been at the inauguration of Foster's Folly. *The Ski Bulletin* immediately reported that "nowhere in New England did skiers enjoy so much delightful downhill skiing with so little uphill effort." The New York Amateur Ski Club tried the Woodstock "ski way" too but found that it required some skill and considerable strength. It was worth the effort though because "one gets almost as much of a thrill going up as coming down."[27]

Naturally there were mechanical problems, most of them connected with engine burn-out. At Woodstock the next season Bunny Bertram operated a more efficient rig on Hill 6 and managed to stop the rope from twisting,[28] which was a problem that had also plagued Ted Cooke's "rope hoist." The White Mountain Ski Runners had shown him a perfect hillside meadow near Gilford, New Hampshire. To his surprise they wanted his tow to rise up the mountain above the meadow. Here mechanization aided the Arlberg downhill ambience. Cooke went back to his tinkering and came up with a "Tow-Way," the longest rope tow in the world, which made possible down-mountain thrills of one-thousand-foot vertical in three thousand feet.[29]

Homemade tow contraptions appeared in Brookline, Rochester, Lisbon, and Franconia, New Hampshire; at Shrewsbury, Corinth, and Putney, Vermont; at Pittsfield, Massachusetts, and Fryeburg, Maine. Each seemed to have something special about it: Putney advertised that its tow was supported at a uniform height, Brookline's 320-foot claim to fame was that two youngsters had had twenty-five thousand feet of downhill running in one day, which was trumpeted as comparable with any Swiss ski center. In Pittsfield, Bousquet's rope was said to carry fifty at a time.[30]

Other plans for tows were in the works. Transporting goods by wire cables had been fairly common; American Steel and Wire Company was well known in this country for such cables, and there were various material "lifts" in Europe that were also known. One early cable lift in the United States was the "new ski tramway" near Dartmouth College. It was what is now called a J-bar and was meant to hook around one's waist, but even the editors of the *Ski Bulletin* first advised skiers "to hold onto the safe convenient handles" that hung down waist high from the cable. The experts did not realize that the bar was intended to go behind so that one could lean back against it and be drawn up the hill. Dartmouth men closed their eyes to the "immorality of the machine" as the numbers of skiers increased one hundred percent in the first year of operation.[31]

Experiments with the first chairlift for Sun Valley in the Union Pacific Railroad's yards in Oklahoma. They soon put straw on the concrete. (Sun Valley Company, Sun Valley, Idaho)

The Uncanoonucs Cable Tramway out of Manchester, New Hampshire, was put into winter service, and Bill and Betty Whitney hung shovel handles from an overhead cable at Jackson on the eastern slope of the White Mountains. The T-bar made its first appearance as the He-and-She-Stick at Pico near Rutland, Vermont.[32]

In this same period small mountain towns in the Rockies looked over their old mine hoists, bought up surplus material, oiled old bull wheels that had last carried ore buckets, and constructed a variety of lifts. Aspen's boat tow, a cable run, jig-back tram comprised two sleds holding about ten people. As the skiers ascended in one boat, the empty one came down. In the Northwest, skiing on Mt. Baker was delayed when the owner of the twenty-skier sled called the "Escalator" was killed in an avalanche while he was trying to get the whole contraption going in 1936. At Yosemite's Badger Pass a boat tow began that ski region's up-ski era in 1938.[33]

The chair tow which was to capture the skiing public's imagination made its first appearance at Averell Harriman's quickly built ski paradise of Sun Valley, Idaho. A group of Union Pacific engineers had been asked to gather information on mine hoists and cable-lifting devices. Jim Curran was impressed by the "banana" hoist used on the docks in Honduras to load fruit. What if chairs replaced the hooks? Sketches were circulated to prominent skiers and ski clubs, and in the Omaha railroad workshops an experimental chair was hung from the side of a truck in July 1936. Harriman's assistant tried getting on and off with little success—skis would not run on hay-covered concrete, so roller skates were substituted. "We then ran the truck up and down the shops in Omaha . . . at various speeds to test the ease of pick up and getting off." Practical engineering discussions of the spacing of chairs, the angle of climb, and the actual positioning of the lift followed, and by December 1936 the world's first chairlift rose up Dollar Mountain at Sun Valley.[34] It was copied in New Hampshire at the Belknap Recreation Area near Cooke's rope tow. "The modern . . . tramway of the sit down variety" was to the East what Sun Valley's was to the West.[35] It started operations in late January 1938, the year Roland Palmedo began soliciting investors for a six-thousand-foot chair up Mt. Mansfield in Stowe.[36]

Americans who skied in Europe experienced mechanical lifts on a far-larger scale. Cog railways and funiculars made it possible to spend all day at downhill running by eliminating the tedium of any up-hill climbs. In one day at Zell-am-See a skier could actually ski for the equivalent of three or four Sundays spent going up (and down) Cannon Mountain in New Hampshire. Some travelers told of eleven thousand feet of downhill skiing in one afternoon above Innsbruck while others talked of the skiing made possible by the Davos-Parsenn cable railway. It was all too obvious: skiers needed aerial tramways up America's mountains. Plans were laid for Mt. Hayden (near Aspen) in Colorado but they were not completed before the war broke out. Alex Bright had his eye on Cannon Mountain. "No avenues of contact with the mountains for the old or the physically untrained offer so much, so intimately and with so little encroachment of civilization on the sanctity of mountains," he argued, and, it must be added, nothing else would serve the newly cut Richard Taft Racing Trail so well. All bases were covered. In 1938, four years and one-quarter of a million dollars later, the state of New Hampshire found itself providing "The Sky Route to Ski Fun" at sixty cents a ride.[37]

Before the Second World War broke out, the East could boast of the first aerial tramway in the United States, chairlifts that competed with Sun Valley and the West, and T-bars, J-bars, and rope tows dotting the landscape of the Green and White mountains. With so many and varied up-ski devices, a Ski Tow Owners Association was formed. It made initial inquiries into how the ever-increasing crowds were to be handled. There were at least one million skiers in 1940 (some put the figure as high as three million) and operators discovered that there was a pattern: 25 percent of their trade was on Saturdays; 75 percent on Sundays, mostly on Sunday afternoons.[38] In an effort to even out their business the owners started to advertise ski weeks rather than day trips.

Ski Trails

Where were all these skiers actually going to ski? In Europe and the western United States skiing was easily possible above tree line, but in New England there was hardly an unforested mountain. The development of ski trails in the modern sense—in contrast to farmers' meadows, logging roads, and the AMC's winter tramping trails—was a direct result of the mechanization of skiing. The Depression also had a significant impact on this development; funds were channeled from various New Deal recovery programs to organizations like the Civilian Conservation Corps to provide labor.

After the first snow train season it became obvious there was an acute shortage of terrain for Alpine skiing. Informal discussions among leading skiers took place before John Carleton called on James E. Scott, the supervisor of the White Mountain National Forest, sometime in early 1932. As a result, the New Hampshire Development Commission, which already promoted skiing in the state through the *Troubadour,* a fifteen-page booklet extolling the joys of country living, called a meeting of recognized ski club leaders and interested hoteliers. A committee was formed to supervise the building of trails specifically for skiing. The Marquis d'Albizzi and Duke Dimitri of Leuchtenberg were engaged to lay out trails in the Franconia area. Charley Proctor laid trails in Pinkham and Crawford notches.[39] As with earlier innovations, it was a small elite group that was responsible for initiating trail development. Carleton and Proctor were both Dartmouth Olympians with European experience and connections to the Boston and New York clubs, and the status of a skiing marquis and a duke seemed obvious.

Survey work began in June 1932. Trails were marked, and when Carleton received state funds, the CCC was put to work on fifteen trails that made for a total of forty miles of skiing. Although they were specifically announced as "not the usual narrow slits," Carleton's and Proctor's trails were criticized for their toughness. The AMC called for more suitable paths for the noncompetitive skier. There was also an effort to make them more accessible from highways. Some hotels and clubs built their own trails. In 1932 Peckett's started construction of the Richard Taft Racing Trail, and the Newport Ski Club built its own trail on Mt. Sunapee. The CCC completed both those trails the next year.

There was continued discussion of what constituted a good trail. The ideal minimum width was twenty feet for any gradient more than 5°, but many were not that wide. One of the astounding facts about the Taft trail was its width—all of sixty feet. When local regions began to advertise their delights, frequently they featured the width of trails. From the start, New Hampshire planned a substantial booklet with maps and details of the trails. First published for the 1934 season and issued free, the statistics for the ski trails were impressive. The New Hampshire maps of 1935 marked 50 ski trails (total miles, 115) and of 1936 marked 90 ski trails (total miles, 200). In 1939 there were too many to mark (total miles, 1,000).[40]

Since New Hampshire was the first state to capitalize on the labor of the CCC for trail construction, that was the place to ski in 1934. Vermont lagged behind principally because there was a "lack of general winter sports enthusiasm."[41] Trail design and cut in Vermont was based upon Proctor's work in the White Mountains. When the CCC did construct trails in the Green Mountains it did so in areas where skiing had some foundation: Stowe and Brattleboro. Whereas New Hampshire could boast fifty trails in 1935, Vermont listed fifteen. In spite of the increasing localized interest in winter sporting, there was still a question of whether it would take hold in the Green Mountain state.[42]

Vermont lacked trail mileage, but various communities in the state saw themselves as ski centers. Brattleboro, with its jumping heritage, made on-going efforts to keep that ideal foremost. Although the town's outing club had CCC help with trails, patrician Woodstock and New York–favored Stowe became more popular in the 1930s. Woodstock, which acted as if it had invented winter sports, owed its skiing popularity to the Woodstock Ski Runners Club, founded and promoted by J. Dwight Francis in 1932.

Promising open field running near an established inn with good rail and road connections, and close to Dartmouth College, this club guaranteed lively activity. Francis imported Fritz Steuri, a well-known Swiss racer-instructor, and invited the wealthy to make Woodstock an Alpine skiing success.[43] Two poor snow seasons damned his hopes, so he took to promoting the first ski cruise to the Alps in 1935—a forerunner of the ski vacation package.[44] Woodstock owed its survival as a ski center to the various rope tows dotted around the neighborhood. But the future belonged to the areas where trails, tows, lifts, and villages all came together—however unharmoniously—and one of those areas was Stowe.

The Amateur Ski Club of New York "discovered" Stowe. One of the club's objectives was to pool information of newly explored skiing opportunities. President Roland Palmedo took a spring trip in 1932 and reported not only to his club but also to the wider skiing fraternity served by *The Ski Bulletin* that the Stowe area offered various possibilities for a week or ten days. The toll road from the top of Mt. Mansfield, he judged, was probably not exciting enough for the experts. In 1935, as a challenge to such experts, the CCC cut the 1¾-mile, 14° Nose Dive, the slightly shorter and steeper Barnes Run, and five other trails radiating down the mountain.[45]

Besides the actual ski slopes, a ski center needed communication links, inns and restaurants, parking lots and on-site instruction. Two hostelries remained open in Stowe for the 1934 winter: the Green Mountain Inn in the village and The Lodge at the bottom of the mountain. Buses met trains arriving at Waterbury, and up at the mountain a large sign announced a ski school with "Herr Sepp Ruschp—In Charge" for the 1937 season.[46] The Stowe-Mansfield Association maintained an office with a phone so that late arrivals could find room and board at one of the lodges or farms listed with the association.[47] This service was paid for by a five-cent-per-person tax, a charge similar to the European *Kurtaxe*. Palmedo began interesting investors in a six-thousand-foot chairlift up Mt. Mansfield in Stowe and as this single chairlift was being readied for the 1940 season, the ski area already had a following who appreciated both the variety of down-mountain thrills and the amenities provided. In 1938 Stowe played host to the United States National Alpine Ski Championships, competitions that confirmed Stowe as one of the most important areas for testing the downhill and slalom sporting fraternity.

9 / *The Sport of Skiing*

> On steep pitches, casting form, technique and control to
> the winds, he adopted the simple expedient of sitting on the
> tails of his skis. We are told it is within the rules.
>
> —*The Ski Bulletin* (1933)

> Men worshipped perfection in tempo, vorlage; were conse-
> crated to mastery of controls and schusses, corridors and
> flushes; talked of waxes and edges, ski-meets and records.
> Men now ski superbly. But what have they lost?
>
> —*Sierra Club Bulletin* (1938)

The university and college outing clubs had promoted the skisport and in
the 1920s it was they who first began to domesticate the attraction skiers
felt for speed on skis into the sport of skiing. When those clubs' members
graduated, sometimes hardly breaking stride, they formed similar organizations in order to continue their winter pleasures: a Dartmouth Outing Club
member could join the Alumni Club of the DOC; fifty Harvard fellows
bought a hundred acre farm so the Schussverein had a base. Most of these
were male clubs. Women were permitted as guests or as members' wives
and took part in both the athletic and the social activities. The names of the
clubs indicated their interest in Alpine skiing: Hochgebirge, Skidreiverein,
and the women's Hoch Alm of Smith College. "Ski Heil!" became the
greeting.

In the 1930s these clubs set the tone for American skiing. Members were
frequently old European hands, already versed in Arlberg technique and a
generally British way of enjoying a clubby winter. The clubs were responsible for many of the major down-mountain racing events; they brought over
particular European instructors; they patronized Arlberg personalities;
they interested themselves in safety; and some financed lifts and developed
ski centers. There was hardly a facet of the modernization process in which
they did not play a major role. They existed easily within Eastern partly
because individual members came to control the organization, and uneasily
within the Nordic-minded NSA although they made efforts—some successful—to move the national organization toward the Alpine disciplines.

In 1930 Eastern's club roster stood at 38. By 1935 it rose to 112, and in
the winter of 1940 it was up to 181.[1] Even in out-of-the-way villages it was

This Arlberg stylist's *Vorlage* flashes him through the small flags of the slalom course. This is how every club skier would have liked to look. Front cover of the new glossy *Ski Bulletin* of 1936. (New England Ski Museum, Franconia, N.H.)

presumed that the local skiing organization "will be a racing club." Roger Langley, long-time official in Eastern and the NSA, judged that "you more or less had to belong to a club if you wanted to be a competitor."[2] When Eastern put out its first modern annual in 1934, 31 of its 174 pages were devoted to "Results of Competitions." They ranged from the United States National Championship to the Junior Intra-Club Meet of the Lebanon Outing Club.[3] These statistics are overwhelming proof of the increasing popularity of Alpine skiing.

If its racing was one mark of a good club, social activities became an increasingly important aspect and were sometimes actually written into constitutions. Franconia's ski club, for example, was specifically for "social recreation and the improvement of members."[4] Improvement could be assessed by the children achieving the Boy Scout's merit badge in 1937.[5] Women were encouraged to get out on the slopes: "Ski Widow?" asked Delphine Carpenter in a *Leisure* article of 1935, "never!"[6] The new skiers took to skiing for both its personal and its social appeal. They enjoyed adventuring in winter because it offered an antidote to urban living. Seriousness was not the main consideration; they thought in terms of merrymaking both on and off the trails.

Alpine Instruction and Terminology

The first instruction in the new Arlberg style of skiing for these social skiers was provided by clubs who often hired immigrants like Schniebs, as the AMC had done. Hardly any American really understood the Arlberg technique, let alone knew how to teach it to others. But at this time, as fascism spread over Europe, there were an increasing number of immigrants from Germany, Austria, and elsewhere, who had experience in European ski schools. These men became instructors in the Arlberg method, especially in New England. The lack of ski knowledge in the urban centers of the East gave some immigrants who only had the rudiments of ski technique a chance at employment. Styling themselves "experts," holding forth in fascinating broken English, they were able to teach skiing just by being European.

Eastern's executive committee cast a jaundiced eye on these developments as "the number of these self-designated ski instructors . . . reached serious proportions and the fraud on the novice is almost a scandal." Eastern set in motion the idea of certifying professional instructors by an examination "similar in nature but less difficult" than any European exam.[7] Some of these European instructors really were stars. "To see Siegfried Buchmayr" (Peckett's resident ski impresario), was "to see skiing advanced to the realm of a fairy tale."[8] Another side of the legend was demonstrated in the evening when accent, pipe, and lederhosen provided authentic European ambience, a fascinating attraction for the *Skihaserl* ("snow bunnies"). Benno Rybizka, one of Schneider's disciplinarians, was in charge of the "Eastern Branch of the Hannes Schneider Ski School" on the eastern slope of New Hampshire's White Mountains. When Otto Schniebs left Dartmouth, his place was taken by Swiss *Kanone* Walter Prager, winner of the famed Kandahar and Parsenn Derby.

These men were part of the second wave of immigrants who changed American skiing and gave it its Alpine ambience. It may be uncharitable to say that they took some of the joy out of skiing, but the conclusion seems inescapable. For a start, ski instruction was based upon the different techniques which the European nations had developed in their own competitions for winter tourism. The differences had little relevance in America but the national techniques of the immigrants were defended with such zeal that Eastern saw it necessary to let each candidate for the professional

The magic of a name and a ski technique: Hannes Schneider's Austrian Arlberg was jealously guarded east and west by *Skimeisters* Benno Rybizka and Otto Lang. Poster by Tyler Micoleau, one of Rybizka's instructors. (New England Ski Museum, Franconia, N.H.)

certification know that no one "need fear the examination because the technique he teaches differs from . . . one of the examiners." It was understood, Fred Nachbaur told me, that if Rybizka—who had been named as one of three examiners—were present, few would turn up for the test because "he was obsessed with the Arlberg system" and would not be impartial.[9]

The major criticism of professional instructors, and especially of the Arlberg specialists, was leveled at the prevalent theory that pupils should absolutely perfect each stage of skiing technique before being permitted to advance. Rybizka's "whole idea . . . was perfection. It was going to be absolutely correct or you just didn't go on to anything else until you did it."[10] Economic motives undoubtedly account for some of the emphasis on slow progression. The beginning skier would need several seasons of lessons. The "ski larks" expected to be told what to do and "going to ski school" became such a rite of passage for a new skier that if a student arrived late, he or she might simply not attempt the hill alone. "The middle Europeans," sniffed Erling Strom, Lake Placid's Norwegian expert, "were brought up to look upon skiing as a business."[11]

One requirement of the professional examination was that the instructor had "sufficient English," but it was better if it was not too polished. One of Schniebs's attractions was his broken, syntactical explanations. Fred Nachbaur, an American whose parents were Austrian and who himself was fluent in German, was once refused a job as an instructor because he had no foreign accent. American instructors were known to assume an accent for the sake of business.[12]

If an accent authenticated Alpine instruction, an ability to use the terminology granted an aura of its mystique to those who skied. The German language came to best express the new fashion in winter enjoyment. As the Norwegian Telemark style of skiing was replaced by the Arlberg crouch, so the language of *Idraet* lost its sway. By the 1930s there was an almost wholesale defection to German. Although the Norwegian "*Langrenn*" virtually was never used in the United States to announce a cross-country race, once the Alpine disciplines were embraced in this country, even cross-country was given its German name of "*Langlauf*." Official results in American ski publications may be found under such a heading up until the Second World War.

Many *Ski-laufers* (a club in Eugene, Oregon) might have to *stemmbogen* on the *Steilhang* especially if their *Vorlage* did not permit a secure *Geländesprung* before starting their *Schuss* over the *Firnschnee*. If they made a *Sitzmark*, they would still be able to attend the *Preisverteilung* in the hope that the *Amerikanerin* of the *Damenmannschaft* might add *gemütliche Stim-*

mung to the occasion. These words are drawn at random from articles in the *American Ski Annual* from 1934 to 1939. The educated audience that enjoyed skiing also delighted in the titillations that the new language provided. The vocabulary separated those whose special world was the Germanic Alpine high country from the rest. "Gott sei Dank!" Jack Durrance cried when he arrived in the Tetons, "I've brought my skis."[13]

All of this emphasis on language may appear as dilettante superficiality and it probably was. But underlying the language shift was a denigration of the Norwegian heritage. "Ski Heil!" ran the advertisement for Nordic [its brand name] downhill skis sold by a New Jersey shop in 1936.[14] Was the owner cleverly latching on to both traditions or did he simply not know one from the other? If language is, as the German romantics used to say, the soul speaking, then collegiate New Englanders' skiing soul was no longer Norse but German.

This Germanizing was viewed at times as nationalistic and ideological. David Bradley, one of Dartmouth's globe-trotting skiers (at various times "teams" had gone to Europe, South America, and Australasia) whose articles often charmed through the use of foreign words, objected to the efforts to purge American skiing of its "hereditary Europeanism."[15] There were those who wanted to rid American skiing of "'schuss,' 'vorlage,' 'langlauf,' and even the venerable 'Ski Heil!'" The problem was that a yodel in the late 1930s might indicate an ace, an exhibitionist, or a Nazi. Bradley argued that foreign terminology added joie de vivre, something which American skiing badly needed; it made nonsense of trying to nationalize what had become a international sport. But "Ski Heil," however special to skiers in the 1930s, was soon tainted by that other Heil, and it is hard to realize now just what a wholesome, almost sacred skiing world once was bound up in that greeting.

German was passed on to the snow-train crowd, at first by the instructors. Then, as the manuals appeared, it became "necessary for the understanding of a ski lesson" to list and explain *Langlauf, Dauerlauf, Geländesprung, Quersprung, Bahnfrei,* and *Vorlage,* and this was done in a book specifically written for beginners in 1937.[16] *Abstem[men], Schuss,* and *Stemmbogen* were frequently used, and *Passgang, Vorläufer,* and *stemmfahren* could also be found. From *Stemmbogen* the semi-anglicized "stem turn" emerged. Others, like *Quersprung,* meaning a jump turn, were so strange that they disappeared quickly. *Vorlage,* already associated with a forward kick in soccer, remained the term for a forward lean long after the period covered in this book.

Teachers, for whom skiing was a business, used technical terminology. Serious instruction did not sit well with many who remembered skiing as part of a care-free collegiate youth; learning to ski had become a chore.[17]

Certainly part of the antagonism to the German involvement was political but even without that consideration there were objections. Any beginning skier would be confused and could validly object to a French instructor describing in halting English a Swiss stem using Austrian terminology. There was a need for an American ski technique.[18]

Downhill and Slalom Racing

As more people became proficient they took to racing and, as *Appalachia* noted as early as 1933, "all the traditional machinery and panoplies of organized athletics" would soon spoil the sport. "There will be the U.S.N.A.A.A.E.A.U.," the article continued, besides "official ratings, official tests, sanctioned tournaments, judges, umpires, starters, time keepers, flags, badges, cups and insignia; food canteens and contestants with pages off the calendar stuck to their backs prancing around on a windy slope waiting interminably for zero hour." If that was not bad enough for the competitors, far worse were the "nonskiing, thrill-seeking spectators restrained by roped-off sidelines; parked automobiles, and hot dog stands. Thus appears the mountain trail when competitive skiing pitches camp."[19] Overcivilization was a real fear. The truth of the matter was that speed had become the lure and the more beginners skied and the more lessons they took, the sooner they began to feel the attraction of the wind in their faces. With a modicum of control, beginners might enter club races of downhill and slalom.

These two Alpine disciplines had grown to prominence at Dartmouth, and it was fitting that the college sponsored the first United States Downhill Championship on its own Mt. Moosilauke in 1933. There had been down mountain races before this, even an Eastern Downhill Championship in 1932, at which the winner of one race was forty-two minutes ahead of the last man home.[20] These events had an unsophisticated experimental quality to them in which a hell-bent dash down the trail counted more than any aesthetic style. One of the best Canadian downhillers described his race as a "straight, easy gradual descent. First turn—a Christiania. Then steeper, and next an 'S' curve, narrow, banked like a race track, with a solid line of spruce along the top. Instinctively I braked . . . fell inwards, my skis crashed against the lower branches of a tree. . . . Up again, and once more gathering speed along the 'Devil's bumps,' hard banks of drifted snow, where the very vitals seemed to be shaken out of me."[21]

It is understandable that skiers in the Nordic Midwest might wonder about this newfangled Alpine sport. In 1932 the Hochgebirger Alex Bright and Lake Placid administrator John E. P. Morgan lobbied NSA to accept downhill and slalom. John McCrillis took along a film he had made of

Finish of First United States National Downhill Championship on Dartmouth College's own Mt. Moosilauke, 1933. There were no surprises: Dartmouth, the AMC, and the Hochgebirgers all placed well. (New England Ski Museum, Franconia, N.H.)

down-mountain racing as an added persuader. The NSA did not like downhill and slalom much, and accepted them only grudgingly; they were "not to be thought of as of equal importance to jumping and cross-country."[22]

"Not to be thought of as of equal importance" is a significant caveat. Since this was an Eastern proposal, it was viewed as a political threat. If downhill and slalom ever became popular, the USEASA might become more powerful and have more control of the sport than the national organization itself. More important still was the obvious challenge the Alpine disciplines presented to the Norse heritage. Whereas jumping and cross-country were perceived as part of Norse culture, downhill and slalom were recently invented disciplines that could be changed at will. The NSA simply did not care to accept the Alpine disciplines as true skiing.

Whereas the old Norse ski songs came from a peasant heritage, the downhillers chorused theirs from the Yale song book:

> Heil to the skier; point them down the hill;
> Cut all the corners, to get the greatest thrill.
> Here's to the skier who skis without a fall!
> We'd like to drink to him, but there's no such guy at all.[23]

The 1933 National Championship ensured official acceptance of downhill racing. One hundred and seventy-six clubs were invited. About eighty competitors started, of whom sixty-seven finished in three classes: A and B open to all seniors; C open to those under eighteen. Over the 2.8 mile course Bem Woods of the Dartmouth Outing Club won in just over eight minutes, thus becoming national and collegiate champion; second was Harry Hillman of the Hanover Ski Club; third was the ubiquitous Hochgebirger Alex Bright. The first three in Class C were all from the Hanover high school. There were, then, no surprises. The course was "more dangerous than drilling due to its narrowness with both sides thickly wooded." Otto Schniebs regretted that there was no women's class and suggested it for the next championship.[24]

In 1934 "young Richard Durrance made his appearance," as *The Ski Bulletin* put it, giving "a further stimulus to speed" along with a demonstration of smooth technique copied from Toni Seelos, Austrian *Slalommeister,* and learned in six years of schooling in Garmisch, Germany. Durrance consistently broke his own record on the Taft trail and shone even more brilliantly in the slalom; at Woodstock he was twenty-four seconds ahead of the second man in a race won in just over 1¼ minutes.[25] Excellent technique—often dubbed Durrance's "tempo turn"—provided a winning margin that no amount of dash could beat.[26] Technique marked off the first-class racers from the hundreds who began to think of themselves—not unhappily—as permanent "also rans." As the courses became steeper and more exacting, the difference between the small group of top-notch experts and those who tried to follow in their tracks grew wider. Dartmouth team members thought of racing as a game where you "cut out a tree, put it on a short cut, and get a buddy to pull it out so *you* got the short cut and the others didn't," as Durrance remarked. Ed Wells, another Dartmouth student and an alternate on the aborted 1940 Olympic team, remembered that "we never really trained; we just skied for the hell of it. And once in a while we'd race. . . . The race was sort of incidental. . . . We loved to beat the Hochgebirgers because . . . they were older."[27] These were the first-class skiers who could afford to be cavalier about the way they skied. But for the majority, whose technique was not sufficient for safe skiing at high speeds, racing became dangerous. Schniebs left Dartmouth to start his own ski school and business in upstate New York, partly because he was shocked at the increase in ski racing but also because he felt it no longer exhibited sport "but peaceful war." Schniebs called for giant slaloms and no-fall races— both of which were run as experiments in the spring of 1938.[28] Certainly one of the problems was that the downhill courses were, as one man remembered, narrow "slits cut through the trees"; another recalled they were "like a toboggan chute."[29] Speed became the ideal, and the new heroes of the ski day were the trail and hill record holders.

"We got off early from school because we knew the Taft was in good condition," Norwood Ball told an interviewer. "I got number one starting position which I didn't really want [because] we each had our own little secrets as to actually running the trail." Ball turned in a time that showed two minutes and thirty-five seconds on both watches, but the timekeeper did not believe it and announced two minutes, forty-five seconds. Only when the next man had tried to follow in Ball's tracks—they were straight—was the timing verified and Ball awarded the record for the Taft.[30] After 1945 the record was down to two minutes and four seconds. In these attempts there was no set course, just a starting point and a finishing line. Hill records were important because record holders and times were used as advertisements for ski hills.[31] Speed was such an attraction that it was even important in tows. The Underwood rope-tow manufacturing company advertised its tow's possibilities as 100 mph on level ground.[32]

International Racing and the Olympics of 1936

This fervor for speed and especially for racing was stimulated by tales of the competitions in Europe; the Galtzig, Schilthorn, and most of all the Parsenn were familiar to eastern American skiers through written accounts and to international skiers from experience. It was natural, almost, that American skiers who happened to be in Europe in 1933 entered international races for downhill and slalom. With only three weeks of downhill experience, a midwestern cross-country man, Al Lindley, still managed to finish twenty-ninth in a field of 150 runners, some four minutes behind the winner—an indication of the general low standard of Alpine racing as well as the fact that someone with no record at all could enter such a prestigious international meet. Another American was fifty-first.[33]

At the FIS meet two years later three members of the Hochgebirge sent in their entries at the last moment. They were met in Switzerland by a fellow member who "gasped at the sight of so much talent" and decided then and there that this was "America's first international ski team!" Two others joined as well. So, in the words of James Lowell, who was picked as an "alternate," "the team was never chosen; like Topsy it just 'growed.'" In competition with Europe's *Kanonen,* the two top Americans, Alex Bright and Tony Page ran well enough to draw occasional favorable comments.[34]

This FIS team was "frankly a pick up affair," but there was more care in the selection of the Olympic team for the 1936 Games at Garmisch, Germany, the first to include Alpine events. Men of "good character and unquestioned sportsmanship" were to be selected, so Avery Brundage instructed the NSA's convention. Three try-outs for the team were decided upon: combined cross-country and jumping at Lake Placid; slalom and downhill on Mt. Rainier; and jumping on Ecker Hill, near Salt Lake City, Utah. A manager was selected from nine candidates, and Dr. Joel H. Hildebrand from California was given a budget of $9,000—$450 per skier for the thirty-five-day period of travel and participation in the Games.[35]

The jumping and cross-country events at Lake Placid and in Utah produced no surprises; on Ecker Hill, Sverre Fredheim, Roy Mikkelsen, and Caspar Oimen took the first three places, as they had at the 1935 national tournament in Canton, South Dakota. The competitors for the combined cross-country and jumping were more difficult to select but the list contained regular winners: the Satre brothers, a Dartmouth contingent, and other consistent performers. In all, fifteen were chosen for the squad with another eight who would compete if funds were found.[36]

The Alpine trials on Mt. Rainier also produced no surprises with three Dartmouth students and one Hochgebirger taking the first four places. Hannes Schroll, just over from Austria, had not been on the try-out list, however, and he trounced the field. The best western skier, Don Fraser, was injured so could not compete. He was chosen for the team anyway.[37]

Since a number of likely candidates from the east were unable to travel to Mt. Rainier, the Eastern Downhill Championship doubled as the eastern Olympic trials. Alex Bright won the event and was chosen for the squad.[38] The team for Alpine competition was made up almost entirely of New Englanders, as might have been expected, and the region's wealthy clubs supported their men financially with the Eastern, the DOC, AMC, and Ski Club Hochgebirge supplying much of the money.[39]

Voices were raised against American participation in these Nazi Games, and for a while it looked as if American teams would not compete. When word was received from Brundage that the International Olympic Committee would brook no discrimination and—for what it was worth—Hitler had personally assured IOC president Baron de LaTour that all antisemitic placards would be removed from Garmisch, the NSA voted for participation.[40]

These winter Olympics were the first to have ski events for women. There were few competent women skiers in the early 1930s. When the AMC ran a "Women's Experienced" event in 1932, three women competed. One male observer's "biggest disappointment" was "the quality of skiing among the local fems."[41]

There was, in fact, a small cadre of experienced women, but they were little remarked upon because they went to Europe for the season. In one sense the creation of a women's team for the 1935 Fédération Internationale de Ski Championship was simple because of the limited number of qualified women. In another sense it was difficult to gather a team together because it was a novel idea and men would have to interest themselves in such an undertaking. A women's team appears to have been of little interest to women skiers in general.

Alice Pennington, a member of Amateur Ski Club of New York, first had the idea for a United States Women's Ski Team. Her house at St. Anton in the Arlberg of Austria was a home-away-from-home for friends and friends of friends; she knew all the expert skiers. She talked to club president Roland Palmedo, who immediately suggested wealthy and influential contacts among his Boston friends.[42] Palmedo—"our Arnold Lunn"—suggested borrowing Helen Boughton-Leigh, an American who was racing for the British, to act as captain of the team. Feeling "like a small boy reverentially writing President Roosevelt," Palmedo asked Arnold Lunn for the loan of Helen Boughton-Leigh.[43] The rest of the team was chosen according to availability and record, which meant there were no try-outs or funds to send them to Europe. Four wealthy New Englanders crossed the Atlantic to join two expatriates living in Switzerland and Italy.[44]

The men's team "provided a good foundation for the future"; the women's team was thought to be "too good looking to know how to ski."[45] Training began in January 1935, and none too soon. Betty Woolsey was on the team on the strength of wins in recent slalom and downhill competitions—"more by good luck than ability."[46] Hannes Schneider proffered advice now and then, and a week of racing with the British at Wengen added some spice. Every member of the team was awed by the German women, but Helen Boughton-Leigh showed well with tenth and twelfth placings. The European women, however, won handily. "I don't honestly think it was a bad last," one member of the team said, summing up the team's effort.[47] It was, as Palmedo had realized, the last moment to gather international experience before the real test: the Olympic Games at Garmisch.

The attempt to regularize the selection for the team was not a success. Twelve competitors, none from New England—hardly a representative field—raced in the trials on Mt. Rainier.[48] The team was largely chosen through the "old girl" network. Invitations were sent to prominent skiers and to those who regularly skied in Europe. It was hoped, somehow, that the team would have three westerners and three easterners from which the final four would be selected in Europe.[49]

Three from the 1935 team were chosen along with a newcomer, Clarita Heath, whose amateur zest provided an antidote to the seemingly unstoppable Germans. Times and placings in these politicized Olympics mattered and the American women did not fare well. Arnold Lunn, always generous to the amateur tradition, wrote that results were not everything; American teams raced for the joy of racing, not to prove one political system better than another. "A cheery team that doesn't take skiing . . . too tragically is a very valuable element at these meetings."[50]

Lunn was also referring to the participation of the men's team, which was dismissed by the American public as a failure.[51] Indeed, the Alpine events for the United States were hardly a success but Durrance, who was "guide, coach and trainer simultaneously," gained eighth in the slalom and eleventh in the downhill. Still, for many "the season of skiing was more of a disillusionment. The standard in Europe is so high that one despairs of ever reaching it and it seems silly to go into competition where one is entirely outclassed."[52]

American teams, men and women, continued to race in Europe, more on the basis of who was there than on who was distinctly chosen. An advertisement for members was put in the *Paris Herald* in 1938.[53] Once they were entered in an event, the individuals represented the United States. The women, particularly, showed much improvement, but when Clarita Heath came in fourth in an FIS race in 1937 there was general disbelief among spectators and officials.[54] Marion McKean was America's star the next season. The foundation of American women's racing—and postwar success—was laid in the 1930s.[55]

The National Ski Patrol System

Racers were skiing ever faster and suffering breaks (three prospective team members broke a back, a hand, a foot, and a leg),[56] and so were the thousands of recreational skiers. As early as 1931 Roland Palmedo, who had seen the Parsenn patrol at Davos in Switzerland at work, suggested a ski patrol at Stowe. Three years later an informal group of local skiers agreed "to be around" on weekends.[57] Until downhill skiing became prominent there were in fact very few accidents and danger was associated with jumping, not with recreational skiing, where bindings were loose and speed was hardly a factor. But the new conditions created by the speed involved in downhill skiing, the tightly clamped boot, and the greater number of weekend skiers made for more and more accidents.

Articles on safety began to appear in the ski literature in 1934 with descriptions of what local groups were doing, diagrams of how to lash four skis together for a makeshift toboggan, and discussions of plans for the location of first aid supplies. To the present safety-conscious age it may

The message of this National Ski Patrol poster was clear: have some marvelous skiing and serve others at the same time. Dwight Shepler was the leading American ski artist of the 1930s. (New England Ski Museum, Franconia, N.H.)

come as a surprise that safety was given so little consideration. "I don't really remember anybody getting hurt," recalled Roger Peabody of the early 1930s. "We had no provisions for anybody that was injured," remarked Ted Cooke, who had put up one of the early rope tows in 1935. "The first year we operated we didn't even have a toboggan; in those days people accepted the risk—considered it their own risk." Surprisingly, insurance was advertised as early as 1933.[58] Nothing was done until the situation became a real concern.

Two serious accidents in 1936 brought the problem wide attention. Charles Minot Dole, member of the Amateur Ski Club of New York, broke his leg on the toll road on Mt. Mansfield, Vermont. A so-called instructor refused to help him on the grounds that "anyone fool enough to hurt himself on this dumb trail deserves to break his leg." Two months later a fellow ASC member, an African safari hunter and Greenwich socialite, Frank

Edson crashed in a race and died of his injuries. Roland Palmedo, president of ASC, announced that "the time [has] come for a general study of safety in skiing." Dole chaired a committee which sent out questionnaires aimed at finding out the causes of accidents and about how casualties were handled. Although widely circulated in the Northeast, the questionnaire drew only a few hundred replies, a few of which, from the Boston area, wondered who these "sissies" were and how the "spoilsports" were going to wreck their winter fun, suggesting these mother-frighteners would probably keep all daughters at home.[59]

Nevertheless, a number of local patrols were formed as the ski slopes became more crowded. At Stowe in the spring of 1936, Mt. Mansfield ski patrol members helped "to clear up traffic snarls" by marking dangerous spots on the trail and giving directions to those unsure of their way. *The Ski Bulletin* editorialized: "While the patrol idea is still in the experimental stage, it seems to have a great deal of merit, and might well be adopted in other ski centers." Overcrowded trails were seen to be the biggest problem; trails "must not be allowed to get overcrowded, . . . groups must not stand at the top of a steep slope together." Naturally trying to enforce such restrictions earned the ski patrol the reputation of cops of the trail.[60]

The Amateur's report was published in the *American Ski Annual,* and increasing attention was paid to patrol work. For the 1938 National Championship held at Stowe, a special patrol was organized, and all spectators were given a copy of *How to Behave While Watching a Race.* Toboggans stood ready at appropriate intervals and splints, bandages, and hot coffee were available. Roger Langley, president of the NSA, was much impressed, and in March the National Ski Patrol System—the NSPS—was founded with members qualifying after thirty hours of Red Cross classwork. One member from each of the NSA's divisions served on a national committee, of which Dole was the chairman. By the spring of 1940, there were 153 patrolmen and statistics began to be accumulated on accidents. Subcommittees were at work developing rescue toboggans and lobbying for trail improvements. An educational-promotional film was in the making and, since there was no official financing (the Amateur Ski Club of New York had bankrolled the initial efforts), a Broken Bone Club produced $1.50 from each skier.[61]

The increasing concern for safety paralleled the growth of the sport. Control became essential, and the process of that control was also the process of modernization. Patrolmen (there were no women) were specialists selected by the NSPS whose bureaucratic organization ensured standards of first aid along with competence in skiing ability. The NSPS offered courses and administered tests.

The concern for the physical safety of skiers on the practice hill did not mitigate the devil-may-care attraction of trails named to create the daring ambience. One raced, perhaps as a Black and Blue Trail Smasher, on Hell's Highway, down the Nose Dive, over Devil's Dip, and along Shincracker. Some trails had "every corner . . . named for someone who had gone off in the woods. But Ritchie, he had two or three corners," reminisced Roger Clapp, a Schussverein member. Quite complacently Al Sise, an old-time racer, remembered that last corner—that was where "Andy Marshall had left his teeth."[62] Hill 6 near Woodstock, Vermont, gained some fame through the rope tow, but the skiing world of the 1930s already knew it as Suicide Six.

Tuckerman and the Inferno Races

In New England there was one great test for all people who characterized themselves as skiers in the 1930s. As skiing became more mechanized and popular, the great glacial cirque on Mt. Washington known as Tuckerman Ravine drew the collegiate and club crowds in spring as regularly as swallows return to Capistrano. In order to get to the ravine, would-be skiers had to climb for two and a half hours. The *Idraet* ideal involved with this hike combined with the camaraderie of making the trip with other "hair-shirt" youth gave the adventure the status of a tribal rite. The Tuckerman Ravine and Bowl were first entered on skis in 1914. After 1926 winter visits became more regular. The attraction towering nine hundred feet up was the headwall, a 50° steep first climbed and descended on skis in 1931 by Olympians Carleton and Proctor. The first to *Schuss* the headwall was Norwegian Sigmund Ruud, who was in America for the 1932 Lake Placid Games.[63] In the meantime prominent skiers like Arthur Comey had climbed Mt. Kathadin, the highest mountain in Maine, on skis and had described how he had negotiated the changing conditions on his descent: a true down-mountain testing. Comey also learned of a mad-cap, no-holds barred English adventure at Mürren called the Inferno Race from the top of the Schilthorn to the Lauterbrunnen valley with no flagged course, just a pure down-mountain dash. He published verbatim the report of the race from the *British Ski Club's Year Book* because it beggared description. He added that in New England there were also some little Inferno runs available.[64] For the Hochgebirge (Hochies) Ski Club of Boston, Easter Day, 16 April 1932, seemed appropriate for such a "Suicide Race." Each racer absolved the Hochies from any responsibility. For Mt. Washington the weather was pretty fair; one racer did, indeed, lose his way in the fog but found his bearings quickly. Another broke a ski but there were no accidents

SPRING SKIING

NEW HAMPSHIRE
STATE PLANNING AND DEVELOPMENT COMMISSION, CONCORD

State and federal governments promoted skiing in depression America. This poster combined the attraction of the Tuckerman headwall with sun and sociability. (New England Ski Museum, Franconia, N.H.)

for the thirty Nansen Club members and their three toboggans. Flags were posted at crucial spots but the fog was heavy enough to make them scarcely visible. It was said skiers gauged their direction more by the wind.

Racers were started at one minute intervals (which was safer than the mass start at Mürren) and were timed by radio telephone—an innovation. The winner, who went from the top of Mt. Washington, over the headwall, down the Sherburne trail, to the AMC hut at the bottom, made his run in 14 minutes, 41.3 seconds.[65] The race was deemed a grand success, a worthy off-spring, this American Inferno, of its English sire. In the 1934 Inferno (there was none in 1933 because of bad weather) Dick Durrance took the time down to 12 minutes, 35 seconds. "You couldn't see one flag from another," remembered Al Sise whose red strings trailed from his pants so that if he set off an avalanche he might be more easily found. "It was like an ocean race in a fog."[66] People were stationed along the way with bells and whistles.

The descriptions of the 1939 Inferno with Toni Matt's headwall *Schuss* have been told so many times that it is difficult to distinguish what really happened, but he halved the time for the descent by simply going straight down the nine-hundred-foot drop and ended at the AMC hut six minutes and twenty-nine seconds later, adding to the lore of Mt. Washington and the mystique of the Inferno.[67] There were attempts to resurrect the Inferno in 1952 and 1983 but they foundered on weather and safety concerns. Robert Monahan, stationed on the summit in 1932, had been right when he wrote that he did not believe the race could become a fixture, for skiing "up here is decidedly unsatisfactory, except during a very brief period, which the Hochs so fortunately struck."[68]

However, weather and danger did not spoil the thought of spring in the Tuckerman bowl. As skiing became more mechanized, the long trek up to the ravine floor was valued as an "authentic" experience. And then the challenge of the headwall! As Tuckerman's fame spread, the spring ritual would bring two thousand people into the bowl. What had once provided glorious seclusion for the ski fraternity, a special place that did not have to be shared, now seemed spoiled and somehow sullied by the hoi-polloi. Where then could one go for untracked powder, for the camaraderie of sun and snow with a few friends? With Europe embroiled in ideologic invective, the answer lay two and three thousand miles from Boston, in America's western mountains.

10 / *Western Idylls*

> Then for four miles downhill running, carefree and as
> happy as the winds that flew with us. Not even the beasts of
> the forests trespassed upon this ground we were skimming.
> Forgotten all the petty sordid things that surround one in
> this greedy rush to exist among the smokestacks of the city,
> for here, in the covert of the towering, unchanging moun-
> tains, for a few brief days, we *lived*.
>
> —"In the Northwest," *American Ski Annual* (1934)

As the ore veins in the California Sierra petered out, miners' race meetings became sporadic; the last major meeting was in 1911. By that time the
Lake Tahoe region was already known as a winter resort for city people.
Some took ski trips from Tallac to Fallen Leaf Lake, a few of the more
adventurous skied into the snow-buried hostelry at Glen Alpine when it
could only be entered by the dormer window. Skiing, wrote one enthusiast,
is "the chief method of locomotion . . . and the novice soon becomes expert
in the milder forms of the sport."[1] One could rent skis at Truckee where the
local club operated "a haulback" for tobogganists and skiers who wished to
return to Hilltop Lodge. The standard of skiing was poor. "Your feet and
ankles . . . acted in a steering capacity," and if they failed you swayed your
body to determine your downward path. The occasional expert appeared.
A short clip in the documentary film *Legends of American Skiing* shows Mrs.
Birkin's fast and graceful telemark style on the Donner Pass in 1917. When
a small group of enthusiasts explored the area two seasons later, locals
wondered at their short skis and flimsy bamboo poles. The few trappers and
railroad men still using skis of gold-rush vintage turned out for a good
laugh, but ended with "loud hurrahs and shouts" as the new skiers turned
their telemarks and swung into their Christiania turns.[2] When Otto Lirsch
immigrated to California in 1927, he too came upon old-timers using long
skis with slip-in bindings. They simply could not believe he used wax—it
was still called dope—to go up hill.[3] Even as late as the spring of 1935, a
group of Arlberg devotees found locals on "home-made skis, straight-
edged and eight to ten feet long with more or less elaborately carved
points."[4] Several carried ornamentally carved staves. Only two years later
the toe-strap-only skis were a curiosity in California.[5]

This photo celebrating the vastness of the western mountains is one example from a rare album designed to attract easterners to Alta, Utah, 1940. (New England Ski Museum, Franconia, N.H.)

In the Idaho hills, shepherds of Basque origin clutched stout staffs as they skied on their long boards to which their boots were nailed.[6] Colored moving pictures of these herdsmen taken in 1938 give a lasting image of the sort of skiing that had created such carnival fun among the nineteenth-century miners. In the back valley ranches of Colorado snow country the traditional wide and long ski was used until the time of World War II.[7] These home-made skis and the utilitarian nature of their use offer a contrast to the sporting nature of Alpine skiing that had taken hold in the colleges and clubs of New England.

In California and the Rockies local clubs were formed in the 1920s but the recreational emphasis was on cross-country trips and, for the men, on jumping. Members left Denver, for example, for expeditions to Estes Park where Erling Strom had inveigled a hotel owner into staying open over the winter in 1920, about the same time that NSA president Torguson predicted that the "Rockies will become the center of skiing in the U.S."[8] The sort of one-hundred-mile cross-country expeditions such as Strom and Lars Haugen made in 1926 from Estes Park to Steamboat were obviously not for most skiers.[9] Strom was upholding the *Idraet* ideal; it was "real" skiing as opposed to the downhill and slalom which were merely pastimes.

Little by little, though, reports of skiing above timberline filtered back to the board rooms in Boston and New York. Californians believed they had snow comparable to Europe's, and Coloradans knew that their peaks provided some of the finest ski running grounds. It took ten days to cross the Atlantic by boat and another twenty-four hours to reach the Alps by train; easterners naturally began looking to America's own mountains for their winter enjoyments.

Californians were first to advertise skiing in their state. When Los Angeles was awarded the Summer Olympic Games for 1932, the state expected to be granted the Winter Games too; after all, no one could dispute the guaranteed heavy snowfalls and marvelous terrain. Ample housing and adequate transportation facilities were planned, and capital was raised by issuing bonds. Instead, Lake Placid was awarded the Games because the IOC realized that Californians had no experience in staging events of Olympic magnitude and had no governing ski association—nor, indeed, any winter sport association used to handling the management of such a festival.

Not everyone in the state was unhappy with the IOC's decision; business had spent huge sums of money touting California as the "Land of Sunshine and Roses" and did not wish to cool and whiten that image. The California Chamber of Commerce, sensing a new economic possibility, took a hand and began to advertise the Land of Sunshine as a winter sports paradise as well.[10]

Yosemite put California on the skiing map. On the initiative of the Yosemite Winter Sports Club, a California Ski Association was formed in 1930 which immediately affiliated with the NSA. In February nineteen thousand visitors came to Yosemite, up from three hundred in the same month in 1923. This spectacular growth was due to the "All-Year Highway," which opened in 1926. Ernest des Baillets, a Swiss with experience in ski developments in Canada and at Lake Placid, became director of Winter Sports in Yosemite in 1929. He built up the park's trail system, called for small ski huts stocked with provisions, and hired ski guides to take the growing clientele into the back country. The conditions were ideal; no better could be found in Europe.[11] But skiers of the 1930s wanted Alpine skiing, so Charley Proctor and other eastern and European instructors were brought in to run the ski school while the Park Service planned various improvements: a permanent "up-ski," reliable water supply, efficient drainage, and sufficient parking. A new lodge was on the drawing boards with headquarters for a ski school and a waxing room. Yosemite had swapped the *Idraet* ideal for "Alpine ambience." Prominent European skiers like Otto Steiner and Hans Thorner, both of whom had skied in New England, began advertising that in Yosemite one found Europe in America. In 1935 Yosemite took out a full-page advertisement in the *American Ski Annual* showing Hannes Schroll, who had recently trounced the field in the U.S. Olympic try-outs and had become director of the ski school, saying "Yosemite National Park Ski Slopes are more like those in my own country, in the Austrian Tyrol, than any other I have visited in America." The next year Yosemite proclaimed itself the "Snow Capital of California," and in 1937 it boasted that it had the state's "most *complete* winter program."[12]

It was true. But there were plenty of other ski venues; the state Chamber of Commerce issued 250,000 copies of a winter guide covering all resorts in 1938 and splashed the glories of winter sports on five hundred highway billboards and the temptations of winter in the sun and snow on city streetcars. Newspapers and radio stations were furnished two releases every week as well as regular reports of snow depths and road conditions. A winter sports film was available with an accompanying lecturer in the metropolitan areas and with mimeographed cue notes for outlying districts. Fresno's ski membership drive, the new "pull-back" installed by the Auburn Ski Club, Tahoe activities, and the Winter Sports Carnival held in the Sacramento auditorium in January 1939 all received much attention. The Forest Service opened up a new area; the Mt. Shasta Snowmen were active; programs for children were started by the Placer County School Board. These random items indicate a growing interest in skiing; it became *the* winter sport by the war years.[13]

Yosemite, however, held pride of place with its average twelve-foot snow depth and its spectacular Ahwahnee Hotel. An application was pending for an aerial tramway. Yosemite and the Sierra Club sponsored the "Sierra Skyway," a crest trail planned to run along three hundred miles of the Sierra range. When Arnold Lunn visited for the first time in 1938 he was so impressed with the terrain and facilities he said he would try to induce the Kandahar Ski Club of Mürren to put up a replica of their cup to be raced for annually. The first Far West Kandahar took place in March 1939.[14] It seemed to certify that America had found its own Europe.

Coloradans too believed that their state was a sporting winter heaven. The aptly named Colorado Arlberg Club promoted Alpine skiing from its founding in 1930, and even Europeans like Otto Schniebs judged that Aspen's "climate and the snow conditions surpassed anything I have seen in this country or Europe." André Roche, brought over from Switzerland to survey the Aspen area in 1935, said the slopes which "lead down into Ashcroft can be compared to the best of the Parsenn," and that here was the possibility of a resort "that would in no way be inferior to anything in the Alps."[15] In 1936 Averell Harriman's resort complex at Sun Valley, Idaho, was called the St. Moritz of America even as it was being built.

There was growing excitement for Alpine skiing, and the test—just as in Europe and New England—was in downhill and slalom racing. The cognoscenti were those who had been to Europe: Frank and Lee Ashley, for example, had been schooled at the exclusive Le Rosey in Switzerland; Ted Ryan and Billy Fiske, Cresta bobsled champion, had spent winters in Europe; Bob Balch, another early supporter of the joys of Alpine skiing was a transplanted Hochgebirger and full of downhill verve. But the standard of skiing was low. Lee Ashley entered a slalom comprising six turns over a hundred-yard course and managed a fourth or fifth place by using telemark turns. Local lad Barney McLean, already well known as a jumper, managed to win his first slalom even though he could hardly turn. Ned Grant, who in the West was admired as a technician, could only place forty-sixth in a field of fifty-eight when he raced in the U.S. Eastern Downhill Championship. Skiers used a wide stance, recalled Lee Ashley. In those days you got "your skis as wide apart as you could without scraping your privates in the snow." Whenever anyone with eastern experience joined the Arlberg Club outings, "we get a new angle on skiing . . . and usually learn we are far behind in . . . technique."[16]

Berthoud Pass was the most favored skiing grounds for the Arlberg Club whose clubhouse held up to thirty members on weekends. During the week it was available "to desirable parties."[17] One of the attractions of Berthoud was that it was accessible by train and car. West Portal, where the actual skiing took place, was at the western end of Moffat Tunnel. At first, skiers had to jump from the train as it slowed near the summit, but the Arlberg Club eventually persuaded the Denver and Salt Lake Railroad to run ski specials that left Denver on Saturday noon and returned on Sunday evening. Berthoud "became so crowded that there was scarcely room for skiing," one correspondent reported, let alone for parking four to five hundred cars every Sunday.[18] Something had to be done.

The Forest Service commissioned a survey of possible areas where additional trails could be cleared. There was a call for more overnight accommodations, better transportation facilities, and more ski trails, but, although some cutting was done, most of the pump-priming New Deal money that went to the CCC was spent on "picnic grounds for local grocers," as one disgusted skier reported.[19] The first rope tow at Berthoud, financed by a department store, was ready in February 1937. It was followed next season by another one at Loveland which inevitably brought greater crowds.

By that time Aspen's "boat tow" was in operation although the real development of Aspen was planned for Mt. Hayden's slopes with a prospective resort in the ghost town of Ashcroft. While a four-mile tram was being contemplated and financing arranged, André Roche cut one run on Aspen's Ajax Mountain, and Roland Palmedo, Sig Buchmayr, and Otto Schniebs—one could hardly find three more influential easterners—came to test the region's delights and found them quite exceptional. The first real downhill race was held on the Roche run on Ajax in February 1938, and spectators marveled at the "beautiful high-speed controlled running" of the winner and the seemingly "continuous front somersaults" of the other competitors. Jarvis Schauffler's time of two minutes fifty-three seconds was faster than anticipated, and it was generally believed that his record would stand for several years. But when the German universities' team arrived, top man Ulli Beutter "brushed down the course in 2.20," over a half-minute better than Schauffler. The Roche, he announced, was the finest competition course he had seen in the United States.[20] Many believed that skiing in the Rocky Mountains had entered a new phase, that it was about to become one of the leading attractions of Colorado.[21] In 1931 Tom Cabot of Boston had called Colorado the ideal country for those who could not afford the time to visit Switzerland. Now Ted Ryan and Billy Fiske were planning a resort larger than Zermatt.[22] With all plans—political and economic—in order, development was stalled by the war in Europe, and when Fiske, flying for the RAF, was shot down in the Battle of Britain, the hope of the Hayden-Ashcroft resort died with him.[23]

In the West there was a belief, advertised in strikingly similar phrases, that America's mountainous terrain was more than equal to Europe's Alps. The Northwest's "high altitude skiing [was] comparable to the best . . . that can be had in Switzerland," and furthermore could be enjoyed for six months out of the year. Mounts Rainier, Hood, and Baker provided the main focus for skiing in the Pacific Northwest. Rainier gained special attention because the National Championships of 1935, which doubled as try-outs for the 1936 Olympic team, were held on its slopes. Mt. Baker's growing reputation received a boost when 20th Century Pictures filmed Jack London's *Call of the Wild* there. After Clark Gable and Loretta Young frolicked on Mt. Baker, its popularity was assured. Mt. Hood in Oregon gained considerable favor because it was only fifty miles from Portland. The main road to Mt. Hood was first kept open during the winter of 1928. The Portland Winter Sports Association steadily promoted Mt. Hood as a skier's paradise. Skiing was established as a regular winter activity with an estimated 120,000 people participating in the 1938 season.[24]

In fact, if the city promoters had done a little historical research, they would have discovered that since the beginning of the Great War parties made up from the Portland Snowshoe Club and the Mazama and Multomah ski clubs had enjoyed outings like "a week's romp" on the north side of the mountain. At Government Camp a guide gave ski instruction as early as 1913 and some of the Mazamas "became quite adept at the sport."[25] But except for a few Scandinavian immigrants and occasional excursionists, skiing petered out in the 1920s. When the mountain became accessible by car, however, winter sporting began to appeal to those with money and leisure time. Hans Otto Giese, who had been part of the pack in Schneider's 1923 film *The Ski Chase,* arrived as a law student at the University of Washington and found himself one of the very few Arlberg specialists who could be relied upon to give instructions in the rudiments of skiing.[26] Reed College eagerly anticipated a Viennese racer. The Cascade Club of Portland took to downhill and slalom competition, and the first Northwest Championships were held on Mt. Baker in 1935. Just as with Colorado's Arlberg Club, the Cascade Club called for increased huts, cabins, and lodges. There seemed to be endless members who joined up to ski; the select Mazamas, for example, had over one thousand members in 1935 and had already built their own cabin near Government Camp. The Washington Ski Club could take fifty in its hut on Mt. Baker, and the Forest Service had plans for opening a stone hut to the public that year too. The Wy'east Climbers— known for their selectivity (maximum twenty-five members) and for their mountain rescue work—also completed a new winter cabin in 1935 and, in order to extend their service, took to skiing.[27]

It would be wrong, though, to think only in terms of these major skiing grounds. The CCC work force, along with civic groups, opened up part of the Whitman National Forest. A typical depression-era development was at Anthony Lake: the lake itself was readied for skating, a fifteen-hundred-foot rope-tow area was created, fifteen miles of road were kept open and

Timberline Lodge
Mt. Hood, Oregon

Historic Preservation USA 14

Today there is enough concern about historic preservation to put public works of the depression era on the Historic Register. This 1986 prestamped postcard brought Timberline Lodge on Mt. Hood, Oregon, to public notice. (New England Ski Museum, Franconia, N.H.)

plans, contingent upon government subsidies, were made for a 120-bed guest lodge and cleared slopes, some lighted for night skiing.[28] Depression money channeled into the CCC and other agencies provided some of the essential modern skiing facilities which became the structural foundations for the postwar skiing boom.

One million dollars of Works Progress Administration money was budgeted for the Timberline Lodge development on Mt. Hood which outpaced all other areas as the Northwest's answer to Europe. It boasted "The Skiing Thrill of a Lifetime" in "Perfect Snow Conditions for 8 Months of the Year," under the tutelage of Otto Lang, one of Schneider's top lieutenants. In this way Schneider's Arlberg technique was adopted as the way to ski in the Northwest where Lang operated the western branch of the Hannes Schneider Ski School, just as Rybizka was running the eastern branch. One could get more skiing in in a single day because of the "World's Longest Chair Type Ski Lift." What more could any devotee of the snow game want for twelve dollars a week and a "skier's lunch" for thirty-five cents?[29]

Leavensworth's two-hundred-foot jumping hill near Timberline was famous in the 1930s, but more and more attention was paid to community ski developments such as that at American River. Clubs opened up what they considered "their mountain"; some areas were proclaimed to have excellent terrain for beginners. Mt. St. Helen with its limited accommodation offered the continuing charm of touring.[30] In the Northwest of the 1930s, then, there was a trend to capture the increasing neophyte market but at the same time there was a push to prove to the experts that American skiing was equal to that of Europe.

California promoted Yosemite, Colorado its Aspen area, and Oregon, Mt. Hood and Timberline, but they all were measured against America's first destination resort: Sun Valley. It is difficult to separate myth from reality in Sun Valley's history. The man who found the site, Count Felix Schaffgotsch, bon vivant and ardent Nazi (he was later killed on the Russian front), was the one who wired Averell Harriman, "This is the place." He was not much of a skier, something which Harriman (also not much of a skier!) recognized, "but he knew resorts." Sun Valley—from the outset conceived as a ski resort to boost Harriman's Union Pacific Railroad—was even more important as a magnet for high society. Harriman was determined to attract the wealthy. He chose public relations man Steve Hannigan to orchestrate the resort. Hannigan, who had earned a reputation by making a sun-drenched paradise out of a Florida sand spit called Miami Beach, created a marvel of rustic-chic living with Harriman's money.[31]

Schaffgotsch was hired to investigate "the present centers of sport in our territory," the areas served by the Union Pacific Railroad of which Harriman was chairman of the board. According to all accounts Schaffgotsch traveled throughout the West: too crowded at Alta, too rainy on Mt. Hood, too many weekenders at Yosemite, too windy on Berthoud Pass, and so on. He wandered the Ketchum, Idaho, region for three days before wiring Harriman, who came to look in February 1936. By the end of March nearly four thousand acres had been bought for $10.04 an acre, and Charley Proctor from the 1928 U.S. Olympic team was hired to select ski runs.

Hannigan arrived in Ketchum in his Miami clothes and turned those snowed-in Sawtooth Mountains into Sun Valley. "This is one city," Hannigan noted of the old Brass Ranch, "in which roughing it must be a luxury."[32] Work on the lodge was under way in June, with everything just completed for the opening on 21 December. This was truly the first instant million-dollar resort and it drew stars of stage and screen, who brought a swirling glamour to the Idaho hills. In 1980, when Dorice Taylor published a book chronicling the progress of Sun Valley, she chose four photographs for its back jacket, which appropriately documents the range of visitors: Jacqueline Kennedy, Groucho Marx, Satchmo Armstrong, and the shah of Iran.

The fact that there was no snow before Christmas in 1936 hardly mattered. Sun Valley was a theater where actors such as John Wayne, Claudette Colbert, Tyrone Power, and Arlene Dahl could play in a new setting. Sonja Henie starred in *Sun Valley Serenade,* which brought world renown to the resort. Hemingway had a house, Clark Gable and Gary Cooper once rented the Ruud lift for a day. Antelopes and a St. Bernard rubbed noses while German chefs prepared the cuisine, steam swirled from the outdoor heated pools, and Austrians manned the ski school. One disgusted instructor wrote:

> It takes patience to be a skilehrer at Sun Valley because the inmates are about what you'd expect. You know the idle rich up all night and asleep all morning and "I'm simply exhausted darling" after one ride down a two foot hill.[33]

In fact, Sun Valley was more than a showplace for glamour. Proctor and Dollar mountains provided excellent skiing; the resort simply made the best of everything available. True skiers ensured its skiing reputation. Visiting European teams always included Sun Valley on their circuit, top American racers competed there regularly—Durrance retired the Harriman Cup in 1940.

Ketchum, at the end of a Union Pacific Railroad spur was about as isolated a destination as there could be. Everything had to be brought in. Sun Valley, geographically in a world by itself, ensured a social selectivity that marked it off from all other skiing regions in the United States. In a curious way, even as it retained its exclusivity it influenced and gave impetus to the image of the *Skilehrer* in lederhosen and Tyrolean hat and, with its chair lift, to the mechanization of skiing. The press and the resort's own publicity office capitalized on the affluent who came "from the four corners of the social world." Photographers caught handsome and bronzed faces athletically arranged for skiing by day and après skiing by night. It all made "the sport" even more attractive to office workers in Boston, Washington, and Los Angeles.[34] Sun Valley had no competition, hence it attracted all the attention, but it did become the model when the Salt Lake City Winter Sports Association started a resort at Alta in Utah's Wasatch Range in 1936.[35] On the East Coast, one New England hotel, already known for its luxurious accommodation "was made over into an eastern 'Sun Valley Lodge'."[36]

The West was beginning to affect skiers back east at the same time that it attracted the wealthy few to its vast and pristine snowfields, its pure air at ten thousand feet, and its lonely, dizzying two-mile descents. The mountain settings held an extraordinary appeal for those caught up in the bustle of Boston and noise of New York. In the years after the war many more would be able to visit the sites of their western dreams.

11 | The Economics of Pleasure

> Asa Osborn has moved to a new shop, four times the room.
> This is good news because a major portion of Asa's clientele
> has always regarded the shop more as a club than a store.
>
> —*Boston Herald* (1936)

> For Digestion's Sake ... Smoke Camels! "That tells one
> big reason why I smoke Camels," says SIG BUCHMAYR,
> skiing wizard.
>
> —Advertisement, *Collier's* (1937)

> Billy Fiske brought us all to the Aspen area and we made
> plans to develop an entire ski resort the size of Zermatt. We
> had plans laid—political, engineering and every possible
> way. We were on the go! And boom comes World War II.
>
> —Ted Ryan, oral history interview for
> *Legends of American Skiing*

How much did it cost to ski? Who put up the money to construct lifts and create ski centers? What profits were made? What effect did money have on skiing and on communities? Simple questions, but impossible to answer. There are many facts about the economics of skiing but they rarely provide enough information to give a firm understanding of the ski business. Data can be organized to indicate trends but the evidence cannot be pushed beyond suggestion. Most histories of sport—except the more leftist oriented—shy away from economic evaluations. I offer here only considerations.

The problem in discussing the economic history of early skiing is that no consistent records exist. In the 1930s most who built rope tows did not really care whether they made money. There was little thought of profit and for the most part little effort was made to reap financial gains. This was not the case with those who began to manufacture skis, but I have not located a single series of account books. The first ski shops are gone and with them their ledgers. Although oral histories can provide a sense of the economic ups and downs, they offer only impressionistic revelations that do not count as hard evidence. It may be that the reason most sport history is social rather than economic is that most studies suffer from a paucity of economic sources upon which to draw. Stephen Hardy has recently exhorted historians to look at sport history from the inside out, analyzing the role entrepreneurial activity played and how managers organized the business.[1] I was tempted to use this approach to get at the economics of skiing in my study, but came up against a dearth of information.

I find the most persuasive case can be made by adapting Rostow's "take-off" thesis, which is an analysis of the momentum reached when an economy is so driven that it does not falter and decline. Although applying this Kennedyesque international economic model to skiing might appear to be stretching it, my contention is that all the parts to modern skiing were in place, ready for the "take-off" when the war intervened and put everything on hold. Extrapolating from Rostow, this chapter amplifies the following observations: there were both local and wider populations of consumers and an industry with a major successful product—the ski—to sell in vast quantities; there was a transportation network that allowed local, national, and even international travel everywhere, from ski hills to resorts. There was a political climate that promoted skiing and coincided with a philosophy determined to keep alive the health and morality connotations of the sport. Small-time tinkerers, individual entrepreneurs, clubs, communities, states, and the national government all sponsored ski activities.

The New Consumer

In 1920 a young American learned to ski in Norway. He returned to live in Boston, and for three years he could not find a soul to join him on ski excursions. If he had gone to Lincoln, New Hampshire, he might have found a couple of people in town who knew how to ski.[2] By 1940 one authority estimated the skiing population of the United States at three million. The Red Cross's estimate was two million and *Time* magazine put the figure at one million.[3] The truth is that no one knew the number, and few thought it was important, but it was all somehow rather exciting that so many were on skis all across snow country. Some of the business minded may have given thought to appealing to these people, but no statistical foundation was forthcoming. One study on vacation travel expenditures showed clearly that increasing amounts of money were spent in the United States.[4] One difficulty in getting valid data lies in the fact that no one studied vacations by season. Even if it were possible to separate statistics by seasons, winter vacations were not always spent doing winter sports. For many, the attraction of winter vacations was sunshine rather than snow, as California discovered when, in trying to publicize its skiing potential, it ran up against strong resistance from those who advertised the state as the land of sunshine and roses.

Numbers of skiers, in fact, may not have been the most influential factor in certain aspects of the ski business. Furthermore, the depression, which the graph shows had a great impact on the travel of the general population, did not have much effect on wealthy skiers. We have already had occasion to mention Tom Cabot's 1933 trip to Europe. The men who instigated the Woodstock tow in 1934 had just returned from the Alps; Alex Bright and his friends advocated the tram after they returned from Austria in 1935, and so on. The first ski cruise to Europe—an express sailing to Austria!—was advertised in 1934 and was followed by an accompanied trip to the 1936 Olympics and by other cruises in 1937 to Europe and Chile.[5] The "snow plane" from Boston to Laconia, New Hampshire, a regularly scheduled weekend flight, was advertised as "something new" in the winter of 1935. This let the White Mountain Ski Runners avoid the fatigue of driving north to their club farmhouses. Weekend tri-motor aircraft charters of the Boston-Maine-Central Vermont Airways were available the next winter.[6] Although these services were inconsequential in the 1930s, they demonstrate, yet again, that some were willing to pay extra to enjoy their sport as comfortably as possible. Only after the war did Colonial Airlines offer daily and weekly scheduled services from New York to New England's skiing grounds.[7]

These were opportunities that only the wealthy could take advantage of. The Hochgebirge Ski Club of Boston had forty members in 1938: seventeen members (42.5%) had skied in Europe; fifteen (37.5%) had skied in the West, the Canadian Rockies being favored; and one member had South American experience.[8] The president of the Amateur Ski Club of New York, Roland Palmedo, had his photograph—"How Roland Palmedo Carries His Skis"—in the *American Ski Annual* of 1935.[9] It showed his skis strapped to the fuselage of his biplane. The Schussverein, recalled Roger Clapp, was "the most diverse group of people you'd ever want to meet in your life from world famous surgeons and physicians, to top Boston lawyers and industrialists, government officials, businessmen of course. You name it and you'll find them in the Schuss."[10] Count Schaffgotsch found Sun Valley, the marquis d'Albizzi was at Lake Placid, the duke of Leuchtenberg, at Peckett's, count de Pret, at the Broadmoor.[11]

Although skiing was an elitist sport, it was also available to the less wealthy. The vast majority of these skiers came from cities. Statistics from the snow trains are evidence of this vast and mostly new clientele. Between 1931 and 1935 the Boston and Maine carried 59,305; between 1936 and 1940 the number tripled to 174,622.[12]

Many of these thousands joined ski clubs: in 1922 the United States

Estimated expenditures for vacation travel (millions of dollars)

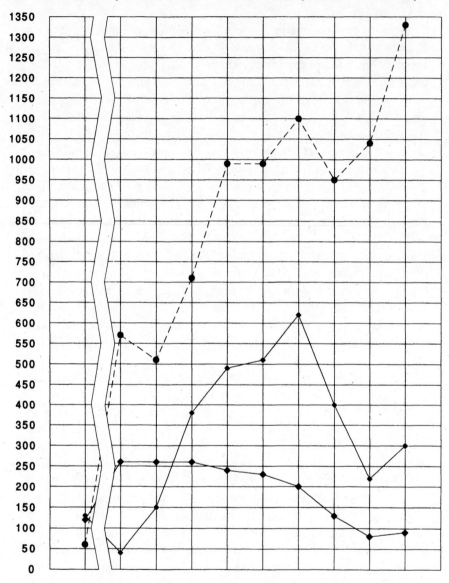

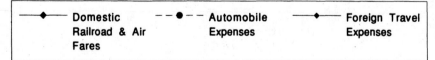

Eastern Amateur Ski Association was founded with 7 clubs; in 1932 there were 67; in 1935 there were 135; and in 1940, 181.[13] The clubs were extremely varied. If we look at two typical cases, the Onondaga Ski Club of Syracuse, New York, whose membership was solely interested in getting out of the city to ski, and the Ski Club of Plymouth, New Hampshire, which was dominated by merchants who hoped for winter prosperity, two pictures emerge that can serve as general economic indicators of 90 percent of the clubs.

The Onondagas in 1939 had a membership of thirty-five with annual dues of twenty-five cents. This was a low-keyed club whose January accounts reached a total of $8.55, which they quickly reduced by $6 when they rented a film. Yet they tried to interest the state in channeling the CCC into cutting ski trails, and there was a hope that the State Conservation Department might follow up on it.[14] This was a club whose leaders experimented in trail cutting, slalom work, and social activity. It is representative of many small enthusiastic groups who saw skiing as both a physical activity and an occasion for socializing; economics were unimportant.

A different picture emerges from the account books of the Plymouth Ski Club, one that is typical of a larger group. Contributions from merchants formed a substantial financial foundation; the local theater subscribed thirty-five dollars, the two banks in town, twenty-five dollars each, and many of the businesses ten dollars apiece. Membership in the club was one dollar, with some paying five dollars; youngsters paid twenty-five cents and "Old Members," twenty cents. In the 1938 and 1939 seasons the income and expenses were remarkably stable with the club running minute deficits, although these were always made up by donations from the ski school, chamber of commerce, or others. In fact, at the end of the 1938 season, the ledger showed a balance of $36.58 although actual expenses just exceeded income.

	Income	*Expenses*
1938	$1,262.71	$1,272.53
1939	$1,012.00	$1,046.17

The Plymouth merchants saw the economic advantage in promoting skiing. Over half the club's expenses was for advertising. Brochures were published, the Boston and Maine carried the town's advertisements, as did the local Lakes Region Association and the four Boston papers, the *Globe, Herald Traveler, Post,* and *Evening Transcript,* as well as New Hampshire's *Manchester Union Leader.* Besides appealing to local and regional skiers, Plymouth also ran an advertisement in the national *Sports Illustrated,* an indication of the town's play for major attention, which did, indeed, bring the Women's State Slalom Championship to one of its five hills in 1938.[15] It is impossible to gauge whether the business community benefited—and if so, by how much.

On the other side of the continent, largely because the state of California had failed to obtain the 1932 Winter Olympic Games, the State Chamber of Commerce was extremely active. It initiated the development of the higher regions of the state as an economic asset for all of California. A general study estimated that skiers were going to spend over $1 million that season. In 1933 more than a million skiers visited various California areas, and the ski industry expected a $6.5 million business, which was nothing compared to Switzerland's annual $50 million.[16]

These statistics come only from the Northeast and California because the Midwest and the Rockies did not have to cater to the skiing population, nor were many ready to inveigle nonskiers into the sport. Fred Pabst, the brewery heir, tried; he had a total of seventeen rope tows in areas as diverse as Wisconsin, Canada, and New England. All but the one at Big Bromley in Vermont failed. "I had the hills, but where were the skiers?" he asked.[17]

In the 1930s there were both local people interested in sporting on skis and a larger population in urban centers near mountains who enjoyed the new thrill. At the same time there were international connections; the 1924 and 1928 Winter Olympics held in Europe had virtually no appeal except to a tiny minority of enthusiasts. The 1932 Games at Lake Placid—enormously unsuccessful from the point of view of weather and economics— also did not do much for skiing although they did raise people's consciousness of winter sports.[18] The 1936 Games generated more interest—partly because of the political presence of fascism, but also because Alpine skiing and women's events were presented for the first time. An increasing number of Europeans were skiing on slopes and trails in the United States, and American skiing was becoming part of the international skiing world. The best book on skiing in the 1930s—certainly the most impressive in English—was Roland Palmedo's *Skiing: The International Sport*.[19]

The first of Rostow's conditions for business take-off—a local, national, and international clientele—was present by the late 1930s.

The Equipment Market

Skiing as a sport of a million people created an extraordinary market for skis, boots, poles, and accessories. Again, expenditures for ski equipment were only occasionally itemized as such, so it is difficult to know exactly who was buying what and who was reaping the profits.

The well-established midwestern ski manufacturing companies of Strand and Lund continued to dominate the market in the 1920s. By 1934 Strand advertised his as the "largest ski factory on the earth," and C. L. Lund's Northland Ski Company promoted itself in the same year as the "World's Largest Ski Manufacturers" and claimed "90% of America's Expert Skiers" used Northlands. To take advantage of the growing numbers of skiers in New England, Lund opened up a second factory in Laconia, New Hampshire, four years later.[20] In the 1920s there were one or two other companies, for instance Tubbs in Maine, which also made snowshoes, sleds, and ice hockey sticks. But in the 1930s small-time manufacturers began to capitalize on the demand for skis. First only Groswold of Denver and Strand of New Richmond, Wisconsin, advertised in the USEASA *Annual,* but they were soon joined by Schniebs, Northland, Gregg, Craftsbury Common, and Anderson and Thompson. The last publicized a laminated model.[21] The list grew to include Spalding,[22] Nordic, Peterborough, Adirondack Products, Alpine Sporting Goods, and Winner's Hydrocyl. In 1937 Farr-West, Trailmate, and Broadmount too began marketing skis. It is significant that of the newer manufacturers, only Gregg was based in the Midwest; the others spread from Seattle to Schenectady, from Craftsbury Common—in Vermont, although difficult to find on a map—to Trenton, New Jersey. A number of these domestic ski manufacturers gave their products authenticity by advertising that their "old country craftsmen" made a ski of traditional quality but charged a domestic price. Among the many imported skis the Norwegian ones were preferred. The choice was among Johansen, Nilsen, Tangvald, Norge, Gresvig, Amundsen, Holmenkollen, Hagen, Erickson, and Gresshoppa. Attenhofer and Zogg competed for a share of the sales from Switzerland.[23] There was an all-metal-bottom Swiss ski on display at the New York World's Fair in 1939.[24]

The price of skis varied according to wood and craftsmanship. Hickory was best. Ash and maple were considered adequate. In the chic New York store of Abercrombie and Fitch a pair of hickories cost $16.50 in 1935, whereas maple was $6. There were children's skis, frequently of pine, for $3.50. A specialists' shop like Hambro's of Boston sold a variety of skis from $7 to $18 that year. In 1936 Macy's models ranged from $10 to $16 for domestic skis and $17 to $20 for imported ones. In 1931 sales of skis and snowshoes had totaled $163,032; by 1937 the figure totaled about $1.25 million.[25]

The case of Darby and Ball of Waterbury, Vermont, offers an alternative view. The company made scythe handles, but with the increasing interest in skiing in the area around Stowe in the early 1930s, one of the company's carpenters fashioned a ski from an old model. The skis seemed to work, and a friend wanted fifteen pairs to sell in Stowe. It was a catch-as-catch-can effort as manufacturers tended to keep their operations secret. The problem Darby and Ball ran into was not in the manufacturing but in the selling. Ski Sport, one of the new ski shops, was looking for skis to market, and in a mutually beneficial arrangement, Darby and Ball became their supplier. Partner and general manager Bill Mason's rationale for ski making was simple: there was local interest and it offered a chance to survive the depression.[26]

Up to the 1920s bindings were not given much attention. Dartmouth's first coach, Anton Diettrich, echoed a common perception when he stated that with any but the worst bindings, it was possible to learn to ski.[27] As people began to ski faster and required more control for the new Alpine technique, bindings became increasingly important. Men experimented with rubber rings from pickling jars and old tires to keep the heel on the ski before imported "Amstutz Springs" and, then, the copied "Heel Springs" from Ski Sport became available.[28] At Macy's bindings began at $2 and increased to $9 for the most sophisticated. Hambro's models sold for $3.50 and $4.50; Abercrombie and Fitch's were only $1.50. In 1934 Ski Sport offered three bindings: a standard touring and, responding to the Arlberg enthusiasm, a Schuss downhill and a Christie. By 1937 the shop listed the Gold K (reflecting the British influence of the classic Kandahar downhill race), three models of the "New Seventy" (reminding buyers of "Hill 70" in the Laurentians), and one with Hannes Schneider's autograph. The nomenclature was chosen to attract the newer skiers with connotations of speed, venue, and technique—along with a touch of international snob appeal. The Ski Sport touring was an established favorite. Junior models came on the market, reflecting an increase in youngsters taking up downhill skiing.

There were plenty of imported bindings besides Amstutz: Bildstein, Thirring, Sandstrom, Almonte, Eckel. The firm of Dovre advertised its domestic bindings as "Austrian precision type." There were some experimental safety devices too. Northland's Micromatic and Gerber's "cable tested to 2000 lbs." gave a scientific veneer; here were the beginnings of high-tech equipment.

Boots also changed. In the 1920s boots of all sorts served for skiing as long as they were "stout, flexible, waterproof, and very loose," meaning that they offered room for at least two pairs of thick socks.[29] The Alpine type of skiing required a specialized boot, thick-leathered and stiff for more control and with a grooved heel to keep the binding cables from slipping off. In the 1930s all boots were so styled. The choice was based on quality, an expert's recommendation, and price. As with skis, Norwegian boots were preferred, but Bass and L. L. Bean, both well known for their stout working and hunting boots, began to capitalize on the growing ski market. In 1932 L. L. Bean, "believing there is a demand for a high grade Ski Boot," charged $6 for one with a "hard box toe, solid leather concave heel," and a "heavy wool felt top . . . to keep out the snow." Bass had a model for women in 1935. In 1937 Bean competed with a "fine grade smoked Elk leather model with a two inch lambskin collar" for $6.10. For the specialist there was Bean's Seamless for $8.85 patterned after an expensive Austrian model, but Bass supplied the boots to the U.S. Olympic squad for Garmisch-Partenkirchen. Sandler of Boston had endorsements from Birger Ruud and Hannes Schneider for two handsome and rugged models. The Limmer boot, however, was the top of the line. Before coming to the United States Peter Limmer had been in charge of a boot factory in Garmisch. He offered ski boots made to order for men and women.[30] A Limmer boot was a status symbol in the years before the war. It was of the highest quality and its price reflected this.

Tough, steel-shanked boots spoiled carpets and hardwood floors. Innkeepers provided slippers for the thé dansant, and one manufacturer made gargantuan slip-ons, forerunner of the indoor après-ski boot which appeared in Europe in 1934.[31]

The last essential piece of equipment was a pair of poles. They cost between $2 and $9 at Macy's, at Abercrombie and Fitch, $3.50, and at Hambro's, between $1 and $6. The single stave of an earlier time had been made of any wood that was handy. Hazel poles were still being sold by Hambro's in 1934, but tonkin cane and bamboo were the most common. By 1935, poles manufactured from metal alloys offered more durable support. Gerber shrank a fiber over tonkin cane and called it unbreakable. By 1938 Swedish steel was used in Tangvald poles, and an all-metal model was available for $7.50 from the L. A. Young Golf Company of Detroit, a nice example of a company diversifying to profit from a winter sport.

The basic equipment of skis, bindings, poles, and boots changed in the 1930s to cater to those who schussed in Arlberg style. The offerings reflected the market. The companies that survived before the war were able to capitalize on the ever-expanding number of people taking to skiing. Manufacturers encouraged the trend by marketing special equipment for the youngest generation of skiers, just as the occasional ski school geared itself for children's classes.

Four of the major sources used in this analysis of equipment have been Northland, Strand, Hambro, and Ski Sport. The first two came out of an early twentieth-century midwestern background: Martin Strand and C. L. Lund were both Norwegian immigrants and put much effort into promot-

Oscar Hambro catered to skiers in the 1920s. In the 1930s he expanded his Boston business with fashion wear. *American Ski Annual* (1937–38). (New England Ski Museum, Franconia, N.H.)

ing skiing for its *Idraet* ideal. They were pleased that their successful businesses made skiing popular because it was physically, morally, and in every way right for individual, club, and country. Hambro and Ski Sport were different.

Oscar Hambro, also a Norwegian immigrant, had come to Boston by way of Canada in 1925 and had turned his factory and shop into something resembling a club; his customers were more like members of a ski fraternity who talked skiing in front of a roaring fire in a Norse-like cabin. "These ski addicts," reported the *Boston Evening Transcript,* made Hambro's a focal point for skiers before clubs like the AMC and Hochgebirge made their contributions. The outstanding fact was that Hambro's personnel were all involved in skiing themselves. In 1933, for example, on the shop floor or in the factory one might find an American 1932 Olympian and two Norwegians, one of whom had just spent a year in the old country catching up on the latest manufacturing processes. There was Eddie Boeck, well known in the White Mountains of New Hampshire as an instructor, two other Norwegians known for their cross-country and jumping expertise, and Christine Reid, a photographer and journalist who was able to discuss the Parsenn in Davos, Switzerland, with the same familiarity as the Taft trail in Franconia. "If you're looking for sociability and not high pressure salesmanship . . . drop in sometime," finished the *Transcripts* report. Although Hambro opened another store in New York, had his own factory in southern New Hampshire, and was financially successful, it was the sport aspect of his business that attracted clientele to his shop in Boston. This social way of conducting ski business came to an end with the war.[32]

Ski Sport was founded as a result of "chew[ing] the rag with Charley Proctor" at Asa Osborn's, the other ski shop in Boston. "We took some time off," recalled Rockwell Stephens, "and wrote a little ski book, and then another." When good equipment was difficult to obtain, the two "stumbled into Bill Mason and his partner." These were the depression years but "some people in Boston put up some money for us . . . and off we went." There were eight or ten stockholders—all skiers—who "decided to take a fling more or less for the hell of it." When Ski Sport needed financing "the nature of the stockholders was such that one of them told us to go to a certain bank and we could probably get a little credit there. He apparently swung a big enough stick so that anything he wanted his friends to do, they did and the bank did, so we had no trouble getting credit." Here was the same wealthy old-boy network that was quite prepared to help out a few friends who enjoyed entrepreneurial experimentation. Even if plush skins, inner boots, and the first steel pole to be domestically made never were successful, "it was fun . . . breaking new ground all the time." It required finding a shoemaker in Maine, figuring out how to avoid 40 percent import duties on metals, discovering a tonkin cane wholesaler in Hoboken. "We had a great time!"[33]

It was a great time until Charley Proctor left for Yosemite, and the war changed the nature of leisure. Ski Sport's operation, based upon a love for skiing rather than an accountant's audit, closed because of the war and, like many other such ski businesses of the 1930s, never reopened.

The simple equipment of the 1920s was improved upon for Alpine skiing. A more sophisticated ski with steel edges, tighter bindings, and stiffer boots was needed for the dash of the downhill descent.

Skiing in Style

Hambro's, Osborn's, and Ski Sport sold skis and skiing; Saks and Abercrombie and Fitch sold fashion to the elite, Jordan Marsh and Filene's to the middle-class skiers. The growth of Alpine skiing as a social activity was paralleled by the growth of the ski fashion industry. Just as Alpine skiing was imported from Europe, so were Alpine skiing clothes, and early advertisements literally instructed the neophytes in the right apparel. "Kitzbuhel [sic]," advised Sporting Tailors of Boston in 1934, "the smartest skiing place in the world, sends this information: Ski Clothes, for men and women are cut alike. Black, Dark Blue and Grey are definitely THE colors."[34] John Wanamaker's in New York City transplanted a Swiss winter village into its auditorium and engaged a Swiss ski instructor to exhibit and teach on an eighty-foot indoor slide. The place was a beehive as yodelers yodeled and customers thronged to inspect the newest and most fashionable styles in winter sports attire.[35]

Things had certainly changed since the turn of the century and the decade of the twenties when clubs decked themselves out in ski uniforms. Flannel shirts, heavy pants, sweaters, outing suits, and toques, that is, normal winter clothes, had been the usual attire.[36] Women wore long heavy skirts. Photos of 1920s skiers show a huge range of winter clothing and, with the exception of the college crowd which tended to baggy trousers and heavy sweaters with occasional Norfolk jackets and women in breeches, there appeared to be no set style at all. However, toward the end of the decade B. Altman offered "a smart ski costume" by Patou,[37] and from then on nattily dressed skiers advertised Coca-Cola, tires, cars, and wool products. Although there were no ski clothing advertisements in the Ski Annuals of 1928, 1929, 1930, or 1931, there were plenty of fashion plates in the New York Times. Most ads were obviously aimed at the elite who might actually see Princess Lleana, the attractive daughter of the dazzling queen

Two different appeals: Slalom Ski Wear, "skier designed and made in the North Country," used authenticity to appeal to the city skier. Bjarne Johansen relied on his Norwegian heritage, with a skiing figure that implied the cross-country world (note the raised heel). Even so, Johansen's skier obviously is making a fast descent, possibly even a slalom! The *Ski Bulletin* (1936). (New England Ski Museum, Franconia, N.H.)

of Romania, splendidly dressed to enjoy her time in the snow. The major shops—the expensive, large emporia—sent representatives to Europe. Katharine Peckett, dubbed as the foremost authority in America on both skiing and ski clothes, assembled incomparable European styles for B. Altman whose shop had a Dartmouth graduate on hand, who "adds to the atmosphere by wearing a skiing costume." Saks had "combed Holmenkollen, Kitsbuehel [*sic*] and Davos." Of course, some clientele were more interested in the effect created than in actually using the ski slopes: "Another spot for breaking out is around your waist. Here you can wear those wide stone studded Mexican belts or a band of imported linen with embroidery, more European House loot."[38] No wonder a cynical observer of the social scene would comment that skiing had been "taken up by those with nothing in particular to do, and who like to see their pictures in the paper and themselves in interesting costumes."[39]

Hambro's in Boston was quite different from these New York stores. Among the "unusual articles" for sale in January 1931 was a "parka" which, a couple of years later, was "accepted" by the AMC's equipment committee. B. F. Moore outfitted the Byrd Antarctic expedition in 1933, Sporting Tailors promised "no flighty or untried styles." In the East, Moore's Slalom Ski Wear was particularly popular; in the West, Hirsch-Weiss's White Stag line was what many skiers tried to find. Colorful costume was considered infra dig by the cognoscenti. "Concerning ski costumes there is one school of thought which favors a rather flamboyant use of color, possibly in an attempt to acquire the graceful swoop of a bird by imitating its plumage. In contrast to the sombre garb affected by their less original fellow, these riotous figures give a startling, though not unattractive, tone to the snowscape." On the slalom hill, the article continued, "one such skier blazed gloriously in scarlet and white . . . until the countryside quivered with reflected color. Naturally this lad was the focal point of the spectators' interest." This was a fair-minded appraisal by the *Mt. Mansfield Ski Club Bulletin,* a pamphlet that in 1935 had to take care not to upset the growing group of regulars to Stowe. The trouble was that the lad "came down through the flags smirking at the ladies and nonchalantly twitching his rear."[40] Clothing of bright hue was thus linked to flirtatiousness, which in turn hinted at an immoral enjoyment of what had begun as a moral-making sport.

The Boston and Maine Snow Train Guide for 1936 had a long instructive section on how important "warm and adjustable" costumes were.[41] Women had to be assured that trousers and sweaters were as acceptable for them as they were for men. In a 1933 New Hampshire Development Commission's *Troubadour* there is an article entitled "The Trail Was Gorgeous." As the author's party snow-shoed up, a group of skiers came down. "Whiz! Whir! He was by. No, she was by. Which? One couldn't tell. Men and women were dressed alike, and were equally skillful."[42]

Money was made by the traditional ski shops that dealt in equipment, but there was far more profit in gabardine trousers and colorful fashion sweaters for the new skiers. Fashion experts and live models presented style shows, Hollywood stores advertised skiing with a Sun Valley theme, and the Ski Wear Alliance show, as early as 1936, drew 150 store representatives.[43]

A Bon Marché's advertisement from 1938 serves as an example of the trend toward fashionable dressing. Drawings of handsome men and women in ski clothes accompanied the text.

> The gentleman surrounded by his two ski queens is happily waiting to do justice to his taste in women and clothes. The cap ([$]2.00), two-tone parka (8.95) and downhill skipants (10.95) are all gabardine. The sox (3.50) and mitts (2.50) are imported from Norway and match. The boots are made by Bass (14.50).
>
> She who looks so jaunty under her gabardine cap (2.00) wears ribbed trousers of tricardine (10.50) and a jacket to match (12.95). She carries her make-up in a rucksack (2.00) and her overmitts are poplin (2.00). 7.50 buys the boots. The sash is Norwegian and bright (5.95). . . .[44]

There was no telling when you might be picked to double for Tyrone Power or Sonja Henie. In the East the logging-road tramp and health of the skisport had given way almost entirely to Arlberg attractions. The equipment market provided the means to enjoy Alpine skiing; the fashion industry glamorized it.

Getting There and Getting Up:
Development of the Ski Center

Sport geographers spend much of their time accounting for the places where sports occur. To date, they have not tackled skiing. I suspect the reason is that there is little to say: the sport is carried on in snow country. However, skiing in New England, in the Midwest, the Rockies, and the West has geographic factors that forced the development to emerge in particular ways. The major question was always one of getting to the skiing grounds. The two basic ways, by road and rail, have already been discussed. Here, though, I want to suggest some economic considerations of travel which became increasingly important as the number of skiers rose in the 1930s. .

The beginning of the development of a ski center (the term "ski area" did not exist until after the war) was tied closely to its accessibility. Snow clearance of the roads—for automobile traffic the move from rollers to plows was essential—greatly concerned East and West and had been discussed only in Colorado. Up to 1930, snow removal in New York State depended on particular local needs: ski enterprises cleared the way from the railroad station to their own hill. As skiing became more popular, counties took on an increasing role. Eventually the state legislature was persuaded that, besides Speculator and Lake Placid, there were so many centers "cropping up in the Adirondacks" that snow removal benefited everyone, and the state took over responsibility in the early 1930s.[45]

On the other side of the country, the California Chamber of Commerce presented some statistical foundation. Based on careful car counts, in the 1940–41 season the state expected almost a million and a half ski days, which would generate just over $15 million in revenue, or $10.71 per capita. Certain areas required immense funds to make them accessible. The fifteen miles between Pine Grove and Antelope Springs averaged out to be $3.62 per one thousand vehicle miles over the three seasons, of 1936 to 1939. In 1939, when the state kept the Emigrant Gap road open, it cost $61.82 per thousand vehicle miles to maintain. Even so, the report concluded, considering many other factors such as the amount of business generated and taxes that accrued to the state, skiing was paying its own way by the time of the Second World War. The Chamber of Commerce report showed that if California were to enjoy a winter economic boom, government should really support the businesses of the state in making it happen.[46]

In New Hampshire snow removal was especially vital because there were so many skiers. The major road arteries from Boston to the Franconia and

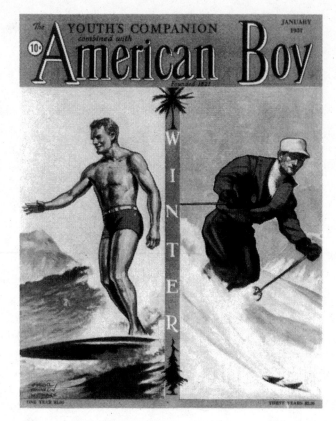

The question for boys with vacation money: Sun or Snow? *American Boy*, 1937. (New England Ski Museum, Franconia, N.H.)

Pinkham notches were both kept clear of snow by the state from 1927 on. Therefore Cannon Mountain in the first notch and North Conway in the second saw such major developments as the first American aerial tram and the first ski town in the eastern United States.

The eastern slope welcomed the "ski larks" aboard the Eastern Slope Express from Grand Central, but the majority of people traveling north came with the Boston and Maine snow trains. Even with the remarkable increase in passenger numbers in the January to March period, total annual passenger revenue actually decreased, as it did virtually all over the United States as a result of the rise in automobile use and the depression. Boston and Maine revenue declined 20 percent in 1931, lost a further 29 percent the next year and 18 percent in 1933. Only in 1934 was there a 2.54 percent increase, and until the war passenger revenue varied little. Perhaps it was this small increase that spurred Edward F. French, the chairman of the Boston and Maine, to refer to snow train activity for the first time. But the number of winter passengers were so impressive that "snow train tie-ups" with ski shops were stressed.[47]

From Boston a round-trip ticket to snow country cost between $2.50 and $4.50. If a stenographer's weekly salary was about twenty dollars, a day's outing every once in a while, or even regularly, was possible to afford, and the snow train excursion broke the routine of city living.

Cannon Mountain's reputation as a skiing center was based on the renown of its Taft Racing Trail and its various tows, which culminated in 1938 with the opening of the tram. Rope tows were originally thought of as movable. The early tows were put up by artisan tinkerers. Find a convenient meadow, drive an old automobile to it, rig the contraption up, and you had a place to ski with a tow to pull you up. But soon the tow stayed where it was located and skiers went to it.

One fairly complete record of a 1935 tow, Ted Cooke's Gilford "ski hoist," erected for the White Mountain Ski Runners near their farmhouse, gives at least a glance into economic aspects. Numerous published contemporary remarks, an oral history memoir, a film of the tow's construction, and the account books, if not always clear, survive. There are checks from 1934 drawn on a personal checking account to buy timber and hoists. In November 1936 accounting begins:

	Revenue	Expenses
Nov 1936	0.00	0.00
Dec	0.00	102.76
Jan 1937	0.00	12.52
Feb	0.00	2.52
March	127.02	81.66
April	24.70	25.70
Jan 1938	312.64	305.33
Feb	?	29.18
March	98.40	55.52
Jan–Feb 1939	215.31	153.71
March	30.00	49.88

Clearly, this ski hoist was not a money-maker. Even in a good skiing month such as March 1937, Cooke only cleared $45.36. In January 1938 he barely broke even. The first two months of 1939 show slightly more than a $30 profit. Cooke also patented and sold rope-tow grippers. The accounts show that in the big month of January 1938 he sold $35 worth.

Unfortunately it is not clear what capital was invested, although there are notations of capital stock from November 1936 to May 1937. It appears that Cooke had one major stockholder—his brother-in-law—to whom thirteen hundred dollars in one- or two-hundred-dollar installments were paid irregularly from December 1934 to November 1935.[48] In comparison, the first Woodstock, Vermont, tow was said to have cost about five hundred dollars.[49] Unsatisfactory as these figures may be, they are from the only ledgers that I have been able to find. From several oral interviews I conclude that early rope-tow entrepreneurs tinkered with their machines for their own pleasure and a club's benefit with little regard to finances.[50] When the Hussey Manufacturing Company began marketing tows commercially in 1936, clubs and individuals who bought them began to charge the skiers who used them. At the first meeting of the Ski Tow Association in 1938 there was unanimous agreement to charge a dollar a day and seventy-five cents for those arriving after 1 P.M. Some planned to charge twenty-five cents or fifty cents for admission to the ski hill.[51] Operating tows was becoming a winter business.

Rope tows dotted the mountain meadows but from 1936 on, other contraptions also appeared on New England slopes: the J-bar at Oak Hill, New Hampshire; the T-bar—known in the early days as the he-and-she-stick—at Pico, Vermont; the already mentioned Skimobile at Cranmore, New Hampshire; and, finally, the chair lift at Belknap, New Hampshire, "the tram way of the sit down variety." All offered a glimpse of the future technological developments of skiing.

Dwarfing these in conception and cost was the Cannon Aerial Tram. In May 1934, the executive secretary of the New Hampshire State Development Commission appointed a committee (three Dartmouth men, two Olympians) to look into possible financing for a tram, and hearings were held in the New Hampshire House of Representatives in August. House Bill 171 spent 1935 winding its way through judiciary and appropriations committees and, with the understanding that Works Progress Administration money would be made available, was passed into law. But federal financing was not forthcoming, and it was not until 17 June 1937 that the new House Bill 474 funded the $250,000 state project. The tram opened on 28 June 1938 to almost universal acclaim.[52]

Skiers came to the same place to ski over and over again. They found a congenial place to stay, came up from the city with the same group of friends, knew the trails from top to bottom: it became their mountain. This sense of belonging helped to give each place a particular character. There was even an indication of the condominium world to come. What was touted as America's First Ski Village near Peterborough, New Hampshire, was "a project . . . organized along club lines . . . primarily devoted to winter sports lovers." One acre parcels of land had a "rustic sportsman's lodge" on each and all looked to the commissary, clubhouse, ski shop, and shelters.[53] The geographer's "sport place" emerged because of the ease of access to the favored spot. Put in skiers' terms, here was the beginnings of the ski center.

Many centers developed from cooperative ventures of local ski clubs, hotels, chambers of commerce. For instance, in 1936, Plymouth, New Hampshire, boasted of being the Snow Bowl of New England with resident Swiss instructors. That same season the Winter Sports Committee of Fryeburg, Maine, created one of the largest open slopes in New England, cut a novice trail, and ran a ski tow, all under the auspices of the Western Maine Sports Association, comprising twelve local towns.[54] Vermont had some philosophical problems with development. Advertising itself as "Unspoiled Vermont," it claimed thirty-nine winter resorts, but it also wondered whether it should break its own Sunday blue laws and allow skiing on the sabbath. "The State," commented the *Boston Herald* as the 1937 season got under way, "is taking this whole winter sports furore in its stride, refusing to be stampeded into skiing," and thereby economically lagging far behind neighboring New Hampshire.[55]

Regional cooperation also emerged as a way of presenting a strong front in the competition for the increasing clientele. In the White Mountains, the Newfound region's five villages promised excellent terrain, excellent instruction and hospitality; eight advertisers extolled the Dartmouth Open Slope region. The most aggressive promotion was done by the Eastern Slope region. Four hostelries advertised in the 1934 *Annual*, sixteen in 1936, and twenty-six in 1937. The Eastern Slope region had rail connections to North Conway, the famous branch of the Hannes Schneider Ski School, ski tows and the extraordinary skimobile, Dr. Shedd (the only well-known ski-country doctor before the war), and Carroll Reed managing a branch of Saks Fifth Avenue (eventually he opened his own shop). Its proximity to the Tuckerman Bowl kept skiers coming well into spring.

Skiers had a range of accommodations to choose from: there was Pinkham Notch's year-round mountaineering camp run by Joe Dodge, an individual whom everyone knew and everyone respected;[56] the Glen House, which as late as 1937 still thought it important to advertise that the highway was open all winter; Whitney's with its shovel handle tow and "good food, good beds and good books." The Eagle Mountain House held two hundred people and charged $4.50 and up. The Guptill House charged $2.50. Murphy's could take fifteen and promised pick-up from the station. There were flood-lighted skating rinks, toboggan chutes, "Commodious Lounges with Huge Fireplaces," ski rooms, ballrooms, special rates for parties, home-cooked food a-plenty, afternoon teas, a ski jumping hill, private chalets, steam heat, ping-pong, and dancing—what more could anyone want for a week or a weekend? If one wished for the rougher life of the outing club a skier could be "badgered by two Dartmouth men" at the Glenwood:

> Our Beds are Hard
> Our Steam is Cold
> We Cook with Lard
> The Rooms are Sold—But
> A Skiers' Welcome Awaits You.[57]

As skiers crowded into ski centers, "management" had to organize the sport. In one center tobogganists were separated from skiers;[58] the first law suit was in 1939;[59] Mount Greylock, Massachusetts, graded ski trails to "path and lawn-like smoothness;"[60] night skiing was made possible in the 1936 season;[61] roads were closed to Bertram's Suicide Six when he ran out of parking space and Franconia issued a blanket warning that reservations were necessary.[62]

Politics and Development in the Depression

The political climate was certainly right for the development of skiing in the 1930s. Ski trails became easily available in the East because depression-spawned agencies such as the Civilian Conservation Corps provided the labor to build them. In the West, because much potential ski terrain was in the national parks or on national forest land, a capitalistic entrepreneurial agency such as the California Chamber of Commerce had to persuade and cajole the federal government into opening up national land to skiers. The National Park Service organized an advisory committee on skiing in late December 1937.[63]

The California Chamber of Commerce made the case that it should receive government support. In 1938–39 parks in Washington and Oregon received 224,972 and 169,265 visits in comparison with California's 745,170. The Forest Service spent $115,200 on shelters, ski runs, and novice slopes in the Pacific Northwestern states, excluding developments on Mt. Rainier. By 1939 the Timberline Lodge alone had cost $768,000. Clubs and other private investors such as the Chicago and Milwaukee Railroad had put up over $320,000, and the total came to $1,365,000. Economists worked out that it cost $3.46 to get one skier to a center for a day on the slopes.

California received about $100,000. The state in 1939 had thirty-nine private tows worth $125,000. Each skier to California's centers only cost just over three cents. The conclusion was obvious: the federal government owed it to California to support ski development. By 1940—exclusive of snow removal—the cost per visit was up to seventeen cents, and the state benefited through various gas and sales taxes and license fees totaling

$289,707. It appeared then, the report concluded, that the state "could qualify for further investment by government." After five years of lobbying, the highway department allocated funds to keep Route 50 open from Placerville over Echo Summit to the south end of Lake Tahoe. By then there were sixty-four tows in the state.[64] The skiing business was well launched in California and, just as in New England, gave evidence of all the conditions Rostow found favorable for "take-off" when the war intervened.

Publicizing Skiing

NSA's publication of *The Skisport* played a major role in the association's efforts to control the sport; Eastern's domination of the *American Ski Annual* after 1934 had the same effect. Far more influential for the New England ski fraternity, however, was the correctly named *Ski Bulletin,* published in Boston, a 6-by-9-inch weekly pamphlet full of information, comment, and in-group news. Starting in 1930 with six pages, it expanded to an 8½-by-11-inch glossy sixteen pages and by 1939 had a circulation of four thousand.[65]

There was competition from *Skiing* (a supplement of *Sports Illustrated*), *Ski Illustrated, Ski West, Ski-Week, Central Ski Sport,* and *California Ski News,* most starting between 1936 and 1938. However much *Ski Illustrated* might have aimed "faithfully to chronicle all the main skiing events, how and where to enjoy the sport" and to give highlights of ski organizations, in fact "Technique, Humor, Fashions and Cartoons" were what it mainly covered. There was an equipment review section, Forest Service ideas on cabin building, and an article entitled "Are Skiers Going Pansy?"[66] Here was a glossy, photo-filled magazine aiming at neophytes and offering just enough information to be useful.

At least the ski publications had their skiing matters correct. When the less-specialized magazines began to exploit this new thrill theme, they offered such a mish-mash of coverage that real skiers quickly ridiculed such popular magazines as *Life,* for example. Readers of the weeklies were told that experts were making their own secret wax formulas, that Buchmayr's jump turn on the Tuckerman headwall, which had been used as a Camel cigarette advertisement, was done at 40 MPH, and that "imported Buggie Snuggies will keep you warm as you sail over the ski jumps." The ski jumping depicted on the cover of the January 1929 *Youth's Companion* shows perhaps a *Geländesprung,* perhaps a jump from a structure, and the man has only one pole. *Collier's* cover of 11 January 1930 has a young woman in a ridiculous yet possible snow-plow position. She has at least six feet of scarf flowing behind her and another three feet in front. The happy and healthy threesome descending a slope on a *Saturday Evening Post* cover in February 1931 do so without poles, and *American Girl* has a red-suited girl who looks as if she is coming off a jump with two poles. The artists had not troubled to be correct nor to record the truth. Perhaps most curious of all, and certainly the most widely circulated, was the 1932 postage stamp designed to commemorate the Lake Placid Olympic Winter Games. Just over a million and a half stamps of a "ski jumper" were printed. In fact the man is neither shown in the correct style for a competition jump, nor is he even doing a *Geländesprung*.[67]

The production of ski books, most of them manuals on how to ski, was a summer occupation for skiers. My working bibliography shows, from the end of the First World War to 1929, a list of eight books. From 1930 to the beginning of World War II twenty-eight were published, 61 percent of them in the years 1936, 1937, and 1938. The figures for popular magazine articles are equally astounding: I have counted sixty articles in the decade 1918–28; in the following decade 215, 35 percent of them published in the years 1936, 1937, and 1938. The Sierra Club—not one to think of itself as a ski club—reviewed twenty-one books in its June 1939 *Bulletin,* ten of which were on skiing.[68] This extraordinary popular publishing topic was aimed at men, women, and children, and an ever-increasing market seemed to keep on buying: Schniebs and McCrillis's *Modern Ski Technique* first appeared as a book in 1932; its eighth edition was selling in 1937.[69]

Newspapers, especially in Boston and New York, became important sources of ski news. Of course, skiing was written up in the papers before the 1930s, but from 1935 on ski columnists such as Frank Elkins in New York and Henry Moore and "Old Man Winter" in Boston, provided regular information. Skiers read the Friday newspapers for announcements of snow train destinations. More up-to-the-minute news was relayed on a radio winter sports program which made its Friday evening debut in Boston on 3 January 1936, jointly sponsored by the state of New Hampshire and other winter organizations interested in promoting the White Mountains as a winter sports paradise.[70] These radio efforts were essentially regional, but Lowell Thomas broadcast from all across ski country U.S.A., although he disclaimed that it was to promote skiing: "I did it just for fun." Since he had to pay the line charges when he was away from New York, skiing was an expensive hobby for him.[71] It is impossible to tell what effect any of these promotions or the broadcasting from the top of Cannon Mountain, from the Green Mountain Inn at Stowe, or from the Wheeler Opera House in Aspen had on the growth of skiing.

Although the influence of films from Europe and Hollywood cannot be measured, it cannot be discounted either. It was evidently thought worthwhile for Sun Valley's representative of the Union Pacific to show Schneider's *Ski Chase* to the Jordan Marsh Ladies Home Journal Sub Deb Club in 1939. My feeling is, however, that skiing, when presented on film as entertainment (e.g., *Adventures in the Engadin* and *Sun Valley Serenade*) or as farce (e.g., *Dr. Schlitz on Mount Washington*), provided a vicarious experience for those who lacked any personal involvement. The Engadin was so spectacularly Alpine and Sun Valley so superlatively Hollywood that many viewers were more struck with the unreality of the snow world than drawn to it. Movietone News also covered skiing but only when it had a wide appeal. Thus most newsclips are of jumping events, of wild ski-joring, or of Sun Valley's novel chair lift.[72] Collectively though, books, magazines, newspapers, radio, and films reached a market of interested buyers who turned to them for promotion, information, ideas, instruction, and entertainment.

The "Take-Off" Phase

In the late 1930s the ski business was ready for "take-off." Since the sport began to expand rapidly, wrote one commentator, "it has developed into a 20 million dollar industry." The ski business put itself on show, first in Boston, then in Madison Square Garden in New York. In 1935 at the Boston Garden's three-day Winter Sports Show, over thirty thousand viewers enjoyed the event, thirteen thousand alone turned up for the finale and thirty-five hundred had to be turned away. More than twenty manufacturers, dealers, hotels, clubs, community developments, and travel bureaus advertised. A representative of Garmisch-Partenkirchen, host city of the 1936 Olympic Winter Games, came to Boston too. An indoor slide was used for ski performances, for showing off "fancy turns," somersaults, and jumping with torches. By 1938 five days of showmanship had turned the ski show into a travel and vacation attraction; with each succeeding year fewer skis and bindings were on view but more and more hotels were represented. One European country advertised nothing but its railways.[73] The market competition had changed to enticing the seemingly unending supply of customers to the new ski centers.

When the Ski Show moved to Madison Square Garden in 1936, about eighty thousand people saw seven shows, and more than $200,000 was said to have been spent in the exhibiting hall. The owner of the New York Giants even planned to convert his arena into a ski slide and toboggan run. As had been the case in Boston, one of the attractions was the indoor slide where ski jumpers performed. These indoor slides, used by experts, also

Serious ski promotion was combined with show business when skiing went indoors in 1935 at the Boston Garden. Crushed ice provided the surface for torchlight descents and a finale of leaps through wheels of fire. (New England Ski Museum, Franconia, N.H.)

appeared in the big New York stores. Whereas at the Boston, Seattle, and New York shows, crushed ice had provided the surface, at Saks, Wannamaker's and Macy's borax was sprinkled over a tough carpet.[74] Sig Buchmayr was engaged for Saks's sixty-three-foot high, sixteen-foot-wide slide. Overheard in the Club Room of the Laurentide Inn at Ste. Agathe des Monts were two New York women: "Where did you learn to ski?" "At Saks, Fifth Avenue, my dear."[75]

Newsweek judged that the borax slide really brought in business in 1935. The article, accompanied by four photos, credited the New York City area with selling $2,400,000's worth of equipment, much of which would be used by an estimated 150,000 snow-train riders. At the end of the 1936 season, the *New York Times* reported that city department stores' ski business had risen 250 percent more than the previous year. Before the next Christmas, department stores were glowing over their "almost fantastic sales of equipment and clothing"; two large stores had already sold four times as many skis as in the previous year and a third had tripled its sales of equipment. In order to satisfy the extraordinary demand and to be ready for the season, one fashion buyer had bought eight times more clothing and accessories in Europe than the previous year.[76]

Business kept increasing but there were warning signals that it could not go on forever. There were by then "Stormy Horizons" in Europe, as Roland Palmedo titled the lead article in the 1938–39 *American Ski Annual,* in which he warned that European imports might soon be hard to obtain. More important (and first detected in California) was the beginning of market saturation. In 1940, 25 to 30 percent of ski clothing and equipment was being sold to high school and college students going on their first ski trip.[77] Except for the very wealthy, America was not ready to indulge in an annual change of ski fashions.

In spite of the looming world problems, ski manufacturers and retailers continued to enjoy a rise in business. In the 1940 season, skiers spent approximately:

$3,000,000	skis, bindings, and accessories
6,000,000	clothes
3,000,000	transportation
3,000,000	lodging
500,000	instruction
4,500,000	incidentals[78]

In 1926 a Sierra Club member wrote: "[I] tried every sporting goods store in town and couldn't get skis in any of them. Finally I got the name of a mail-order house from a power company lineman and sent away for them. When they got here nobody could show me how to use them. I had to learn skiing from a book."[79] Fifteen years later skiing had become a $20 million business. Only something as cataclysmic as a war could change its bright future as an exploding industry.

12 / Epilogue: To the Future

> We should all look on skiing as an art akin to ballet—
> dancing to imaginary music. It is not only "exercise" or
> merely "sport," but revelation for body and soul.
>
> —Lang, *Downhill Skiing* (1936)

Fridtjof Nansen, our guide to *Idraet,* would have been delighted to hear Arlberger Otto Lang call skiing a "revelation for body and soul," but he would have been horrified to see how much of a society pastime it became. The difference was one of quality: *Idraet*'s skisport was a life philosophy, skiing was merely a leisure-time amusement. The skisport had contained a pantheistic connection and held out hope for its regenerating effect on individual body, soul, club, and even nation. There was nothing remotely connected with these notions in the 1930s crowd waiting in line to grab the rope tow, however pleased the folks were with themselves for having such a healthy sporting weekend. A secular, modern way of skiing had developed by the outbreak of the war.

By then that same crowd had made skiing, according to a prominent sporting goods executive, the fastest growing recreational activity in America.[1] The equality of opportunity to ski—to use Allen Guttmann's second point in his paradigm of modernization—had been confined by ethnic restriction and geographic place. Both the numbers of skiers and the places they could ski had increased as Americanization and mechanization made the skisport more popular. When collegiate skiers first took it up in New England, skiing was limited to those with the inclination, leisure time, and wealth. They retained what suited them of the *Idraet* ideals. Many then found the new craze for Arlberg speed attractive, but *Idraet* remained part of the lore, even as the sport was modernized for the urban office-bound.

Thousands took advantage of the opportunities when they became available because the brand-new sport held the promise of healthy sociability: the club car on the snow train, two-by-two on a T-bar, communal dining and singing in the lodge. By 1940 the new ski centers, open for business all across the country from Maine to California, appeared to make for a new *Gemeinschaft,* but in fact economic competition was too strong to allow much sense of community.

In the era of skisport, beginning skiers eagerly sought advice from heroes of the wooden blades, and the recommendations were put to commercial use. Many skiers might recognize Lars Haugen giving exhibitions, retailing advice, and promoting Northland skis on the professional ski circuit. The jump, skisport's centerpiece, was measured, however, as much for lucre as length. In the 1930s the circuit failed financially and was replaced by the momentary film clip of this or that jumper—it hardly mattered—seen on Pathe News by thousands who never knew what the "real riding" was all about.

Cross-country skiing was physically demanding and boring to watch. Cross-country racing lacked the dare of the leap or the exhilaration a *Schuss* might bring. Those who guarded the *Idraet* ideal lamented the loss of all-round skiing ability and worried that the skiers' bodies were no longer being toughened by the vigorous exercise demanded by cross-country. The only true enthusiasts who remained, it seemed, were the few who sought lonely and challenging mountain peaks.

If cross-country was the poor cousin to jumping, it was also the aging uncle to the Alpine disciplines. Hannes Schneider had gauged the wealthy public correctly: they were lured by speed. Obviously speed had also been part of the attraction in the Californian gold-rush frolics, but one-on-one competition was far more important. In skisport's heyday, speed was noted only if it added to the daring and hardy quality of, say, a group of Dartmouth men returning to their base after an expedition on Mt. Washington. But Alpine skiing was epitomized by speed. In one sense the graded instruction method was meant to ensure that skiers could control their speed, the down-mountain *Schuss.* The term was German, but the English made this new skiing a social sport. This was the mix that was brought back to the United States along with a variety of *Skimeisters* whose rule was law. But the orderly progression, the step-by-step disciplined learning proved too much a mirror of daily urban routine, precisely what people were seeking to escape. Shouldn't ski school be fun?

In fact, the whole business of skiing was becoming too much like the day-to-day business of life: parking lots filled up, the line for the ski tow paralleled the one for train tickets earlier in the day. An extra rope tow had to be put into operation to handle "rush hour."[2] Advertising presented all this as an integral part of social skiing: sober blues and blacks of the 1920s gave way to smartly fashioned ski togs just as the glossy ski magazines superseded the skiing fraternity's bulletin. *Gesellschaft* wrapped in *Gemütlichkeit* came in many guises in the years before the war.

Yet skiing was by no means fully organized, not by bureaucrats, snow-train schedules, or instructors. However much the *Skilehrer* might have tried to insist upon a perfect Arlberg Christiania, one of the great charms of skiing remained the opportunity it offered for individual expression. The idea may have been to look upon skiing as "dancing to imaginary music," but there were many ways to dance to a variety of tunes. Although not many could reach Otto Lang's aesthetic heights, all could feel that skiing was not just "exercise or merely sport."[3] Skiing might not be quite "the revelation for body and soul" that it was for those who laid perfect tracks through virgin powder glades, but for most there remained in Alpine skiing what had made the earlier *Idraet* so powerful: exhilaration in the unsullied outdoors, far away from the city.

The control of the sport in its pre-1930 years was dominated philosophically and geographically by *Idraet*-based midwestern immigrants. With the enthusiasm for the Arlberg, the control of skiing moved to New England. However, not a few Bostonians and New Yorkers tested and tasted the West. In the Rockies (excepting Sun Valley), in the Pacific ranges, and in the Sierra Nevada, everything appeared so totally untouched, so totally superb, and, with war clouds over Europe, so totally desirable.

"Keep Fit to Fight" was President Franklin Roosevelt's injunction to the nation, and no one was more fit than those who skied. Indeed, it could be argued that the civilian effort, crowned with success, to raise a division of ski troops was an attempt to ensure that sportsmen could get in on the war effort. The recruiting film made at Sun Valley (directed by Otto Lang no less!), the sing-alongs at Paradise Lodge after a day's scouting on Mt. Rainier, the T-bar on Cooper Hill, and the training in the Aspen–Mt. Hayden area all carried the civilian ski ambience into the Tenth Mountain Division's military life at Camp Hale, nine thousand feet up in glorious Colorado ski country.[4] It was almost as if the West had already come into its own, as NSA president Torguson had foretold it would in 1920.[5]

Skiing's infrastructure developed in the prewar years had all the ingredients necessary to handle a mass market. It had taken one hundred years to move from the cross-country world of the Scandinavians to the fast-paced Alpine downhillers. Just as Americans had enjoyed the immigrant skisport and channeled it from its Scandinavian base into regional settings, so did they take the Alpine immigrants' technique, flair, and lore to make skiing part of a week or weekend of winter fun in depression-scarred America. The growth in the number of places to ski was equaled only by the variety of terrain and price. All the facets of modern skiing were in place before the outbreak of the war.

NOTES

1 / The Skisport

1. Allen Guttmann, *From Ritual to Record: The Nature of Modern Sports* (New York: Columbia University Press, 1978), 15.
2. Two persuasive writers on the reorientation of American culture in this period are T. J. Jackson Lears (*No Place of Grace: Antimodernism and the Transformation of American Culture 1880–1920* [New York: Pantheon, 1981]) and John Higham ("The Reorientation of American Culture in the 1890s," in *Writing American History: Essays on Modern Scholarship,* ed. John Higham [Bloomington: Indiana University Press, 1972], 73–102).
3. Higham, "Reorientation," 77.
4. Charles W. Hendel, "Snow-Shoeing in the Sierras," *Mining and Scientific Press,* 3 January 1874, 1, 9. For a synopsis of Hendel's career, see *Reproduction of Fariss and Smith's History of Plumas, Lassen and Sierra Counties, California: 1882 and Biographical Sketches of Their Prominent Men and Pioneers* (Berkeley: Howell-North Books, 1971), 190–91. There are occasional references to skiing in Hendel's diaries, written in German, in the California State Library, Sacramento.
5. William H. Brewer, *Up and Down in California in 1860–1864: The Journal of William H. Brewer, Professor of Agriculture in the Sheffield Scientific School from 1864 to 1903,* ed. Francis P. Farquhar (New Haven: Yale University Press, 1930), 435. See also John R. Gillis, "Tunnels of the Pacific Railroad," *Transactions of the American Society of Civil Engineers* (1874): 114; *Marysville Herald* in the *Sacramento Daily Union,* 24 January 1853; William E. Mills to D. Mills, Norwell, Mass., 17 December 1924, reprinted in *The Skisport* (1924–25): 24.
6. "When Skis Were a Dollar a Foot," an interview with Henry Anderson, *Silver Birches* (Students from Stockholm and New Sweden, Maine, 1976): 14–17. The Historical Society Museum of New Sweden, Maine, displays several pairs of skis of unequal length.

7. Theodore Roosevelt, *The Wilderness Hunter* (1900; reprint, Upper Saddle River, N.J.: Literature House/Gregg Press, 1970), 250–51.

8. *Denver Times,* 11 March 1901.

9. *Downieville Mountain Messenger,* 21 February 1863.

10. *The Field,* 14 January 1883; E. R. Warren MS, 137, uncataloged Natural History Collection, University of Colorado, Boulder. Warren diary, 24 January 1909, Natural History Collection. Warren also wrote an article on racing, "Snow-shoeing in the Rocky Mountains," *Outing,* January 1887, 351–52.

11. Sir A. de Capell-Brooke, "The Skating Soldiers of Norway," *Saturday Magazine,* 9 January 1836.

12. George Crofutt, *Crofutt's New Overland Tourist and Pacific Coast Guide* (Omaha and Denver: Overland Co., 1882), 218; William M. Thayer, *Marvels of the New West* (Norwich, Conn.: Henry Hill, 1892), 261.

13. People in Minnesota tended to pronounce *ski* as *sky,* much to the annoyance of the Scandinavians at the St. Paul Carnival. *St. Paul Daily Pioneer Press* (26 January 1886) told its readers that the word should be pronounced as if it were spelled *she.* Hemmetsveit, said the *St. Croix* [Wisc.] *Valley Standard* (2 February 1888), "is not a skiest but a sheist." There was similar concern in Red Wing, Minnesota, in 1894 (*Advance Sun,* 13 January 1894). As late as 1938, the *Sierra Club Bulletin* printed a letter on the matter (*Sierra Club Bulletin* 31, no. 2 [1938]: 98–99).

14. Fred H. Harris diary, 17 and 19 December 1908. I should like to thank Helen Harris of Brattleboro, Vermont, for permission to use her late husband's diaries, which remain in her possession.

15. Theo. W. Johnsen, *The Sport of Skeeing* (Portland, Maine, 1905), 7. *Skidor* also appears in the *Ishpeming* [Mich.] *Iron Ore,* 3 February 1906.

16. *Ski Notes and Queries* 6, no. 4 (1933): 158. The German and Austrian ski associations had officially sanctioned *Schi* and *Schier* in 1909. "Schneeschuh, Ski oder Schi?" *Der Winter* (1908–09): 9.

17. Erling Strom, "Slalaam," *National Ski Association Year Book* (1930–31): 18. Other terms, *Kneikelam, Ufselam, Svinglam,* and *Uvyrdslam,* indicate a variety of trails. John Weinstock, "Sondre Norheim: Folk Hero to Immigrant," *Norwegian-American Studies* 29 (1983): 347. For an excellent description of one of these trails in America, see the *Iron Ore,* 3 February 1906.

18. *Ski-Wettfahren in Lilienfeld am 19. März 1905,* pamphlet in Zdarsky-Archiv of the Bezirksheimatmuseum, Lilienfeld, Austria. This has been reprinted by Wolf Kitterle, *75 Jahre Torlauf* (Wien, 1980). There is a vast literature on Zdarsky and his contributions. For the first *Torlauf* particularly, see Erwin Mehl in *Oesterreichische Alpenzeitung* (1934): 1141, translated as "The Origin of the Gate (Slalom) Race," *British Ski Year Book* (1934): 597–603, and see the comment by Lunn in ibid., 603–4. For Zdarsky's wish for it to be a testing of expertise rather than a race, see Mathias Zdarsky to Erwin Mehl, Marktl im Traisentale, 3 February 1932, in Zdarsky-Archiv, Lilienfeld, Austria. Arnold Lunn, "Style Competition and Slalom Races," ibid. (1922): 393; idem, "The Modern Slalom," ibid. (1933): 175–84; idem, "Down with the Marxist Slalom," *Ski Magazine,* February 1955, 32–33.

19. Åke Svahn, "Idrott und Sport. Eine semantische Studie zu zwei schwedischen Fachtermini," *Stadion* 5, no. 1 (1979): 20–41. See also Carl J. Luther, "Ski-

touristik und Skisport," *Aarbok* (1913): 76–87. For a slightly different view of *Idraet* see Peter Levine and Peter Vinten-Johansen, "Sports Violence and Social Crisis," *Sport in America: New Historical Perspectives* (Westport, Conn.: Greenwood, 1985), 222–23, where *Idraet* is tied to military efforts. See also the standard dictionaries such as *Novensk Ordbok* and *Norsk Riksmalsordbok*. The only reference found in popular literature defines *Idraet* as "Back to Nature." Milana Jank, "Back to Nature," *Physical Culture* 67, no. 2 (1932): 22.

20. Fridtjof Nansen, *Paa Ski over Grønland* (Kristiania: Aschehoug, 1890), 78.
21. *Stockholms Tidningen,* 5 September 1937, cited in Svahn, "Idrott und Sport," 31.
22. Ibid., 36.
23. *Dagens Nyheter,* 24 August 1867, cited in ibid., 30.
24. Aksel H. Holter, "A Short Sketch of the Skisport in America," *The Skisport* (1912–13): 72–73.
25. See, for example, *Hutchings' California Magazine,* February 1857, 318–24; *Frank Leslie's Popular Monthly,* January 1893, 64–67; *Harper's Weekly,* 9 June 1883, 365; *St. Nicholas,* February 1883, 304–11; *Outing,* January 1913, 492–99; *Scientific American Supplement,* 12 April 1902, 21,972; *Munsey's Magazine,* February 1900, 665–68; *Scribner's,* January 1911, 92–102; *Popular Mechanics,* January 1910, 860. For an analysis of magazines, see Frank L. Mott, *A History of American Magazines,* 5 vols. (Cambridge: Harvard University Press, 1957–68), especially volumes 2, 3, and 4, which cover 1850 to 1905.

2 / California Gold Rush Snow-Shoeing

1. Most of the sources for this chapter have been local newspapers whose parochial quality was—and is—their strength. They provide the only body of material with a consistent interest in skiing in the Sierra Nevada ranges in the late nineteenth century. It is a remarkable fact that there are so few other sources. In one sense historians looking for ski items are lucky: most local papers had little other news to report when mining activities came to a standstill, so the accounts of races are numerous. Even so, one observer concluded that "in the arrangement of our report errors may have occurred, which were unavoidable, owing to the hasty manner in which they were reported. In some respects, the reports are unintelligible to us, but they are probably plain to those who were on the ground" (*Downieville Mountain Messenger,* 26 [23] February 1867). History is only as good as its sources permit.

   The following newspapers have been researched for the months of November through March: *Alpine Chronicle* (1873–1892; many issues missing); *Daily Alta California* (1849–1857, 1861–1875; some issues missing); *Downieville Mountain Messenger* (1865–1888; many issues missing); *Goldfield Daily Tribune* (1908–1909); *Marysville Daily Appeal* (1860–1874); *Marysville Herald* (1850–1858); *Nevada Journal* (1854–1861); *Plumas National-Bulletin* (1892–1904; many issues missing); *Sacramento Daily Union* (1851–1890); *Sierra Advocate* (1866–1867).

Collections of newspaper clippings, retyped clippings, and miscellaneous items have been gathered from: *Auburn Stars and Stripes; Carson City Territorial Enterprise; Dutch Flat Enquirer; La Porte Union; Nevada County Nugget; Nevada Daily Gazette; Nevada Daily Transcript; Placerville American; Plumas Argus*. These may be found in the Western Skisport Museum, Boreal Ridge, California, in the following files: (a) Bill Berry File: "Untitled Americana"; (b) Robert J. Sluyter and Grace J. Sluyter, "Notes of the Early Washington, Nevada County, California Mining District" (a typed MS); Helen Weaver Gould, *La Porte Scrapbook,* comp. and published by Helen Weaver Gould (La Porte, Calif., 1972).

Many of the papers reprinted news items from other mountain camp papers, as did urban newspapers such as the *Sacramento Daily Union*. Many runs of papers, now on microfilm, are incomplete because a comparatively small number were printed in the first place and not all survived. Newspaper was also put to immediate domestic use. When winters were extremely harsh, the high camps were often isolated for months, so only a few "local" items found their way into the valley news columns. See David C. Mills, "California Pioneers on Skis," *American Ski Annual* (1938–39): 35–44. For a historical overview of how newspaper reporting of sports developed, see Susan L. Greendorfer, "Sport and the Mass Media," in *Handbook of Social Science of Sport,* ed. Gunther R. F. Luschen and George H. Sage (Champaign, Ill.: Stipes, 1981), 160–80, and John Stevens, "The Rise of the Sports Page," *Gannett Center Journal* 1, no. 2 (1987): 1–10.

2. Royal Hubbel, "Ski Running," *Frank Leslie's Popular Monthly,* January 1893, 64. "Winter in California," commented a Minnesota paper, "don't mention it. No sleighing, no skiing, no skating, no Minnesota ozone—nothing that makes life worth living" (*Red Wing Daily Republican,* 13 February 1905).

3. E. des Baillets, "Winter Sports in the California Sierras," *California Journal of Development,* November 1930, 7; Wilbur Maynard, "A New Version of King Winter," ibid., 8; Wendell T. Robie, "Formation of the Californian Ski Association," *National Ski Association Yearbook* (1930–31): 36; des Baillets, "California Organizes Ski Association," ibid., 38; Maynard, "Sunshine and Flowers Notwithstanding," ibid., 42; J. C. Carpenter, "Civic Commercial Organizations," *American Ski Annual* (1938–39), 208. The California Olympic Games Committee was so outraged when Lake Placid was awarded the Games that they considered conducting an "opposition" festival (*Nevada State Journal,* 11 April 1929).

4. *Sacramento Daily Union,* 7 April 1869.

5. "The Canadian snowshoe . . . was never used in the mountains," recalled one pioneer in *Charles Kellogg, the Nature Singer, His Book,* cited in Dr. Clarence W. Kellogg's diary, 85–86, typed MS in Plumas County Museum, Quincy, Calif.; J. Ross Browne, *Report of J. Ross Browne on the Natural Resources of the States and Territories West of the Rocky Mountains* (Washington: Government Printing Office, 1868), 142. Bill Berry, the most knowledgeable historian of early skiing in California, believes there is no doubt about the dominant role skis played in Sierra camp winter activities (see the documentary film directed by Richard W. Moulton, *Legends of American Skiing* [Huntington, Vt.: Keystone Productions, 1982]. A shortened version of this was aired on PBS).

6. *Marysville Herald* in *Sacramento Daily Union,* 29 January 1853. Scandinavians introduced skis to the mountain communities. It has been suggested that Norwegian sailors jumped ship on hearing of the gold finds and stayed on to follow the gold and silver strikes. Bill Berry and Frank Elkins, "The Outcasts of Poker Flat," *The Ski Bulletin,* 20 December 1940, 5. Other emigrants from Europe's Alps and its foothills could not have initiated skiing because skis were unknown in the Alpine countries at that time.

   A number of men who skied were known to be Norwegian, Snowshoe Thompson being the most obvious example. There were occasional references to (usually) hardy Norsemen and the like who skied on "Norwegian" snow-shoes to and from camps that had Norwegian names like Kongsberg (later Silver Mountain).

7. *Nevada Journal,* 10 March 1854.

8. Hendel, "Snow-Shoeing," 1, 9.

9. *Marysville Democrat* in *Sacramento Daily Union,* 2 December 1859.

10. *Marysville Daily Appeal,* 22 November 1861.

11. *Daily Alta California,* 17 January 1856.

12. *Sacramento Daily Union,* 8 March 1859.

13. *Alpine Chronicle,* 16 February 1878.

14. *Downieville Mountain Messenger* in *Marysville Daily Appeal,* 17 February 1865; also in *Sacramento Daily Union,* 16 February 1865.

15. *Alpine Chronicle,* 11 March 1876; *Sacramento Daily Union,* 29 January 1857; *Daily Alta California,* 31 January 1855; Stephen Powers, "A City of a Day," *Overland Monthly,* November 1874, 431; *Daily Alta California,* 7 February 1859; 20 February 1861; 16 February 1869. On doctors, see the testimony of Alice Holcomb in Gould, *La Porte Scrapbook,* 161; on marriage, ibid., 105; *Daily Alta California,* 20 February 1861; *Grass Valley Union* in *Marysville Daily Appeal,* 30 January 1880. A photo of a funeral on skis illustrates William Mills's published letter in *The Skisport* (1924–25): 25. For three deaths, covering the era, see *Downieville Mountain Messenger* in *Sacramento Daily Union,* 29 January 1857; *Downieville Mountain Messenger* in *Marysville Daily Appeal,* 28 March 1871; *Plumas National-Bulletin,* 12 March 1903.

16. "Crossing the Sierras," *Hutchings' California Magazine* 1, no. 8 (1857): 349.

17. *Sacramento Daily Union,* 9 February 1860. For an evaluation and analysis of women's skiing in the Sierra, see E. John B. Allen, "Sierra 'Ladies' on Skis in Gold Rush California," *Journal of Sport History* 17 (Winter 1990): 347–53.

18. *Downieville Mountain Messenger,* 22 February 1873, in Berry File, "Untitled Americana."

19. *Nevada Daily Transcript,* 6 April 1882, in Sluyter and Sluyter, "Notes."

20. Gould, *LaPorte Scrapbook,* 105.

21. Testimony of Birdie Haun in Berry File, "Untitled Americana." For other examples of skiing double, see *Dutch Flat Enquirer,* 14 April 1866, cited in Paul Fatout, *Meadow Lake: Gold Town* (Bloomington: Indiana University Press, 1969), 58; C. B. Glasscock, *Lucky Baldwin: The Story of an Unconventional Success* (Indianapolis: Bobbs-Merrill, 1933), 105.

22. *Marysville Daily Appeal,* 17 March 1865. Another exploit, equally admired is reported in "She Had Grit," ibid., 4 February 1890, in which a Mrs. Murphy,

on skis for the first time in her life, escaped being snowed in by making a 3½ mile trip to Downieville.

23. Ibid., 26 March 1863.

24. The literature on John A. (Snowshoe) Thompson is vast and hagiographic. The most balanced treatment is Kenneth Bjork, "'Snowshoe' Thompson: Fact and Legend," *Norwegian-American Studies and Records* 19 (1956): 62–88. Since I wrote "Demythologizing a Mail Hero: Snowshoe Thompson 1827– 1876," *Postal History Journal* 63 (February 1983): 20–24, which relied heavily on Bjork, I have read a number of Sierra newspapers and a somewhat different picture of Thompson has emerged. For another view of Thompson, see also Captain J. H. Simpson, *Report of the Explorations Across the Great Basin of the Territory of Utah for a Direct Wagon Route from Camp Floyd to Genoa, in Carson Valley in 1859* (Washington: Government Printing Office, 1876), 96–97. Dan de Quille (pen-name of William H. Wright), "Snow-shoe Thompson," *Territorial Enterprise,* 13 February 1876, is the source for most of the extravagant accounts. On the tenth anniversary of Thompson's death, de Quille wrote another account and this, too, has been used to keep the legend alive ("Snow-shoe Thompson," *Overland Monthly,* October 1886, 419–35).

25. *Daily Alta California,* 16 November 1858; *Sacramento Daily Union,* 18 December 1858.

26. *Placerville American* in *Sacramento Daily Union,* 23 February 1857.

27. *Daily Alta California,* 8 January 1853; 10 February 1855.

28. *Nevada Journal,* 20 March 1852. Bjork, "'Snowshoe' Thompson," 67. See also *Sacramento Daily Union,* 1 December 1854; 24 December 1855; 30 January 1856, for various crossings of the range.

29. Buck Whiting, after reading of polar dog-sled expeditions, appears to have instituted dog-sled mail in 1856–57. Bob Francis, the Sierra and Plumas mailman, also used a dog team in 1860–61. See *Marysville Daily Appeal,* 6 February 1860; 22 November 1861. Although snowshoed horses were known to the Romans, in the Sierra, wooden snowshoes were first put on horses and mules in 1857 (*Downieville Mountain Messenger* in *Sacramento Daily Union,* 29 January 1857). Various people claimed the invention of such snowshoes for horses: Doc Brewster (*Marysville Daily Appeal,* 31 December 1873); Captain Russell of La Porte (*Alpine Chronicle,* 24 January 1874); and Henry Kellogg (Kellogg diary, 85). For the Romans, see Xenophon, *Anabasis,* trans. Carleton L. Brownson (Cambridge: Harvard University Press, 1961), 1, 59.

30. *Sacramento Daily Union,* 19 January 1856; 19 February and 8 March 1856.

31. Ibid., 10 December 1856; 23 February and 6 April 1856; *Daily Alta California,* 25 February 1857. For other crossings and for the respect in which Thompson was generally held, see also *Sacramento Daily Union,* 11, 15, and 30 January and 3 March 1858; *Daily Alta California,* 16 November 1858.

32. *Sacramento Daily Union,* 2 December 1859.

33. Thompson's efforts to secure money may be followed in the *Territorial Enterprise,* 13 February 1876; *Alpine Chronicle,* 10 and 18 January 1874; 18 March and 1 April 1876; a photostat reproduced in Bill Berry, "Old-Timers of the Sierra," *American Ski Annual and Skiing Journal* (1953–54): 50; *Sacramento Daily Union,* 5 February 1876; *The Californians,* November–December 1987, 22. See also my "Demythologizing a Mail Hero," 20–24.

34. de Quille, "Snow-shoe Thompson," 432.

35. Bjork, "'Snowshoe' Thompson," 72 n.16.
36. *Alpine Chronicle*, 10 January 1874; 18 March and 1 April 1876; *Plumas National*, cited in Mills, "California Pioneers," 41.
37. Excerpts of two letters from Thompson to his wife describing his efforts in Washington have been published in *The Californians*, November–December 1987, 22.
38. The most recent Snowshoe Thompson Day was celebrated on 30 April 1988 with special commemorative envelopes from Genoa, Nevada, and Placerville, California.
39. E. John B. Allen, "Skiing Mailmen of Mountain America: U.S. Winter Postal Service in the 19th Century," *Journal of the West* 29, no. 2 (1990): 76–86.
40. *Nevada County Nugget* [1863?] in Sluyter and Sluyter, "Notes." Some contracts had clauses that stated the mail carrier did not have to carry newspapers. H. G. Squier, "Snow Shoers of Plumas," *California Illustrated Magazine*, February 1894, 319; *Marysville Daily Appeal*, 18 January 1861.
41. *La Porte Union*, 30 January 1869, in Gould, *La Porte Scrapbook*, 48.
42. *Sierra Advocate* in *Sacramento Daily Union*, 2 February 1866.
43. *Nevada Union*, 29 January 1866, cited in Fatout, *Meadow Lake: Gold Town*, 57. An advertisement for Granville Zacharian's snowshoe express in the *Downieville Mountain Messenger*, 28 January 1865, is in Allen, "Skiing Mailmen," 78.
44. *Alpine Chronicle*, 1 April 1876.
45. *Sacramento Daily Union*, 26 January 1863.
46. *Nevada Daily Gazette*, 6 and 7 January 1890, in Sluyter and Sluyter, "Notes."
47. *Sacramento Daily Union*, 6 and 15 January 1890.
48. Mills, "California Pioneers," 40.
49. John Muir letter to *San Francisco Bulletin* (1878), reprinted as "Lake Tahoe in Winter," *Sierra Club Bulletin* 3, no. 2 (1900): 119, 125.
50. *La Porte Messenger* in *Sacramento Daily Union*, 7 February 1861.
51. *Dutch Flat Enquirer*, 18 November 1865, in *Sacramento Daily Union*, 20 November 1865.
52. *Alpine Chronicle*, 15 February 1873. See also *Downieville Mountain Messenger*, 14 January 1865.
53. Crofutt, *New Overland . . . Guide*, 218; Thayer, *Marvels*, 261.
54. Bill Berry, in interview with author, Reno, 26 March 1986. Berry's informant in the late 1930s was a retired school teacher.
55. *Sacramento Daily Union*, 14 December 1867.
56. *Butte Record* in *Marysville Daily Appeal*, 26 January 1861.
57. *Sacramento Daily Union*, 30 January 1861.
58. *Butte Record* in *Marysville Daily Appeal*, 26 January 1861. Miners were paid about two or three dollars a day according to Thayer, *Marvels*, 455, 478.
59. *Downieville Mountain Messenger* in *Marysville Daily Appeal*, 29 January 1868.
60. *Marysville Daily Appeal*, 22 February 1861; 29 January 1868; *Sacramento Daily Union*, 4 February 1863.
61. *Marysville Daily Appeal*, 22 February 1861.
62. Ibid.
63. *Downieville Mountain Messenger*, 21 February 1863.
64. *Quincy Union* in *Marysville Daily Appeal*, 3 March 1865.
65. *Downieville Mountain Messenger*, 16 and 26 [*sic* 23] February 1867; *Marysville Daily Appeal*, 28 February 1867.

66. Berry File, "Untitled Americana."
67. *Daily Alta California,* 14 March 1869.
68. Hendel, "Snow-Shoeing," 9.
69. Cited in Gould, *LaPorte Scrapbook,* 153.
70. *La Porte Union,* 6 March 1869, in ibid., 137. Traveling and racing skis are on exhibit in many museums. The principal collection is in the Western Skisport Museum, but small historical societies and town museums exhibit skis and equipment: Bridgeport, Downieville, Johnsville, Quincy, and Sierra City.
71. Mills, "California Pioneers," 42. A grooving plane is on view in the Plumas County Museum.
72. Squier, "Snow Shoers of Plumas," 324.
73. *Butte Record* in *Marysville Daily Appeal,* 26 January 1861; *La Porte Union,* 6 March 1869, in Gould, *LaPorte Scrapbook,* 142; *Daily Alta California,* 11 March 1869; Berry, "Old-Timers of the Sierra," 45.
74. Hendel, "Snow-Shoeing," 9.
75. *Downieville Mountain Messenger,* 3 February 1866; Bill Berry, "Into the Ski Cradle," *Ski Illustrated,* December–January 1938–39, 15; E. W. H. Elmer, "Ski Run to Desolation Lake," *Outing* 33 (March 1899): 600; Squier, "Snow Shoers of Plumas," 319; John J. Wiley, "The Silver Belt," *American Ski Annual* (1948): 143.
76. *Sacramento Daily Union,* 26 March 1869.
77. Gould, *LaPorte Scrapbook,* 162.
78. *Sacramento Daily Union,* 28 March 1868.
79. *Marysville Daily Appeal,* 28 February 1867.
80. Trial in Plumas County Second Judicial Court, 31 May 1869, in Berry File, "Untitled Americana."
81. Speeds were frequently between 40 and 60 mph. Hendel, "Snow-shoeing," 9. Today we are interested in superlative speed, but in those days, despite some notice of speeds, it was who won the race was that was more important. The fastest time ever recorded was more than 87 mph, achieved by Tommy Todd, but it was accomplished on a sheet of ice. There is very little information about this record. It may be that people were simply not that interested; more likely, the race and speed went virtually unrecorded because the winter of 1874 was particularly severe and little news filtered out of the mining camps. Mills, "California Pioneers," 42.
82. *Sacramento Daily Union,* 28 March 1868.
83. *Marquette* [Mich.] *Mining Journal,* 21 January 1905; Harold A. Grinden, "Away Back Yonder," *American Ski Annual* (1936): 138; Bill Berry, untitled MS on early California skiing, 238–43, in Berry's possession.
84. *Sacramento Daily Union,* 26 March 1869.

3/ Utilitarian Skiing and Ludic Enthusiasms

1. Theodore C. Blegen, "Two Norse Argonauts: Ole and Ansten Nattestad," *North Star* 1 (December 1919): 422; Stanley S. Guterman, "The Americaniza-

tion of Norwegian Immigrants: A Study in Historical Sociology," *Sociology and Social Research* 52 (1968): 254.

2. Svein Nilsson, "De skandinaviske Settlementer i Amerika," *Billed-Magazin*, 1 May 1869, 172. Yves Ballu (*L'Epopée du ski* [Paris: Artaud, 1981], 62), maintains that "the first irrefutable evidence of the use of skis in the United States comes from a local paper of 1840," but he gives no documentation to support this. I have had correspondence with M. Ballu but have not been able to find out which newspaper he quoted.

3. Johan Turi, *Turi's Book of Lappland,* ed. and trans. into Danish by E. D. Hutt; trans. from Danish by E. Gee Nash (Osterhout: Anthropological Publications, 1966), 22.

4. Letter, 26 January 1857, in *Land of Their Choice: The Immigrants Write Home,* ed. Theodore C. Blegen (St. Paul: University of Minnesota Press, 1955), 382. The Emigrantinstitutet in Växjö, Sweden, is putting its collection of letters on microfilm. Once the project is completed the letters will be available for research. Other reports of hunting in the United States may be found in *Norsk Idraetsblad* (1884), cited in Jakob Vaage, *Skienes Verden* (Oslo: Hjemmenes, 1979), 237.

5. The ski is on view in the Svenska Skidmuseet in Umeå, Sweden, and accompanying documentation can be found in Svenska Skidmuseet Document File No. 787. I am indebted to the director of the Swedish Ski Museum, Kenneth Åström, for help in translating various letters. See also E. John B. Allen, "Early Canadian Skis: Notes from Europe," *Canadian Journal of Sport History* 17, no. 1 (1986): 88–90. The last report of chasing a deer and felling it with a ski pole is from 1918 (*Montreal Star,* 22 February 1918).

6. Charles F. Holder, "The Skee-Hunters," *St. Nicholas,* March 1900, reprinted in *A St. Nicholas Anthology: The Early Years,* ed. Burton C. Frye (New York: Heredity Press, 1969), 146; Sherwood Davis, "Hunting Elk on Skees," *Youth's Companion,* 23 July 1886.

7. *Reports of the Board and Commissioner of Immigration. 1872* (Augusta, Maine: Sprague, Owen and Nash, 1872), 13–14. For overviews of the colony, see Charlotte L. Melvin, "The First Hundred Years in New Sweden," *Swedish Pioneer Historical Quarterly* 21 (1970): 232–47; Clifford Weden and Marguerite Weden, "The Beginnings of New Sweden, Maine," *Yearbook of the American Swedish Historical Foundation: 1946* (Philadelphia: American Swedish Historical Foundation, 1946), 85–96; Arne S. Menton, "Children in the Woods," *American-Scandinavian Review* 41 (December 1953): 333–37. W. W. Thomas chronicled the New Sweden story in "Historical Oration by Hon. W. W. Thomas, Jr., Founder of New Sweden," in *Celebration of the Decennial Anniversary of the Founding of New Sweden, Maine, July 12, 1880* (Portland, Maine: B. Thurston, 1881), and also at the twenty-fifth anniversary in *The Story of New Sweden as Told at the Quarter Centennial Celebration of the Founding of the Swedish Colony in the Woods in Maine, June 25, 1895* (Portland, Maine: Loring, Short and Harmon, 1896). For an overview of early skiing in Maine, see E. John B. Allen, "'Skeeing' in Maine: The Early Years, 1870s–1920s," *Maine Historical Society Quarterly* 30, nos. 3 and 4 (1991): 146–165.

8. Frederick E. Jorgensen, *25 Years a Game Warden* (Brattleboro, Vt.: Stephen Daye, 1937), 65, 67, 96, 98, 122–23. For other accounts of a game warden on skis in Maine, see *The Machias* [Maine] *Republican,* 5 February 1910; Harold

Day and Adin McKeown interviewed by Edward Ives, 1971 and 1979, North-east Archives of Folklore and Oral History, University of Maine at Orono, nos. 678.037 and 1284.009.

9. John C. Perry diary, 13 December 1885, in New Hampshire Historical Society, Concord. The account he read must have been Hjalmar H. Boyesen, "A New Winter Sport," *St. Nicholas*, February 1883, 304–11. His skiing to school and to the dentist are from entries of 10 and 15 February 1888, in his diary (New Hampshire Historical Society, Concord).

10. Edwin B. Frost, *An Astronomer's Life* (Boston: Houghton Mifflin, 1933), 48.

11. Testimony of Birdie Haun, in Berry File: "Untitled Americana"; Glasscock, *Lucky Baldwin*, 105; letter in Kellogg diary, 19, in Plumas County Museum.

12. Craig O. Burt, "How Skiing Came to Stowe," *Mt. Mansfield Skiing*, 28, no. 4 (1962).

13. The Damariscotta ski is on view in the New England Ski Museum. The New Hampshire skis are documented by Mary A. Gould of Newport, N.H., and given in a letter from Dick Parker to me, in my possession. Evidence of the Massachusetts skier is from an untitled newspaper clipping from 16 December 1940, in New England Ski Museum, L 80.5.1, and from an oral history transcript, "John Ostberg and Leif Nashe aged 74 and 76," in Concord Free Library, Concord, Mass. See also my "'Millions of Flakes of Fun in Massachusetts': Boston and the Development of Skiing 1870–1940," in *Sports in Massachusetts: Historical Essays*, ed. Ronald Story (Westfield: Institute for Massachusetts Studies, 1991), 72–73. The skis from Connecticut are in the Hartland Museum, Hartland, Conn.

14. *Minnesota Pioneer*, 2 February 1853.

15. The president of the National Ski Association was told this by his father. See G. C. Torguson, "Skiing," *The Ski Annual* 18 (January 1922): 4.

16. A. E. Boyum, *Nordmaendene i Amerika, deres historie og Rekord*, cited in Vaage, *Skienes Verden*, 238; Mark Fiester, *Look for Me in Heaven: The Life of John Lewis Dyer* (Boulder, Colo.: Pruett, 1890), 141. For a funeral on skis in Minnesota, see Helen White, *The Tale of a Comet and Other Stories* (St. Paul: Minnesota Historical Press, 1984), 129.

17. *Fergus Falls Journal* in *Minneapolis Tribune*, 7 March 1881; White, *Comet*, 129.

18. Harold Grinden, "World and American Ski History," in *The Complete Ski Guide*, ed. Frank Elkins (New York: Doubleday, Doran, 1940), 15; *Daily Pioneer Press*, 16 January 1886.

19. *Minneapolis Tribune*, 1 January 1888.

20. E. R. Warren, "Snow-Shoeing in the Rocky Mountains," *Outing*, January 1887, 350.

21. Warner A. Root, "Aspen," *Aspen Times*, first issue, n.d., reprinted in *Aspen Times*, 4 January 1979.

22. "In the San Juan Mountains," *Harper's Weekly*, 9 June 1883.

23. Dr. Charles F. Gardiner, *Doctor at Timberline* (Caldwell, Idaho: Caxton Printers, 1938), 55. There is much of interest in Gardiner's book on early Colorado skiing; see esp. 19, 29–32, 42–43. See also John R. Burroughs, *Ski Town, U.S.A.* (Steamboat Springs, Colo.: Pilot Press, 1962), 5; Abbott Fay, *Ski Tracks in the Rockies* (Cordillera, Colo.: Cordillera Press, 1984), 4, 78. For an overview of early skiing in Colorado see Jack A. Benson, "Before Skiing Was Fun," *Western Historical Quarterly* 8 (1977): 431–41.

24. John L. Dyer, *The Snow-Shoe Itinerant: An Autobiography of the Rev. John L. Dyer* (Cincinnati: Cranston and Stowe, 1890), 164–65, 149, 216; George Cornwall, "The Gunnison Country, 1879–1886" (typed MS, Western State College, Gunnison, Colo.), 15; August Fast, "What I Remember 1891 to 1918," in Sarah Platt Decker Chapter D.A.R., Durango, Colorado, *Pioneers of the San Juan Country*, 2 vols. (Colorado Springs: Out West Printing, 1942–1946), 2: 182; Allen Tupper True, "The Trouble-Hunters," *Scribner's*, January 1911, 100; John Irving Hastings diary, January 1872, in James K. Hastings, "A Winter in the High Mountains, 1871–1872," *Colorado Magazine* 27, no. 3 (1950): 230.

25. Letter of Mr. Toll, Del Norte, Colo., 21 February 1876, reprinted in *Eastern Skier*, February 1953, 6.

26. See the letter of Charles L. Beck to his parents, Hot Sulphur Springs, Colo., 20 July 1878, cited in G. L. Cairns, *The Pioneers* (Denver: World Press, 1946), 58. Beck writes that he has taken the job of carrying the mail. "In winter sometimes I shall have to walk on snowshoes 12 ft. long."

27. W. A. Goulder, *Reminiscences of a Pioneer* (Boise: Timothy Regan, 1909), 219–21, cited in Ron Watters, "The Long Snowshoe: Early Skiing in Idaho," *Idaho Yesterdays* (Fall 1979): 19. The article is a documented study based on his *Ski Trails and Old Timers' Tales in Idaho and Montana* (Moscow, Idaho: Solstice Press, 1978), which is undocumented.

28. Thomas C. Donaldson, *Idaho of Yesterday* (1941; reprint Westport, Conn.: Greenwood Press, 1970), 83.

29. *Nordiske Folkeblad*, cited in Jakob Vaage, "Colorado Carries On," *Ski Magazine* (Spring 1976): 69; Kenneth O. Bjork, *West of the Great Divide: Norwegian Migration to the Pacific Coast, 1847–1893* (Northfield, Minn.: Norwegian-American Association, 1958): 363; A. B. Henderson, "Journal of the Yellowstone Expedition of 1886 under Captain Jeff Standifer by A. B. Henderson, Lieutenant of the Company. Also the Diaries Kept by Henderson During His Prospecting Journeys in the Snake, Wind River, and Yellowstone Country During the Years 1867–72," 99, 108. Microfilm of handwritten MS 452 of Western Americana collection, Beinecke Library, Yale University, New Haven.

30. *Ski Bulletin*, 17 March 1939, 12; F. A. Merriam, *My Summer in a Mormon Village* (Cambridge, Mass.: Houghton Mifflin, 1899), 151–52; R. F. Marvin, "An Account of Alta," MS in Lawrence Jones Papers, Special Collections, University of Utah Library, University of Utah, Salt Lake City, cited in Alexis Kelner, *Skiing in Utah: A History* (Salt Lake City: Kelner, 1980), 11.

31. C. T. Stranahan, *Pioneer Stories* (Lewiston, Idaho: Lewiston Branch of the Idaho Writers' League, 1947), 45; Herbert E. Jones cited in Edmund T. Beecher, *Spokane Corona, Eras and Empires* (Spokane: W. Hill, 1974), 260.

32. W. A. Rogers, "Skee-running in Oregon," *Harper's Weekly* (4 March 1899): 225.

33. *Bergens Tidende*, 29 April 1890. I have found no reference to this expedition in the *Washington Post*.

34. Dyer, *Snow-shoe Itinerant*, 163–64.

35. *Colorado Sun*, 31 January 1892; *La Plata Miner*, 20 March 1880. Interviewees recalled frequent difficulties in carrying mail in Decker Chapter, D.A.R., *Pioneers* 1:27, 39, 47, 100–101; 2:116, 184. To follow the development of the

mail service in Colorado, see Joel Barker, "Colorado Mail Service, 1859–85," *Colorado Magazine* 49, no. 3 (1972): 220–37; this article makes little mention of winter delivery.

36. *Denver Times,* 7 and 23 February and 5 March 1899; 20 April 1900; *Ridgeway Herald,* 5 March 1891. The Swan Nilson story was recalled by Brice Patterson, "The Big Snow of 1884," in Decker Chapter D.A.R., *Pioneers* 2:185, and was repeated years later as far away as Michigan in *The Iron Ore,* 28 February 1903.

37. "Will C. Ferrill Scrapbook Collection," 3, 43, Denver Public Library, Denver. See also "Snowshoe Post Routes," *Colorado Graphic,* 18 April 1891, reprinted in *Colorado Magazine* 17, no. 1 (1940): 37; Duane Vandenbusch, *The Gunnison Country* (Gunnison, Colo.: B and B Printers, 1980), 255; Janice G. Jacobs, "Tin Cup, Colorado: A Cup Full of Dreams," (M.A. thesis, Western State College, Gunnison, Colo., 1974), 157.

38. Z. Fuller, "Rocky Mountain Snow-Shoeing," *Midland Monthly* 9, no. 3 (1898): 205.

39. Wilhelm Freiherr von Wangenheim, *Die norwegischen Schneeschuhe (Ski). Das nützlichste Geräth zur Ueberwindung der dem Verkehr durch Schnee bereiteten Hindernisse* (Hamburg: Verlagsanstalt und Druckerei A.-G., 1892), 11.

40. *Idaho World,* 7 December 1883, cited in Watters, *Ski Trails,* 21. For another poetic eulogy, see *Idaho Triweekly Statesman,* 4 April 1882, cited in Watters, *Ski Trails,* 23.

41. "Report of Superintendent of Yellowstone National Park," 20 August 1887, cited in Jack Ellis Haynes, "The First Winter Trip through Yellowstone National Park," *Annals of Wyoming* 14 (April 1942): 91.

42. *Chicago Tribune,* 23 December 1894. Elwood Hofer expressed his opinion in *Forest and Stream,* 5 May 1887, 319. There is a fine photograph of Hofer with Theodore Roosevelt in *Illustrated Sporting News,* 4 July 1903, 12–13.

43. E. Hough, "A Ski Journey through the Yellowstone," *Chicago Tribune,* 23 December 1893. See also Aubrey L. Haines, *The Yellowstone Story,* 2 vols. (Yellowstone Park: Yellowstone Library and Museum Association in cooperation with Colorado Associated University Press, 1977), 2:11, 25, 63, 181, 191, 194, 314; and Haynes, "First Winter Trip," 89–97, in which a number of Frank Jay Haynes's photographs are published. See also William L. Lang, "At the Greatest Personal Peril to the Photographer: The Schwatka-Haynes Expedition in Yellowstone, 1887," *Montana* 33, no. 4 (1983): 14–29, which also has photographs. This article is particularly useful on the Schwatka failure.

    It is not clear on what date soldiers were using Wold skis (from Minnesota) before Martin Strand supplied them. Martin A. Strand, "Ski Running and Jumping" (a sales catalog), 11.

    For army instructions see *Rules, Regulations and Instructions for the Information and Guidance of Officers and Enlisted Men of the United States, and of the Scouts Doing Duty in the Yellowstone National Park* (Washington: Government Printing Office, 1907), 18. For one popular account of patrol duty, see the experiences enjoyed by Lewis R. Freeman, "Skiing through Yellowstone," *Sunset,* June 1922, 12–15, 66–69.

44. Captain Alfred E. Bradley, "The Ski and Its Use for Military Purposes in Yellowstone National Park," *Proceedings of the Association of Military Surgeons* 10 (1900): 403–10. For foreign mention, see "The Use of the Ski, or Skee, in

Foreign Armies" (translated by permission of the Minister of War from the *Revue Militaire des Armées Etrangères*), *Royal United Services Institute Journal* 53 (1900): 375.

45. See the advertisement in *American Ski Annual and Skiing Journal* (1957): 74.

46. K. B. Wiklund and E. Manker have written many articles on skis. Representative are "Nagra tankar om Snoskors och Skidors Upprennelse," *På Skidor* (1926): 1–26, and Ernst Manker, "Fennoskandias fornskidor: Preliminär rapport från en inventering," *Fornvännen* (1971): 77–91. For a summary of the bog skis from a 1980s perspective, see Kenneth Åström and Ove Norberg, "Förhistoriska och medeltida skidor," *Västerbotten* 2 (1984): 82–87. In English, Gösta Berg, *Finds of Skis in Swedish Bogs* (Stockholm: Generalstabens Litografiska Anstalts Forlag, 1950).

47. *Tass* reports of the Russian find in *Stockholm Aftenbladet* and *Svenska Dagbladet*, 25 January 1985, and in *Västerbottens Kurieren*, 26 January 1985. Also noted in *Deutsches Sportmuseum* 3 (Mai–Juni 1985).

48. Albert O. Barton, "The Old Muskego Settlement," *North Star* 3 (November–December 1921): 339–61.

49. *Nevada Daily Transcript,* 22 January 1895.

50. *The Kalevala: The Epic Poem of Finland,* trans. J. M. Crawford (New York: Columbian, 1891), 1:177. I prefer this translation to the one by F. P. Magoun, *The Kalevala or Poems of the Kaleval District,* comp. Elias Lönnrot (Cambridge: Harvard University Press, 1963), poem 13.

51. Letter from Ernest Ingersoll to *The Field,* 14 January 1883, 53.

52. Donaldson, *Idaho of Yesterday,* 83. Skis of unequal length were common in Scandinavia. The early skis in New Sweden, Maine, show less than a one foot difference in length and have no fur underside. Henry Anderson began making them in 1926 and maintained that they were easier to handle than equal-length skis if one hit drifts at speed. Old-timers who knew the ski makers have no explanation for the unequal lengths. The skis are on view in the New Sweden Historical Museum, New Sweden, Maine. See "When Skis Were a Dollar a Foot," interview with Henry Anderson, *Silver Birches,* 15. Interview by author with Ralph Ostlund and Harold Bondeson, New Sweden, Maine, 29 August 1990. See also Allen, "'Skeeing' in Maine," 151–52.

53. Cristel Hastings, "Winter Sports in Yosemite," *Motordom,* January 1933, 15. A moving picture of Basque shepherds opens the documentary film, *Legends of American Skiing.* See also the 1940 photograph of a woman in White Pine, Colorado, in Vandenbusch, *The Gunnison Country,* 398.

54. Knud Leem, *Beskrivelse over Finmarkens Lapper,* Köpenhavn, 1767, reproduced in Anton Obholzer, *5000 Jahre Ski in Bildern* (Innsbruck: Pinguin, 1975), 67.

55. Perry diary, 7 February 1885. The original photo is in the archives of the New England Ski Museum. For these college amusements see also Herman Holt diary, 17, 25, and 27 January 1896 when he had "an out of sight good time" with four friends. I want to thank Barbara Holt of Dover, New Hampshire, for permission to use her father's diaries which remain in her possession. Letter from John W. Ash in *Ski Magazine,* March 1959, 46. See also Dr. J. B. Thomas's remarks recalling his ski experiences in Hanover, N.H., in 1892 (*New York Times,* 3 January 1937).

56. Dale S. Attwood, "Winter Sports at St. Johnsbury," *The Vermonter* 27, no. 9

(1922): 222. The first time skis were seen at Saranac Lake, New York, was on the toboggan track. Tony Goodwin, "Challenge Skiing: High Peaks Adventures," *Adirondack Life*, January–February 1985, 26.

57. Harris diary, 1904–11. See also E. John B. Allen, "The Making of a Skier: Fred H. Harris, 1904–1911," *Vermont History* 53, no. 1 (1985): 5–16.

58. John Muir to *San Francisco Bulletin* (1878) reprinted as "Lake Tahoe in Winter," 125.

59. *Denver Times* (1901), cited in Cal Queal, "Colorado Skiing: A Century of Sport," *Empire Magazine* of the *Denver Post*, 9 November 1969. See also various photos in Envelope 83 A in Aspen Historical Society, Aspen, Colo.; Clippings Collection File: "Skiing Colorado—Aspen," Western History Department, Denver Public Library, Denver; *Grand Lake Prospector*, 25 January 1883; 10 January 1884; *Gunnison Review Press*, 29 March 1884; letter from Alice Denison to her sister Clara, Steamboat Springs, 9 January 1886, in "Pioneering Near Steamboat Springs: 1885–1886," *Colorado Magazine* 28, no. 2 (1951): 90.

60. *Elk Mountain Pilot*, 6 January 1881; Cornwall, "Gunnison Country," 14; *San Juan Herald*, 17 January 1884. For a race challenge in Idaho, see *The Owyhee Avalanche*, 30 December 1865. For a general, contemporary view of racing, see Warren, "Snow-Shoeing in the Rocky Mountains," 350–53. One historical overview is Jack A. Benson's, "Before Aspen and Vail: The Story of Recreational Skiing in Frontier Colorado," *Journal of the West* 22 (January 1983): 52–61.

61. The *Spokane Falls Review*, with changing title, mentions winter sports only occasionally. In one instance it commented on the difficulty of obtaining Canadian snowshoes for a Mt. Rainier expedition. *Spokane Falls Review*, 2 February 1893; 13 December 1894. For the 1913 competition see *The Spokane Sportsman*, 17 January 1913. See also Sam Wormington, *The Ski Race* (Sandpoint, Idaho: Selkirk Press, 1980), 388–95.

62. See the painting *Whaleships in Winter Quarters at Herschel Island, 1893–4*, by John Bertonchini (1872–1947), Whaling Museum, New Bedford, Mass. Bertonchini accompanied the expedition.

4 / Foundation of the Skisport

1. The figures for Scandinavian immigration are:

	Norway[a]	Sweden[b]	Finland[c]	
1871–1880	95,323	101,169	(1872–73)	1,942
1881–1890	176,586	324,285	(1884–93)	27,443
1891–1900	95,051	200,524	(1894–1900)	35,527
1901–1910	190,505	219,249		133,065

[a]Adapted from *Statistical Abstracts of the United States* 1940 and 1960, in Joshua A. Fishman, *Language Loyalty in the United States* (The Hague: Mouton, 1966), 141.

ᵇTable 14, "Svenskarna i utlandet," *Emigrationsutredningens bilaga* 20, 114 which is the base for Table 3 in Florence Edith Janson, *The Background of Swedish Immigration, 1840–1930* (Chicago: Chicago University Press, 1931), 500.

ᶜA. William Hoglund, *Finnish Immigration in America, 1800–1920* (Madison: University of Wisconsin Press, 1960), 152 n.16. See also Reino Kero, "The Character and Significance of Migration Traditions from Finland to America," *American Studies in Scandinavia* 9 (1977): 98. The reason the Finnish figures do not compare is because Finns and emigrants from the Baltic states were all statistically counted as incoming Russians.

Figures for returning immigrants are more difficult to come by but, for example, returning Swedes numbered: 18,766 (1881–1890), 47,138 (1891–1900), 44,029 (1901–1910).

2. Guttmann, *From Ritual to Record,* 26–36.
3. George N. Stephenson, "The Background of the Beginnings of Swedish Immigration," *American Historical Review* 31 (1926): 709; Guterman, "The Americanization of Norwegian Immigrants," 252–53, 256. The Minneapolis newspaper *The North* was judged by one editor to be "one of the most valuable institutions of our state" because it was helping to accomplish "the Americanizing of the Scandinavian races, and the speedy assimilation of our [i.e. American] ideas by the Scandinavians" (*St. Hilaire Spectator* cited in *The North,* 12 February 1890). For another contemporary view see the *Red Wing Advance Sun,* 9 February 1887. The latest scholarly research has broadened the inquiry of ethnicity in America by studying the emigration and immigration of communities. See Robert C. Ostergren, *A Community Transplanted: the Trans-Atlantic Experience of a Swedish Immigrant Settlement in the Upper Mid-West, 1835–1915* (Madison: University of Wisconsin Press, 1988), and Jon Gjerde, *From Peasants to Farmers: The Migration from Balestrand, Norway, to the Upper Middle West* (Cambridge: Cambridge University Press, 1985). Although neither scholar has anything to say about sport, Gjerde's conclusions are borne out in my analysis of the early skisport. The "essential social fabric of their community," he writes of the Balestrand folk, "was retained in the rural communities they settled." New cultural patterns mostly bound up with American economic mores became part of the communities. In spite of the materialism, the core beliefs of the immigrant remained the tie that held communities together (Gjerde, *From Peasants to Farmers,* 239).
4. Nansen (*Paa Ski over Grønland,* 72–127) discusses the history and development of skiing. The book was translated by Hubert M. Gepp, *The First Crossing of Greenland,* 2 vols. (London and New York: Longmans Green, 1890). A long review, taken verbatim from the *London Times* appeared in *The North,* 31 December 1890.
5. S. L. Berens, ed., *The "Fram" Expedition: Nansen in the Frozen World* (Philadelphia: A. J. Holman, 1897), 47.
6. *London Times,* 16 November 1888.
7. Nansen, *First Crossing of Greenland* 1:82–84. I have used the English translation because those are the words—in English, not Norwegian—that had the effect at the time. For the original, see Nansen, *Paa Ski over Grønland,* 78. This

quote set the tone for a long article on Norwegian skiing in the *Red Wing Advance Sun,* 15 February 1893.

8. In Norway: Victor Hansen, *Vinter-Idraetter* (Kjobenhavn: Philipsen, 1893), 771; in Germany: O. Norwerg, *Das Schneeschuhlaufen* (Warmbrunn, 1893), 20; in Switzerland: Krebs-Gygax, "Erinnerungen eines alten Skiläufers," *Schweizer Skiverband Jahrbuch* 9 (1913): 45; in Italy: Oreste Zavattari, *Gli Skj nella Guerra d'Invierno sulle nostre Alpi* (Roma: Enrico Voghera, 1900), 7; in Austria; Mathias Zdarsky, "Unsere Lehrwarte," *Der Schnee* 10 (1906): 2, 5; in England: Captain Howard V. Knox, "Use of Ski, and Training British Soldiers for Duties on Snow-Clad Frontiers," *Royal United Services Institute Journal* 54 (1910): 148.

9. *Brown Company Bulletin* 10 (February 1929): 3. See also letter from Fred H. Harris to *Free Press,* reprinted in *The Skisport* (1910–11): 69–70.

10. Nansen gave short biographies of his team in *Paa Ski over Grønland,* 23–30. Drawings of each are also furnished: Sverdrup, xiii, 15; Dietrichson, 21; Trana, 25; Balto and Ravna, 27. *Samer* is presently the preferred term for those who were called *Lapps* in the nineteenth century.

11. *Red Wing Advance Sun,* 9 and 16 February 1887; *Red Wing Argus,* 10 February 1887. The ski club in Berlin, New Hampshire, remains active and is still called the Nansen. Minneapolis had a Fridtjof Nansen Ski Club in 1893 (*The North,* 8 February 1893; *Red Wing Advance Sun,* 22 February 1893). Following the Ashland, Wisconsin, tournament "three or four of the addresses" at the banquet were in Norwegian (*Iron Ore,* 3 February 1906).

12. *The Skisport* (1909–10): 31–32, 43–46, 54; (1910–11): 18, 70; (1912–13): 63–67; (1913–14): 21–24, 39–41, 51; (1923–24): 8–10. Back home, Norwegians were interested in how their compatriots were skiing in the United States. The Norwegian sports paper *Norsk Idraetsblad* published an account of the Eau Claire competition and showed more than a passing interest in the fifty dollars won by Mikkel Hemmetsveit (*Norsk Idraetsblad,* 11 February 1888).

13. *Literary Digest,* 23 February 1929, 66.

14. Selden Hannah interviewed by Charles T. Morrissey, Franconia, N.H., 8 February 1981, for film, *Legends of American Skiing.*

15. Constitution of the Nansen Ski Club, Berlin, N.H., presently held privately.

16. Nansen Ski Club, Jones Typescript, 4, MS held by Nansen Club. See also E. John B. Allen, "The Development of New Hampshire Skiing: 1870s–1940," *Historical New Hampshire* 36, no. 1 (1981): 3–4, 36, for a critique of sources.

17. Constitution and by laws of the Aurora Ski Club, Red Wing, 1886. Microfilm of handwritten MS held in Minnesota Historical Society Archives, St. Paul. *La Crosse Republican and Leader,* 5 December 1887.

18. Ole Sundlie, cited by James E. Flaa, "Fifty Years at Ishpeming," *American Ski Annual* (1937–38): 22. See also *Mining Journal,* 20 November 1886; 6, 19, and 26 February 1887.

19. Guttmann, *From Ritual to Record,* 40–44.

20. Ishpeming Ski Club, 18 April 1901, Constitution. Handwritten MS in the National Ski Hall of Fame, Ishpeming, Mich. The club was probably an outgrowth of an outing club for promoting "all healthy outdoor sports," which had been founded at the end of February 1901 (*Mining Journal,* 2 March 1901).

21. Typed MS of address by Carl Tellefsen, president, at annual meeting 18 April 1904 between pages 50 and 51 of "Records of the Ishpeming Ski Club of Ishpeming, Michigan." MS in National Ski Hall of Fame. See also *Iron Ore,* 11 January 1902, which invited "all nationalities" to attend an evening tramp.

22. *Iron Ore,* 27 February 1904.

23. Ibid., 10 and 17 December 1904; 4 February 1905; minutes of the officers meeting of the Ishpeming Ski Club, 5 January 1905, 56 (this invitation was to a president who had first attempted skiing in 1888 in Washington during a blizzard and had gone on to use skis recreationally at his home in Sagamore Hill); *Minneapolis Tidene,* cited in Jakob Vaage with Morten Lund, "America: Meet Your First Skiing President," *Ski,* October 1975, 128. See also Theodore Roosevelt to Anna Roosevelt Cowles, Sagamore Hill, 2 January 1897, in *Letters from Theodore Roosevelt to Anna Roosevelt Cowles, 1870–1918* ed. Anna Roosevelt Cowles (New York: Scribners, 1924), 202; and Roosevelt to Cowles, from Washington, 17 February 1895, in *The Letters of Theodore Roosevelt,* vol. 1, *The Years of Preparation, 1868–1898,* ed. Etling E. Morrison (Cambridge: Harvard University Press, 1951), 427.

24. *Mining Journal,* 16 and 25 February 1905; *Iron Ore,* 25 February 1905.

25. *The Skisport* (1906–07): 22, 32; (1908–09): 18; (1909–10): 42.

26. *The Pioneer Press,* 9 and 15 January 1886. Microfilm of Aurora Ski Club Minute Book, 1886–1892, in Minnesota Historical Society. For uniforms, see also *St. Croix Valley Standard,* 19 and 26 January 1888.

27. *New York Times* cited in *Literary Digest,* 24 January 1925, 54.

28. Barnum and Bailey poster and the photograph of Karl Hovelsen in Leif Hovelsen, *The Flying Norseman* (Ishpeming: National Ski Hall of Fame, 1983), 28, 34. An advertisement and drawing will be found in the *New York Journal,* 22 and 23 March 1907, and an article on March 22, titled "Captain Hovelsen's Death-Defying Bird-Like Flight on Skis a Wonder," gives the tone of the reporting. Skiing was first proposed for Olympic competition in 1908 because it was "of great military importance" according to the Italian delegate to the International Olympic Committee, cited by Brian Dobbs, *Edwardians at Play: Sport 1890–1914* (London: Pelham Books, 1973), 161n.

29. *Red Wing Republican,* 6 January and 6 February 1903.

30. *The Skisport* (1906–07): 32–33, 37–38. For women's participation in club tramps, see *Iron Ore,* 9 and 16 January 1904; 17 March 1906; 4 January 1908.

31. *The North,* 29 March 1893.

32. *The Skisport* (1913–14): 15, 45.

33. Ibid. (1906–07): 6, see also 35–37; (1907–08): 2; (1923–24): 26. Aksel Holter, "Inspiration-Work-Attainment," in Harold Grinden, *History of the National Ski Association and the Ski Sport in the United States of America, 1840 to 1931* (Duluth, 1932), 60.

34. *The North,* 22 February 1893.

35. Ishpeming Ski Club MS, 14–15; *Mining Journal,* 7, 14, 21 and 28 December 1901. In Norway, a long-distance race could be decided by physical condition if the runners were tied (J. W. Schreiner, "The Olympic Games of the North," in *A Book of Winter Sports,* ed. J. C. Dier [New York: Macmillan, 1912], 207). For one account of this "health" condition in a Norwegian race, see the *Red Wing Advance Sun,* 1 March 1893. For the occasional continuation of this

Idraet quality, see the *Iron Ore,* 1 March 1902, and the speech to the Aurora Club reprinted in the *Red Wing Daily Republican,* 28 January 1905.

36. *Mining Journal,* 28 December 1901.
37. The race was not much of a success because the Norwegians were not behind the effort. The December 1902 race drew five entrants, two of whom probably cheated (*Iron Ore,* 27 December 1902; *First Annual Report of the National Ski Association* [1906–07]).
38. *The Skisport* (1906–07): 16–17, 20–21. The St. Paul club reported on its "cross-country and fence climbing abilities" (ibid. [1907–08]: 6).
39. *Ely Miner,* 22 February 1907, cited in Morten Lund, "The Way It Was," *Ski,* September 1978, 63. Autio had often competed for money in Scandinavia (Jussi Kirjavainen, *Suomalaiset Suurhiihträjät* [Helsinki: Söderström, 1938], 167–77; Helge Nygrén, Antero Raevuori, and Tarmo Mäki-Kuutti, *Pitkä Latu: Suomalaista Hiihtourheilua* [Porvoo: Söderström, 1983], 222). I would like to thank Merja Heiskanen, curator of the Finnish Ski Museum in Lahti for translations. See also *På Skidor* (1901–02): 138.
40. *The Skisport* (1910–11): 20.
41. Ibid., (1916–17): 8.
42. Some even set themselves up as ski instructors and asked a fee (*Aftenbladet,* 12 February 1881).
43. For a discussion of equality in competition, see Guttmann, *From Ritual to Record,* 26–36.
44. *Mining Journal,* 1 March 1902.
45. *Red Wing Advance Sun,* 16 February 1887.
46. Minutes of meetings of 19 November 1889, and 7 January 1890, Aurora Ski Club Minute Book, 1886–1891.
47. *The North,* 4 February 1891.
48. Minutes of meeting of 19 November 1889, Aurora Ski Club Minute Book, 1886–1891.
49. *Mining Journal,* 23 January 1901.
50. *The Skisport* (1906–07): 4–5.
51. Ibid.
52. *Mining Journal,* 24 February 1906; *Iron Ore,* 27 February 1905. One-time American record holder Gustave Bye fell twice in one meet but was still awarded fourth place (ibid., 26 January 1907). This partiality to well-known jumpers extended to the 1932 Olympic Games. Birger Ruud, knowing he had been treated too kindly by the judges, refused to receive his prize without the runner-up on stage with him. "It has always been difficult for judges," commented Erling Strom, "to penalize the big names sufficiently for their mistakes" (Erling Strom, *Pioneers on Skis* [Central Valley, N.Y.: Smith Clove Press, 1977], 57).
53. Discussion will be found in *The Skisport* (1910–11): 14–15; (1914–15): 4; (1924–25): 35, 72.
54. *Norman County Index,* 21 and 28 January 1887 (I should like to thank Thelma Strand Wegner of Moorhead, Minnesota, for sending me a copy of notes she collected); *Daily Pioneer Press,* 30 January 1887; *St. Croix Valley Standard,* 19 January and 1 November 1888; *Taylors Falls Journal,* 19 January and 2 February 1888; *Stillwater Messenger,* 21 January 1888; minutes of meeting, 19 November 1889, Aurora Ski Club Minute Book, 1886–1891.

55. *Mining Journal,* 16 February 1901.

56. See the advertisement for money prizes of one hundred, sixty, and forty Kroner given by the Christiania Ski Club (*Aftenbladet,* 17 January 1881). Prizes of one hundred Kroner and ninety Kroner were given to the Hemmetsveits for first and second places in the King's Prize competition in Norway in 1883 (*Aarbog* [1902]: end paper). Torger Hemmetsveit won a first prize of four hundred Kroner in a cross-country race near Christiania in 1893 (*Red Wing Advance Sun,* 1 March 1893).

57. *Mining Journal,* 3 March 1888; *Red Wing Argus,* 10 February 1887; *Red Wing Advance Sun,* 16 February 1887. The St. Paul Ski Club offered the following prizes for the first ten places in its 1907 tournament: gold watch, opera glass, gold locket, gold cuff buttons, smoking set, silver pocket flask, watch fob, staff pin, ink stand, and, for the tenth place, a cigar case (*The Skisport* [1906–07]: 14).

58. *Mining Journal,* 16 February 1901.

59. *The Skisport* (1907–08): 4–11.

60. Derived from ibid. (1906–07). In 1904 miners struck for $2.40 a day (*Ashland Daily Press,* 8 March 1904).

61. *Iron Ore,* 9 December 1905; 17 February 1906.

62. Ibid., 24 February 1906; *Mining Journal,* 24 February 1906; *First Annual Report of the National Ski Association of America* (1906–07). The question over amateurism and professionalism caused contentious discussion in the nineteenth and twentieth centuries. Much of the debate was over the definition of an amateur as one whose daily use of hands and body helped in the athletic result but this definition did not concern skiing at all. It was the other definition, whereby no amateur could obtain money for skiing prowess, that was the concern. For a discussion of these two views see Robin L. Chambers, "Sportsmanship in a Sporting America: Tradition, Ideal, Reality" (Ph.D. diss., Temple University, 1984), 205–6. For a contemporary view see "Snobbery of Sport," *Independent,* 6 February 1913, 277–78.

63. *The Skisport* (1910–11): 21; ibid. (1909–10): 56.

64. Ibid. (1908–09): 49. See also ibid. (1909–10): 12.

65. Ibid. (1910–11): 33.

5/ Controlling the Skisport

1. *Iron Ore,* 4 February 1905; *Mining Journal,* 25 February 1905. See also Allen, "The Modernization of the Skisport," *Michigan Historical Review* 16, no. 1 (1990): 1–20.

2. *The Skisport* (1906–07): 25–35.

3. Ibid. (1909–10): 51–53 (for an overview of the club, see David H. Beetle, "The First Kingdom of the Ski," *Ski Time* [1951?]: 29–31); C. H. Blair to C. A. Proctor, 13 January 1937, in Special Collections, Baker Library, Dartmouth College, Hanover, N.H.

4. *The Skisport* (1909–10): 51.

5. Ibid. (1912–13): 16–17. See also, for example, ibid. (1908–09): 3–4 where

it is reported that the newly formed Twin City Ski Club had lured members from the Minneapolis Ski Club with promises of profits from their newly built hill.

6. *First Annual Report of the National Ski Association of America* (as the first *Skisport* was titled), n.p.

7. Examples may be found in *The Skisport* (1905–06): n.p.; (1906–07): 6, 35–37; (1921–22): 21.

8. See the full-page advertisement in *The Skisport* (1912–13).

9. *Mining Journal,* 23 February 1901.

10. *Iron Ore,* 26 January, 23 February 1907.

11. *Mining Journal,* 1 February 1902.

12. Ibid., 2 March 1901; 1 February 1902; 30 January, 20 February, 24 December 1904; 16 and 25 February 1905; 17, 24 February, 15 and 16 December 1906; *Iron Ore,* 4 February 1905; 13 January 1906. Duluth had sent an orchestra to Ishpeming as part of its effort to secure the national championship. Ibid., 17 February 1906.

13. *The Skisport* (1907–08): 2.

14. Ibid., 19–20.

15. Ibid. (1908–09): 27.

16. *New York Times,* 25 January 1909.

17. K. H., "Skisport in America," *Der Winter* (1909), reprinted in *The Skisport* (1909–10): 54–55 (see also ibid., 10, and ibid. [1910–11]: 69).

18. *The Skisport* (1909–10): 10. This aspect of Americanization had received public comment in the *Red Wing Daily Republican,* 3 February 1905: "When the sport was transplanted to the Northwest, the American instinct for the exceptional and extraordinary naturally emphasized the jumping feature as the most sensational."

19. C. Egger, "England und Amerika," *Ski* [Swiss] 5 (1909): 144; *The Skisport* (1910–11): 78.

20. *The Skisport* (1911–12): 25.

21. *New York Times,* 17 February 1913; 19 February 1916; 10 February 1921; *Steamboat Pilot,* February 1916, cited in Hovelsen, *The Flying Norseman,* 56–59, 63, 75; *Aarbok* (1920): 170; *The Skisport* (1920–21): 17.

22. Mrs. L. F. K. von Thiele, "The Norwegian Olympic Games," *Wide World Magazine* 9 (1902): 465–73. See also *Illustrated Outdoor News,* 17 February 1906, 10–11.

23. Letter Karl Roll to NSA in *The Skisport* (1908–09): 13–14; ibid. (1909–10): 9.

24. Colonel N. R. Ostgaard, "The International Ski Association," *1950 World Championship USA: FIS Lake Placid* (NSA: n.d.), 4–5. There were, though, ten representatives: from Austria, Bohemia, England, France, Germany, Norway, Scotland, Spain, Sweden, and Switzerland. For an overview of the development of the FIS (1910–1924), see Dietmar Hubrich, "Die historische Entwicklung des Internationalen Skiverbandes 'FIS'," Diplomarbeit an der Deutschen Hochschule für Körperkultur, Leipzig (1975), 12–20, TS.

25. Henry Cuënot, "Les jeux d'hiver à Chamonix," *La Montagne* 166 (1923): 281–84. As preparations were made to send a United States team to Chamonix, the *New York Times* frequently referred to the upcoming competition as

Olympic Games (*New York Times,* 7 November and 15, 16, and 23 December 1923).

26. Ostgaard, "The International Ski Association," 5. The sixteen nations that founded the FIS were Austria, Canada, Czechoslovakia, Finland, France, Germany, Great Britain, Hungary, Italy, Yugoslavia, Norway, Poland, Rumania, Sweden, Switzerland, and the United States. The NSA was affiliated with the American Athletic Union, Winter Olympic Games Committee, Intercollegiate Winter Sports Union, Conference on Outdoor Recreation, American Olympic Association, International Olympic Committee, National Ski Alumni, and the Canadian Ski Association (Grinden, *History of the National Ski Association,* 23).

27. The Kandahar Club was founded in 1924 by the British at Mürren, Switzerland, "with the express intention of securing the inclusion of downhill racing in the Olympic Games." Arnold Lunn, "The F.I.S. and Things," *Australian and New Zealand Ski Year Book* (1937): 17. Lunn, *The Kandahar Story* (London: Allen and Unwin, 1969), 21–23.

28. *The Ski Bulletin,* 10 February 1933, 7.

29. Reinhard Straumann, "Vom Ski-Weitsprung und seiner Mechanik," *Ski* [Swiss] 21 (1926): 6–22 and 22 (1927): 34–64. For more on Straumann and his publications, see W. Keil, *Festschrift für Reinhard Straumann* (Stuttgart: Steinkopf, 1950), 3–5, 15. R. Straumann, "Ski Jumping and Its Mechanics," cited in Fred H. Harris, "Building Ski Jumping Hills," USEASA *Year Book* (1928): 32; Charles A. Proctor, "Scoring in Jumping Competition," *The Skisport* (1923–24): 19–21. For an analysis of Dr. Reinhard Straumann's aerodynamic experiments, see *Ski,* January 1968, 30.

30. Fred H. Harris, "The Splendid Sport of Ski Jumping," *Country Life in America,* February 1924, 49; idem, "Building Ski Jumping Hills," USEASA *Year Book* (1928): 32. See also *The Skisport* (1920–21): 18–19; *New York Times,* 27 February 1921; 22 February 1923; 28 January 1924; 8 February 1926; *Springfield Sunday Republican,* 5 February 1922; untitled newspaper clipping, 3 February 1922 (?), in Berlin, N.H., Scrapbook, New England Ski Museum.

31. Information from untitled, undated newspaper clipping, in National Ski Hall of Fame, Ishpeming, Michigan.

32. *Minneapolis Daily Tribune,* 9 February 1885.

33. *St. Croix Valley Standard,* 5 January and 1 November 1888; *Taylors Falls Journal,* 19 and 26 January, 2 February, 25 October, 1, 15, and 29 November, 13, 20, and 27 December 1888; 2 January and 2 December 1890. Another brother, Torger Hemmetsveit, made skis in Red Wing in 1893. *The Red Wing Advance Sun,* 27 December 1893. The skis were similar to the Telemark type on which Mikkel Hemmetsveit had won the King's Cup at the Husebybakken (forerunner of the Holmenkollen event) in 1883 and 1886. *Norsk Idraetsblad,* 17 February 1886, 29; *Aarbok* (1922): 78.

34. The Norwegian Hagen skis were the best known of the foreign imports in the United States. Their manufacture was described for an American audience in *Supplement: The Scientific American* (1911): 4–11. For Holter's factory and business, see *Ashland News,* 16 December 1905; 27 November, 17 December 1906; 4 January 1907; *Ashland Daily Press,* 6, 9, 23 December 1907; *Iron Ore,* 17 December 1904; 10 February 1906. Ingeborg Burnside (Holter's daugh-

ter), interviewed by author. Ashland, Wisc., 26 June 1984. In the *Ashland City Directory* (1907–08), Holter is listed as a travel agent and stationer. There is no mention of any ski manufacture in town. See also *The Skisport* (1923–24): 22, 25.

35. Strand, "Ski Running and Jumping"; *New Richmond News and Republican Voice,* 29 April and 19 July 1911.

36. *New Richmond News and Republican Voice,* 19 July 1911.

37. Ibid.

38. Lyman Johnson interview by author, New Richmond, Wisc., 27 June 1984.

39. Ibid. By the fall of 1911, Strand could turn out about two hundred pairs of skis a day (*New Richmond News and Republican Voice,* 23 August 1911). Strand's records have not been found; the *New Richmond News* building was destroyed by fire (ibid., 22 and 25 January 1913).

40. *The Skisport* (1910–11): 72.

41. Theo. Johnsen Company, *The Winter Sport of Skeeing* (Portland, Maine, 1905). See also Allen, "Skeeing in Maine: The Early Years 1870s–1920s," *Maine Historical Society Quarterly* 30, nos. 3–4 (1991): 155–61.

42. Martin Strand to F. C. Barton, New Richmond, Wisc., 10 March 1914, no. 14   023 in Apperson Papers, Adirondack Research Center, Schenectady, N.Y.

43. Selections are on view at the New England Ski Museum.

44. Johnsen, *Winter Sport of Skeeing,* 21.

45. Herbert Marshall, *How Skiing Came to the Gatineau* (Ottawa: Canadian Ski Museum, [1971?]), 7.

46. Artur Zettersten, "När Började man Använda två Skidstavar?" *På Skidor* (1943): 19–24; Gösta Berg, "De både stavarna och våra skidtyper än en gång," ibid. (1944): 89–94.

47. Charles H. Dudley, *60 Centuries of Skiing* (Brattleboro, Vt.: Stephen Daye Press, 1935), 37.

48. Anton Diettrich, *Ski and Skiing: A Series of Lectures* (Hanover, N.H.: Dartmouth Outing Club, 1924), 18.

49. Betty Whitney interviewed by Arthur F. March, Jr., Jackson, N.H., 2 December 1981, New England Ski Museum, Oral History Archive.

50. *Canadian Ski Annual* (1934): 74.

51. Minutes of meeting, 20 January 1888, in Aurora Ski Club Minute Book, 1886–1892.

52. Johnsen, *Winter Sport of Skeeing,* 53.

53. *The Skisport* (1909–10). For Bass, see *American Ski Annual* (1952): 232.

54. Photographs of early clubs held by the National Ski Hall of Fame show this element of uniformity.

55. For Wold, see *Norvesten* (1888) cited in Vaage and Lund, "America: Meet Your First Skiing President," 95; Timothy R. Manns, "1890's in Yellowstone Park," *Yellowstone Rendezvous* 2, no. 1 (1981). Later, Strand supplied skis to the troops.

56. None of the manufacturers had much influence in shaping the skisport. In 1920 when Martin Strand and Christian Lund (president of Northland Ski Company) wanted to donate $100 and $250 respectively to the NSA, the constitution was changed so that money could be accepted "from those interested in skiing" (*The Ski Annual* [title change of *The Skisport*] [1919–20]: 22).

Stephen Hardy has recently suggested that the sporting goods industry played a major role in shaping nationally standardized sports, but this was not the case with the skisport (Stephen Hardy, "Entrepreneurs, Organizations, and the Sport Marketplace: Subjects in Search of Historians," *Journal of Sport History* 13, no. 1 [1986]: 14–33).

6/ The New Enthusiasts

1. St. Olaf's *Manitou Messenger* 2, no. 1 (1888): 3; *The North* reported on men and women skiing at the Minnesota college in 1891; *Mining Journal,* 3 December 1904; Plymouth Normal School's *Prospect* 2 (January 1907): 114.
2. For Vermont Academy's role see Document Boxes T 7, Folder: Green Mountain Club; and T 11, Folder: Vermont Academy, in Vermont Historical Society, Montpelier, Vt. See also *Vermont Academy Life* (March 1915?), excerpt in Fred Harris, Memory Book, in Dartmouth College History Collection, Baker Library, Dartmouth College.
3. Fred H. Harris to *The Dartmouth,* 7 December 1909.
4. Fred H. Harris, Scrapbook, in Dartmouth College History Collection.
5. Fred H. Harris diary, 10 and 17 December 1910. Harris wrote this trip up in *The Dartmouth,* 12 December 1910. This cross-country outing had the obvious enjoyment of the slides. Distance was also important because it satisfied the *Idraet* requirements of health and morality. Harris was a formidable record keeper: in the winter of 1910–11, for example, he noted the total distance covered by the three leading Dartmouth Outing Club members: Harris, ninety-eight miles, Mr. Goldthwaite, ninety-two, and Dr. Licklider, ninety (*The Dartmouth,* 1 May 1911). Allen, "The Making of a Skier," 9–15, covers Harris's college years.
6. *The Dartmouth,* 9 March 1911. The notes for this are in Harris's diary, 4 March 1911. This experience was given wide publicity in Fred H. Harris, "Up Mount Washington on Skees," *Country Life in America,* December 1912, 63–65.
7. Fred H. Harris, "Skiing over the New Hampshire Hills," *National Geographic Magazine,* February 1920, 151–64. This note is found in a typed list of Harris's articles after the *National Geographic* citation: "Secretary of Dartmouth College stated that this article increased Freshman applications in one year from 800 plus to over 2600 and had a good deal to do with the necessity of organizing the Selective Process of Admission." The date of Harris's note is unknown (Harris Papers, in possession of Helen Harris) but the figures come from David Bradley, "Dartmouth in the Old Days," *Ski* (January 1959): 19. The admissions office at Dartmouth no longer has the records. David Bradley told me he had received confirmation of the figures in 1958.
8. Harris, "Skiing over the New Hampshire Hills," 151–64.
9. Fred H. Harris, ed., *Dartmouth Out o' Doors* (Boston: Crosby, 1913).
10. Minutes of meeting, 28 September 1915, Dartmouth Outing Club, in Special Collections, Baker Library, Dartmouth College.

11. Harris, "Skiing over the New Hampshire Hills," 162–63; Charles N. Proctor interviewed by Richard W. Moulton, Santa Cruz, Calif., 3 April 1981, for the film *Legends of American Skiing; New York Times,* 13 February 1916; *Boston Post,* 23 February 1919.

12. *Springfield Sunday Republican,* 5 February 1922; *New York Times,* 8 February 1926; Newspaper clipping, undated but probably 3 February 1922, in Berlin, N.H., Scrapbook in New England Ski Museum. In 1922 a crowd of twenty thousand watched a tournament in Chicago (*The Skisport* [1921–22]: 23).

13. Undated newspaper clipping (1923?), in Harris Memory Book in New England Ski Museum.

14. Ibid., 28 January 1924.

15. Charlotte E. Wilde, "Reminiscences of the Snowshoe Section," *Appalachia,* June 1952, 54–55.

16. John Ritchie, "On Snow-Shoes at Jackson," *Appalachia* 5 (1887): 212–13.

17. John McDill, "Woodstock, Cradle of Winter Sports," *Vermont Life* 2, no. 2 (1947–48): 14; C. W. J. Tennant, "Ski-ing in the United States," *Year-Book of the Ski Club of Great Britain* (1914): 372. John Martin had experiences similar to those McDill and Tennant reported on his holidays at Woodstock between 1907 and 1910 (John Martin tape recording for film *Legends of American Skiing*).

18. *Littleton Courier,* 16 February 1911.

19. Consumptives, fault-finders, and those who overdressed in elaborate jewelry were among those who along with all Jews, were barred from the club, (*Lake Placid Club Notes,* March 1905; March 1913, 417; March 1929, 2017. For Dewey's antisemitism, see *Petition to the Regents of the University of the State of New York Respectfully Asking for the Removal from Office of Melvil Dewey, the Present State Librarian, whose Tenure of Office is Dependent upon Your Action,* 20 December 1904 (p. 3) and Dewey's reply (pp. 6–20) in New York State Archives, Albany. Antisemitism could be found in some inns and hotels in the East until after the Second World War. For the 1930s see advertisements for "restricted clientele" (*American Ski Annual* [1938–39], [44]) and for "selected clientele" (*New York Times,* 11 December 1938). For the beginning of ski activity at Lake Placid, see Godfrey Dewey, "Sixty Years of Lake Placid Club, 1895–1955," reprint of a talk, 4 August 1955, 6–7, in New York State Archives, Albany, and *Lake Placid Notes,* November 1906, 3; 2 March 1908, 1; January 1910, 206; October 1912, 391. Skiing only became really popular at the club during the 1911–12 season (ibid., December–January 1912–13, 397); Dorothy Clay interviewed by E. John B. Allen, Center Sandwich, N.H., 1 August 1984 (New England Ski Museum, Oral History Archive).

20. John Muir to *San Francisco Bulletin* (1878), reprinted as "Lake Tahoe in Winter," 119–26.

21. Hazel King, "Ski Running: An Impression," *Sierra Club Bulletin,* January 1915, 271–73; J. E. Church, Jr., "Lake Tahoe in Winter," *Sunset Magazine,* reprinted in *Sierra Club Bulletin,* January 1915, 274–77; *Daily Goldfield Tribune,* 27 February 1909.

22. Duncan M. Morison, "Ski-ing in California," *British Ski Year Book* (1926): 513.

23. *Elk Mountain Pilot,* 6 January 1881; Cornwall, "The Gunnison Country," 14; Warren, "Snow-shoeing in the Rocky Mountains," 350–53.

24. In a list of seventeen states where Scandinavians lived in 1890, Colorado was sixteenth. The actual numbers of Norwegian immigrants during the period 1890–1920 never exceeded eighteen hundred, of which about one-third lived in Denver. See Department of the Interior, Census Office, *Report on the Population of the United States at the Eleventh Census: 1890* (Washington: Government Printing Office, 1895), chart between cxxxvi–cxxxvii, 607; Census Reports, *Twelfth Census of the United States, Taken in the Year 1900*, vol. 1: *Population Part 1* (Washington: United States Census Office, 1901), 740–41; Department of Commerce, Bureau of Census, *Thirteenth Census of the United States Taken in the Year 1910*, vol. 2, *Population 1910* (Washington: Government Printing Office, 1913), 211, 216, 218, 220, 222, 224, 226; Department of Commerce, Bureau of the Census, *Fourteenth Census of the United States Taken in the Year 1920*, vol. 3, *Population 1920* (Washington: Government Printing Office, 1922), 149.

25. Hovelsen, *The Flying Norseman*, 49. See also the photograph of skiing at Fern Lake in *The Skisport*, January 1920, 2.

26. *Empire Magazine* of *Denver Post*, 17 January 1954. Graeme McGowan, assisted by Garrat B. Van Wagenen, "The First Chapter in the History of Ski-ing in Colorado," *British Ski Year Book* (1930): 503–4.

27. *Empire Magazine* of *Denver Post*, 17 January 1954.

28. Emil C. Wahlstrom, "Skiing in Colorado," *Outing*, December 1922, 122–23; *Denver Post*, [?] February 1920; Mary Ellen Gilliland, *Frisco! A Colorful Colorado Community* (Frisco: Frisco Historical Society, 1984), 76. Summit County registered fourteen Norwegians in 1890, twenty-one in 1900, fourteen in 1910 when Prestrud arrived in Frisco, and nine in 1920. See *Eleventh Census: 1890*, 614; *Twelfth Census, 1900*, 741; *Thirteenth Census, 1910*, 226; *Fourteenth Census, 1920*, 149.

29. G. C. Torguson, "Skiing: A Wonderful Winter Sport," *Outers' Recreation*, February 1920, 109.

7 / Post–World War I

1. *The Skisport* (1924–25): 22.

2. Oscar T. Oyass, "Our Achievements," *The Skisport* (1924–25): 3.

3. Roger F. Langley, "The Present Status of Skiing in America," *The American Ski Annual* (1939–40): 9.

4. Typed MS of USEASA minutes (1924), 2: minutes from 9 December 1924. The New England Ski Museum holds a run of Eastern's and other associations' minutes, mostly in carbon copies. They are variously dated and some have no pagination.

5. Grinden, *History of the National Ski Association*, 20–21.

6. *Olympic Games 1936. Official Organ of the XI Olympic Games Berlin 1936 and of the IV Olympic Winter Games Garmisch-Partenkirchen*, no. 8, 23; *London Times*, 20 December 1913.

7. Although it had been agreed to hold the Games under IOC rules "champions had no right to medals." Cuënot, "Les jeux d'hiver à Chamonix," 281.

8. *New York Times,* 3, 4, 6, 7, 11, 12, 13, and 14 January 1924.

9. *New York Times,* 31 January and 3 and 5 February 1924.

10. *New York Times,* 5 February 1924; Lt. Col. H. de Watteville, "The Olympic Winter Games at Chamonix," *British Ski Year Book* (1924): 230.

11. *The Skisport* (1924–25): 44; *Skier,* November 1974, 13; ibid., December 1974, 6.

12. *New York Times,* 16 February 1924.

13. Report by Fred Harris on the Twenty-second NSA Convention, 13–14 February 1926, in USEASA minutes (1926).

14. USEASA minutes (1927): 77; (2 November 1928): 116–17.

15. Henry I. Baldwin to author, December 1986 (in author's possession).

16. Charles N. Proctor interviewed by Richard W. Moulton, Santa Cruz, Calif., 3 April 1981; Charles N. Proctor, talk at Hanover, N.H., 23 September 1981.

17. USEASA minutes (1928) and Executive Committee minutes, 1 November 1928.

18. USEASA Executive Committee minutes, 1 November 1928.

19. Charles N. Proctor to his father, reprinted in *Dartmouth Alumni Magazine* (1928): 520. Arnold Lunn, "The International Ski Congress at St. Moritz," *British Ski Year Book* (1928): 475–81.

20. Godfrey Dewey, "The Olympic Winter Games," *USEASA Year Book* (1928): 24.

21. Proctor letter in *Dartmouth Alumni Magazine,* 520.

22. When it was learned that Lake Placid had been awarded the Games, some Californians wanted to hold a rival sports meeting (*Nevada State Journal,* 11 April 1929). For Californian reaction see A. B. C. Dohrman, "California's Opportunity to Invite the World's Best Winter Sports Performers," *California Journal of Development,* November 1930, 5; and E. des Baillets, "Winter Sports in the California Sierras," ibid., 7.

23. There is a vast literature, both official and popular, on the 1932 Winter Olympic Games. See, e.g., George M. Lattimer, comp., *Official Report III Olympic Winter Games: Lake Placid 1932* (Lake Placid: III Olympic Winter Games Committee, 1932). The best popular overview I have seen is P. W. Metzler, "Third Winter Olympics," *Conservationist* 34, no. 3 (1979): 12–16.

24. Published in both *Winter Sports,* February 1933, 4–6, 22, and *The Ski Bulletin,* 10 February 1933, 6–7. See also Fred Harris's reply in *Winter Sports,* March 1933, 4–5.

25. Metzler, "Third Winter Olympics," 12–13.

26. George M. Lattimer, "The Olympics in Retrospect," *Winter Sports,* 3, no. 2 (November 1932, 14–15. Roger F. Langley, "A Survey of Skiing in the United States" (M.Ed. thesis, Fitchburg State College, Fitchburg Mass. 1946), 131–37, is particularly uncritical of the 1932 Games. For one example from the popular literature, see "America Takes to Skis," *Publishers Weekly,* 12 December 1936, 2287. For the Olympic stamp, see U.S. Post Office Booklet, 1937, 84, and letters cited in *The Ski Bulletin,* 20 January 1939, 7.

27. The most satisfactory account of Schneider's early years is the autobiographical article he contributed to Roland Palmedo, ed., *Skiing: The International Sport* (New York: Derrydale, 1937), 87–112. But see also Gerard Fairlie, *Flight without Wings: The Biography of Hannes Schneider* (London: Hodder and

Stoughton, 1957), and Hans Thöni, *Hannes Schneider zum 100. Geburtstag des Schipioniers und Begründers der Arlbergtechnik* (Innsbruck: Tyrolia, 1990).

28. *Ski* [Swiss] (1921): 107; cited in [Arnold Lunn], "The Arlberg School," *British Ski Year Book* (1927): 31.

29. "The Arlberg School," 32.

30. Lt. Col. H. de Watteville, "On Ski-ing Schools and Styles," *British Ski Year Book* (1931): 221.

31. Hannes Schneider, *Auf Schi in Japan* (Innsbruck, Wien, München: Tyrolia, 1935).

32. Nathaniel L. Goodrich, "A Ski Holiday in the Alps," *Appalachia,* December 1929, 336; Wilhelmine G. Wright, "Going to Ski School in the Austrian Tyrol," ibid., December 1931, 372–77.

33. *Ski Survey* 1, no. 9 (1975): 521.

34. One finds remarks in the *American Ski Annuals* such as "The British Ski Year Book . . . is as amazing as ever"; "Again the B.S.Y.B. leaves one rather breathless"; "The British Ski Year Book sort of goes without saying" (see e.g., *American Ski Annual* [1936]: 153). When Alex Bright became the British Ski Club's Boston representative, he signed up more members from New England and New York than from some of the European centers (*Boston Evening Transcript,* 21 December 1934).

35. Arnold Lunn, "Down with the Marxist Slalom," *Ski* [U.S.], February 1955, 32. Idem, "Style Competitions and Slalom Races," *British Ski Year Book* (1922): 393.

36. *Der Winter,* January 1933, 413; Strom, *Pioneers on Skis,* 62. The judgment of Lunn is cited in O. R. Lirsch, "Ski News from Abroad," *Winter Sports,* October 1932, 18.

37. USEASA Report, 1925.

38. Observations by Bill Berry, Reno, Nevada, 1 April 1981, and by Gordon Wren, Steamboat Springs, Colorado, 26 March 1981, recorded by Moulton for the film *Legends of American Skiing. Boston Evening Transcript,* 6 February 1926.

39. Charles N. Proctor, "History and Development of Skiing in America," in Palmedo, *Skiing: The International Sport,* 64; *Handbook of the Intercollegiate Sports Union, with Changes* (1928–30); *British Ski Year Book* (1928): 472.

40. Charles N. Proctor to author, 12 January 1985 (in author's possession). See also an account in the *Boston Herald,* 7 February 1936.

41. *The Dartmouth,* 8 March 1927; Proctor, "History and Development of Skiing in America," 68; *The Ski Bulletin,* 3 March 1939, 5.

42. C. A. Proctor, "Notes on Ski-ing in the United States," *Ski Notes and Queries,* May 1931, 151; Al Sise interviewed by Nick Brewster, Norwich, Vt., 5 November 1979, New England Ski Museum, Oral History Archive.

43. It is hardly known, for example, that a German, Dr. Wiskott from Breslau, was the first to use skis on the highest mountain in the east, Mt. Washington, in 1899. Carl Luther, "Geschichte des Schnee- und Eissports," in *Geschichte des Sports aller Völker und Zeiten,* ed. G. A. E. Bogenz (Leipzig: Seeman, 1926), 2: 527. Even locally, the exploits of Norman Libby in 1905 have received little notice (*Gorham Mountaineer,* 22 February 1905). It is more extraordinary— given his fame—how little it is known that Fridtjof Nansen skied up Whiteface

in the Adirondacks in 1912 (Goodwin, "Challenge Skiing: High Peaks Adventures," 26). This date is not certain. In a 1921 article, Fred Harris recounted how he had been told of Nansen's exploits on Whiteface "several years ago" (Harris, "Up a Mountain on Skis," *Country Life in America,* February 1921, 49). Another source places Nansen's visit in 1919 or 1920 (*New York Times,* 17 April 1937), but I think this unlikely because during those years Nansen was greatly involved in postwar relief efforts. For Irving Langmuir, who later won a Nobel prize in physics, see William M. White, "Mount Marcy—Winter 1911: A First Ascent on Skis," *Adirondac,* January 1984, 3–5.

44. Proctor, "History and Development of Skiing in America," 60–61. *Lake Placid Club Notes,* November 1909, 805, and November 1925, 1,382.

45. Advertisements may be found in *The Ski Bulletin,* 1 January 1932, 3; *American Ski Annual* (1936): 38. See also John Knudson, "The Birth of New England Skiing," *Skiing* (Spring 1974), 117E–18E, 121E–22E.

46. *Appalachia,* January 1929, 285; December 1929, 408–9. The December 1929 issue also translated portions of Schneider and Fanck's *Wunder des Schneeschuhes* and of Ernst Janner's *Arlbergschule,* 369–81.

47. Schniebs's article may be found in the *Boston Evening Transcript,* 7 December 1929. There is an article about Schniebs by E. Bigelow Thompson, "Otto Schniebs Brings the New Technique from the Arlberg and Whole Community Enrolls," in ibid., 21 February 1931.

48. USEASA minutes meeting, 9 November 1931.

8 / The Mechanization of Skiing

1. Trains had carried skiers and their equipment to tournaments in the Northwest. In New England, the Boston and Maine Railroad promoted travel for sleighing, snowshoeing, skating, and skiing as early as 1907 ("The Winter Vacation Habit," *Boston and Maine Messenger,* 1 November 1907, 2). The Canadian Pacific Railway "after much urging" ran "snow specials" to various Quebec venues in 1926 (H. P. Douglas, "Canadian Letter," *British Ski Year Book* [1926]: 507). See also Francis Head, "Early Skiing in the A.M.C.," *Appalachia,* December 1964, 220; USEASA minutes, 6 November 1930; 1 November 1931.

2. W. O. Wright to Henry J. Perkins, Boston, 3 January 1931, in Henry Perkins Scrapbook, and B&M pamphlets, both in the New England Ski Museum.

3. Lawrence H. Bramhall, "The History of Skiing in New England and the Lake Placid, New York Region" (M.A. thesis, Boston University, Boston, 1946), 124.

4. *The Ski Bulletin,* 23 January 1931, 5; Xerox copy of ibid., 13 February 1931.

5. Detailed statistics of snow train passengers may be found for 1931, 1932, and 1933 in *The Ski Bulletin,* 31 March 1933, 3, and see also *Appalachia,* June 1931, 311.

6. Undated, but probably 16 February 1931, Boston newspaper clipping in New England Ski Museum, L81.24.1. Vada Whytlock Martin interviewed by Har-

riet Murray, Concord, N.H., 15 October 1983, for "It Had To Be Done So I Did It," Warner Oral History Project. Tape in Warner, N.H., library.

7. Undated [1931], Boston newspaper clippings in the New England Ski Museum, L81.24.1.

8. George Marshall interviewed by Jerry Urdang, Franconia, N.H., 21 January 1980; Norwood Ball interviewed by Ann Spaulding, Franconia, N.H., 14 October 1979, New England Ski Museum, Oral History Archive. *Appalachia*, June 1931, 312.

9. *The Ski Bulletin*, 20 March 1932. Selden Hannah interviewed by Charles Morrissey, Franconia, N.H., 14 January 1981, for film *Legends of American Skiing*.

10. Olive E. Anson, "The 'Snow Train' as Seen by a Passenger on Her First Trip," *Boston and Maine Employees Magazine* (1933): 9–10.

11. Henning Eichberg, "The Enclosure of the Body—On the Historical Relativity of 'Health,' 'Nature' and the Environment of Sport," *Journal of Contemporary History* 21 (1986): 99–121.

12. *Boston Herald*, 9 March 1939.

13. By Max Barsis, a popular cartoonist-rhymster of the 1930s (*The Ski Bulletin*, 7 January 1941, 12).

14. *The Ski Bulletin*, 1 February 1935, 6.

15. Ibid., 24 January 1936, 10; 28 February 1936, 10–11.

16. Page 16 of typed MS of unfinished history in Harris Papers in the New England Ski Museum.

17. *New York Times*, sec. 10, 5 April 1936.

18. Glencoe [?] *Evening Star*, 3 February 1936, cited in *The Ski Bulletin*, 14 February 1936, 7; *New York Times Magazine*, 18 February 1940.

19. *House Beautiful*, January 1940, 69; *Business Week*, 24 March 1937, 40; *Literary Digest*, 15 February 1936, 39; *Newsweek*, 26 December 1936, 18; advertisement in *American Ski Annual* (1935); Lee Ashley interviewed by Moulton, Berthoud Pass, Colo., 8 April 1981, for film *Legends of American Skiing;* Steve Patterson and Kenton Forrest, *Rio Grande Ski Train* (Denver: Tramway Press, 1984), 18–23; documents on display in the Western Skisport Museum. See also the advertisement from the Peck-Judah Travel Bureau promoting their "Snowball Excursions to Famed Truckee," 15 January 1935. I am indebted to Robert O. Baumrucker of San Francisco for a copy of this advertisement. For the ski plane, see *New York Times*, 22 November 1936.

20. Robert Winterhalde in Schollach, Amt Neustadt, Baden, Patent Application and Drawings, 16 March 1908. MS in Deutsche Skiverband, Luther-Archiv 4.10, Box: Verkehr. See also Alfred Rüsch und Hugo Rhomberg, "Sprunghügelanlagen auf dem Bödele bei Dornbirn," *Der Winter* 3 (1908–09): 29; John Jay, *Ski Down the Years* (New York: Universal Publishing, 1966), 63.

21. "Our First Ski Funicular," *Canadian Ski Annual* (1933): 50; *The Ski Bulletin*, 6 January 1933, 3.

22. *Vallejo* [Calif.] *Sunday Times Herald*, 13 December 1870, cited in Gould, *La Porte Scrapbook*, 136. Interview with Bill Berry, Reno, 26 March 1986.

23. *Reno Evening Gazette*, 12 December 1910. J. E. Carpenter, "Truckee: Pioneer in Winter Sports," unpublished MS for which I am indebted to Robert O. Baumrucker.

24. *The California Ski News,* 17 January 1933, 5.
25. Dartmouth Outing Club Council minutes, 5 February 1915, in Baker Library, Dartmouth College.
26. *Rutland* [Vt.] *Herald,* 28 January 1934.
27. *The Ski Bulletin,* 2 February 1934, 8; Amateur Ski Club of New York, *Ten Winters, 1931–1941* (New York, 1942), 59–60.
28. *The Ski Bulletin,* 29 March 1935, 4–5.
29. Ibid., 28 December 1934, 5; 11 January 1935, 8; 18 January 1935, 11. Ted Cooke, "Ski Tows," *Appalachia,* November 1935, 405. Ted Cooke interviewed by Janet Young, Newbury, N.H., 19 November 1980, New England Ski Museum, Oral History Archive. The New England Ski Museum's film archive contains a home-made movie of the construction of Cooke's tow which shows oxen hauling the rope up.
30. *The Ski Bulletin,* 11 January 1936, 12; 7 February 1936, 2–4; 28 February 1936, 12; *New York Times,* sec. 10, 1 March 1936; *Boston Herald,* 17 January 1936.
31. For all this activity in New England, besides numerous *Ski Bulletins,* see David Hooke et al., "Dartmouth Outing Club History," typed MS, 499; Dan Hatch to author, 26 January 1987, in author's possession; Ed Newell interviewed by Susan Noble, Boston, 29 November 1980, in New England Ski Museum, Oral History Archive; *American Ski Annual* (1936): 158–59; *New York Times,* 1 March 1936; and Jay, *Ski Down the Years,* 63–66. The Hussey Manufacturing Company of North Berwick, Maine, advertised a rope tow in 1936.
32. For the Uncanoonucs tramway, see *The Ski Bulletin,* 29 March 1935, 5; interview by author with Roland Nault, Laconia, N.H., 12 October 1982; interview by author with Betty Whitney, Franconia, N.H., 28 December 1988. For Pico's T-bar, John L. Garrison, *Sun, Snow and Skis* (New York: McGraw Hill, 1946), 218–19, and *Appalachia,* December 1940, 255.
33. The Aspen Historical Society holds photos of early tows in Aspen. See also John O'Rear and Frankie O'Rear, *The Aspen Story* (New York: A. S. Barnes, 1966), 60; Queal, "Colorado Skiing—A Century of Sport"; Fay, *Ski Tracks in the Rockies,* 25; *American Ski Annual* (1936): 9; Charles N. Proctor interviewed by Moulton, and Donald Fraser interviewed by Moulton, New York, Spring 1981, for film *Legends of American Skiing.*
34. John E. P. Morgan to Charles H. Bell, 26 October 1966. I am indebted to Robert O. Baumrucker for a copy of this letter. For a somewhat different view, see Dorice Taylor, *Sun Valley* (Sun Valley: Ex Libris, 1980), 35–36.
35. Boston paper (?) clipping, 14 January 1938, in Fred Nachbaur Scrapbook, retained by Mr. Nachbaur of Gilford, N.H. See also mimeographed MS "Belknap History Excerpts," 7 (in author's possession).
36. *Appalachia,* December 1940, 254–55.
37. For the Cannon tram, see *The Ski Bulletin,* 12 January 1934, 7; 1 March 1936, 6; Arnold Lowell, "The Bright Idea," ibid. (October 1938): 9–11, and Allen, "The Development of New Hampshire Skiing," 32–33 and notes.
38. Langley, "Survey of Skiing," 173.
39. *Appalachia,* December 1933, 600–601; *Boston Evening Transcript,* 22 November 1933.
40. Arthur C. Comey, "Ski Trail Standards," *Appalachia,* June 1933, 428;

Charles N. Proctor, "Ski Trails and Their Design," ibid., June 1934, 88–94; *The Ski Bulletin* 29 December 1933, 4; and December 1939, 16; Proctor, "History and Development of Skiing in America," 70; USEASA minutes, 5 November 1933; *Troubadour,* February 1936, 15.

Although there have been a number of studies on the CCC, none has analyzed its effect on winter tourism in the eastern United States. Even in two 1937 official CCC booklets there is no mention of its influence in this area. See United States Department of the Interior, National Park Service, *The CCC and Its Contribution to a Nation-Wide Park Recreation Program,* and Energy Conservation Work, *Recreational Developments by the CCC in National and State Forests.* The best "insider" knowledge on the CCC and Vermont is contained in interviews and film clips in film *Legends of American Skiing.* For Massachusetts, see Allen, " 'Millions of Flakes of Fun in Massachusetts,' " 90, 93. One contemporary account of CCC work at Rib Mountain, Wisconsin, is Bob Christofferson, "Dynamite and Time," *The Ski Bulletin,* 21 January 1938, 7.

41. A. W. Coleman, "Vermont Ski Runs," *Appalachia,* December 1934, 224.
42. *Winter Sports Development: Season of 1937–38,* 1: 12. (University of Vermont Library, Box U.V.M. Wgw M458s). See also Bramhall, "The History of Skiing," 98.
43. J. Dwight Francis to Natalie Hoyt, Vt., postmarked 28 October 1931 (in Hoyt's possession); "Woodstock Ski Center" brochure and "Woodstock Ski-runners Club" brochure in New England Ski Museum.
44. "The Ski Cruise" brochure in New England Ski Museum. See also J. D. Francis, "Something New under the Winter Sun: Ski Cruise," *Country Life in America,* December 1934, 51–55.
45. Amateur Ski Club of New York, *Ten Winters, 1931–1941,* 55; Roland Palmedo's photo album in the New England Ski Museum; *The Ski Bulletin,* 18 March 1931; Coleman, "Vermont Ski Runs," 224; idem, "Skis Over Vermont," *Appalachia,* June 1936, 39.
46. Photo in *Ski,* October 1961, 99.
47. Jenny Gale cited by George Mazuzan, "Skiing in Vermont: Four Case Studies" (M.A. thesis, University of Vermont, Burlington, Vt., 1964), 65.

9/ The Sport of Skiing

1. *USEASA Year Book* (1929), 74; Thom A. Hook, "Ski Clubs Boom throughout America," *The Ski Annual* (1960–61): 13.
2. Roger F. Langley interviewed by Arthur F. March, Jr., Barre, Mass., 30 January 1980, New England Ski Museum, Oral History Archive.
3. USEASA, *The Ski Annual* (1934): 122–53.
4. Sarah N. Welch, *A History of Franconia, New Hampshire, 1772–1972* (Littleton, N.H.: Courier Publishing Company, [1972?]), 147.
5. Lawrence E. Briggs, "Junior Ski Developments," *American Ski Annual* (1938–39): 10. The scout's merit badge for skiing had been proposed in 1934. See Roger F. Langley, "Interscholastic Skiing," *The Ski Annual* (1934): 99.

6. Delphine Carpenter, "Is Your Wife a Ski Widow?" *Leisure,* January 1935, 26.

7. *Appalachia,* December 1937, 127, 536–37; *The Ski Bulletin,* 28 January 1938, 7–8; Fred Nachbaur interviewed by the author, Gilford, N.H., 3 August 1982, New England Ski Museum, Oral History Archive. For full details of these matters see E. John B. Allen, *Teaching and Technique: A History of American Ski Instruction,* 2d ed. (Latham, N.Y.: EPSIA Educational Foundation, 1987), 7–27.

8. *The Ski Bulletin,* 17 February 1933, 6–7.

9. *The Ski Bulletin,* 9 December 1938, 8; Nachbaur interviewed by author.

10. Arthur Callan interviewed by the author, North Conway, N.H., 24 October 1979, New England Ski Museum, Oral History Archive.

11. Strom, *Pioneers on Skis,* 58.

12. Nachbaur interviewed by author. Douglas Philbrook interviewed by author, Gorham, N.H., 1986.

13. Jack Durrance, "Summer Skiing in the Tetons," *American Ski Annual* (1936): 144.

14. *American Ski Annual* (1936): [6].

15. David J. Bradley, "S.A.S.," *American Ski Annual* (1937–38): 115. "Ski Heil" was probably derived from the German hunters', mountain climbers', and gymnasts' greetings of *Waidmannsheil, Bergheil,* and *Gutheil.* It appears to have been first used as a ski greeting in 1891 by Fritz Breuer of the Ski Club Todtnau in the Black Forest. Fritz Breuer to Dr. Brohl, Düsseldorf, 7 November 1922, TLS in Ski Club Todtnau archive, privately held, and in Breuer, *Anleitung zum Schneeschuhlaufen* (Todtnau: Ski Club Todtnau, 1892), 15.

16. Charles M. Dudley, *When We Ski* (New York: Grosset and Dunlap, 1937), 18–19.

17. Lowell Thomas, "Let's Ski For Fun," *American Ski Annual* (1937–38): 158–59.

18. For the squabble over technique, see Allen, *Teaching and Technique,* 7–27.

19. *Appalachia,* June 1933, 470.

20. *Appalachia,* June 1932, 152; *The Ski Bulletin,* 24 February 1933, 2.

21. Harry Pangman in *Canadian Ski Annual* (1932), reprinted in *The Ski Bulletin,* 13 January 1933, 4–5.

22. The minutes of the Twenty-ninth Annual Meeting of the NSA held in Chicago, 4 December 1932 (typed MS, in National Ski Hall of Fame) only give the fact that downhill and slalom were accepted. The minutes indicate no discussion of this important decision. My interpretation comes from interviews I conducted with John McCrillis, New London, N.H., 16 October 1980, and by Moulton with Roger Langley, Barre, Mass., 26 August 1981, in the film *Legends of American Skiing.* See also *The Ski Bulletin* 4 March 1938, 7–8.

23. Typescript booklet by W. B. Sleigh, Jr., "Ski Songs" (1938), and Sleigh interviewed by James Caron, Marblehead, Mass., 28 October 1979; Roger Clapp interviewed by Susan Noble, Westfield, Mass., 11 November 1980, New England Ski Museum, Oral History Archive. Compare *The Skisport* (1910–11): 44.

24. *The Ski Bulletin,* 10 March 1933, 3; O. E. Schniebs, "First National Downhill Championship: 12 March 1933," *Winter Sports,* November 1934, 5. In these

early races there were timing problems. See Charles N. Proctor, talk to AMC on 5 January 1934, printed in *The Ski Bulletin,* 12 January 1934, 16.

25. *The Ski Bulletin,* 9 February 1934, 4.

26. The tempo turn, often thought to be invented by Richard Durrance and a hallmark of his style (which even spawned a Tempo shop), was in fact a European import. See *Der Winter,* 1 December 1933.

27. Richard Durrance interviewed by Moulton, Aspen, Colo., 23 March 1981, for film *Legends of American Skiing.* Later, short cuts were disallowed. See David Hooke, "D.O.C. History," typed MS, 148, for Dartmouth Outing Club, Hanover, N.H. Ed Wells interviewed by Urdang, Grantham, N.H., 2 January 1980, New England Ski Museum, Oral History Archive.

28. Otto E. Schniebs, "Sanity in Ski Competitions," *American Ski Annual* (1938–39): 149; *The Ski Bulletin,* 3 March 1939, 10–11, and 31 March 1939, 10. The first giant slalom in the United States was tried directly as a result of the death of Frank Edson (Amateur Ski Club of New York, *Ten Winters,* 48–49). See also Richard Durrance, "Controlled Downhill Skiing," in Palmedo, *Skiing: The International Sport,* 84; Robert Livermore, "Giant Slalom," *American Ski Annual* (1937–38): 84–86. The giant slalom was not solely an American experiment. See Franco Dezulian, "Lo 'slalom' gigante alla Marmolada," *Rivista Mensile,* February 1935, xxiii–xxvii, which has an excellent photo of a slalom course in the Italian Dolomites.

29. Clapp interviewed by Noble; Roger Peabody interviewed by Harry Stearns, Littleton, N.H., 28 November 1980; Ed Newell interviewed by Susan Noble, Boston, 7 May 1981; Wallace Bertram interviewed by Michael McQueenie, Woodstock, Vt., 5 December 1980, New England Ski Museum, Oral History Archive.

30. Norwood Ball interviewed by Ann Spaulding, Franconia, N.H., 14 October 1979.

31. *American Ski Annual* (1938–39): [40].

32. Ibid. (1941–42): [13].

33. *The Ski Bulletin,* 17 February 1933, 7–8.

34. James A. Lowell, "More F.I.S.—the Men's Races," *American Ski Annual* (1935): 32; Roland Palmedo, "An F.I.S. Story," ibid., 27. See also *The Ski Bulletin,* 15 March 1935, 4–5.

35. Langley, "Survey of Skiing," 146–47.

36. *American Ski Annual* (1935): 179; *Appalachia,* November 1935, 445.

37. Schroll was twelve seconds ahead in the two slalom runs and seven seconds ahead in the downhill (*Appalachia,* November 1935, 447–48). For an assessment of the 1935 Mt. Rainier championships, see Charles N. Proctor, "The National Downhill and Slalom Championship—1935," *American Ski Annual* (1935): 10–18; Donald Fraser interviewed by Moulton, New York, Spring 1981, for film *Legends of American Skiing.*

38. *The Ski Bulletin,* 29 March 1935, 7. The report of the race as the "Eastern Olympic Trials" is in *Appalachia,* November 1935, 446–47.

39. The Olympic Committee supplied $400 each for Bright, Hunter and Livermore, yet only $125 for Fraser who worked his thirty-three-day passage on a Norwegian fruit boat, chipping paint from Seattle to Le Havre at fifty cents a day. For the funding, see Frederick W. Rubien, ed., *Report of the American*

Olympic Committee (New York: American Olympic Committee, [1936?]), 418. The report on the "IV Olympic Winter Games" is on pp. 307–51. See also D. Moffat, "Mr. Pennyfeather on Skiing," *Atlantic Monthly,* January 1936, 29.

40. The Committee on Fair Play in Sports, *Preserve the Olympic Ideal: A Statement of the Case Against American Participation in the Olympic Games at Berlin* (N.p., [1935]), 36. The discrimination continued; it was alleged that the mayor of Garmisch actually ordered signs saying "Jews are not admitted" to be posted in town (56). See also Carolyn Marvin, "Avery Brundage and the American Participation in the 1936 Olympic Games," *Journal of American Studies,* April 1982, 91–92, 97. The standard book on Brundage is Allen Guttmann, *The Games Must Go On: Avery Brundage and the Olympic Movement* (New York: Columbia University Press, 1984), but it hardly touches the Winter Olympics.

41. *Appalachia,* June 1932, 53; Richard K. Tompkins, "Notes From the Rockies," *American Ski Annual* (1938–39): 199.

42. Roland Palmedo to Helen Boughton-Leigh, 19 June 1934. I would like to thank Helen McAlpin for letting me use her correspondence which remains in her possession. Alice Pennington Wolfe Kiaer was a prime mover in American women's Alpine skiing. For an overview, see Dinah B. Witchel, "Alice in Skiland," *Skiing,* February 1980, 28.

43. Roland Palmedo to Arnold Lunn, 24 October 1934, McAlpin correspondence. "He was our Arnold Lunn!" (Helen McAlpin to author, 24 February 1985, in author's possession). For an overview of women's racing, see Alice D. [Pennington] Wolfe, "Ten Years of Ski Racing for Women," in Palmedo, *Skiing: The International Sport,* 187–200.

44. Roland Palmedo to Helen Boughton-Leigh, 14 December [1934], McAlpin correspondence.

45. Joel H. Hildebrand, "American Skiers at the Olympics—The Men," *American Ski Annual* (1936), 60. Palmedo, "An F.I.S. Story," 20. One paper dubbed the team "a beauty chorus." See also Elizabeth D. Woolsey, *Off the Beaten Track* (Wilson, Wyo.: Wilson Bench Press, 1984), 56.

46. Woolsey, *Off the Beaten Track,* 53.

47. Faith Donaldson, "With the First American Ski Team in Europe," *Appalachia,* November 1935, 404.

48. Proctor, "The National Downhill and Slalom Championships—1935," 17.

49. "Notes and News: the American Olympic Team," *American Ski Annual* (1935): 156; Roland Palmedo, "Plans for the Women's 1936 Olympic Team," *Appalachia,* November 1935, 444.

50. Arnold Lunn to Nathaniel Goodrich, 24 July 1936, printed in *American Ski Annual* (1936): 23.

51. Movietone News commentary in film *Legends of American Skiing;* Ralph E. Miller, "The Olympics—Impressions of a Dub," *American Ski Annual* (1936): 142.

52. Alfred D. Lindley, "Garmisch—1936," in David O. Hooke, "D.O.C. History," MS copy, 495; Edward J. Blood interviewed by Harry Stearns, Durham, N.H., 5 December 1980, New England Ski Museum, Oral History Archive; Fraser interviewed by Moulton; Durrance interviewed by Moulton. For one participant's views written for a wider audience, see Robert Livermore, Jr.,

"Notes on Olympic Skiing: 1936," *Atlantic Monthly*, May 1936, 617–22. Accounts of the Games written for a skiing audience were more reportorial, see Alice Damrosch [Pennington] Wolfe, "American Skiers at the Olympics—the Women," *American Ski Annual* (1936): 7–15; Hildebrand, "American Skiers at the Olympics—Men," 57–61. Representative contemporary articles may be found in many periodicals. See, for example, *Literary Digest*, 15 February 1936, 37–38; *Newsweek*, 22 February 1936, 33, besides the daily reporting in the newspapers.

53. George H. Page, "The U.S. Men's Team at the 1938 FIS," *American Ski Annual* (1938–39): 45; *The Ski Bulletin*, 25 February 1938, 8. The advertisement in the *Paris Herald* drew no response.

54. Woolsey, *Off the Beaten Track*, 99; *British Ski Club Year Book* (1937): 135, 146. See also Elizabeth D. Woolsey, "The 1937 Women's Team," *American Ski Annual* (1937–38): 19–21; and Roland Palmedo, "U.S. Teams in International Competition," ibid., 96–98.

55. Alice Damrosch [Pennington] Wolfe, "The American Women's Team in Europe, 1938," *American Ski Annual* (1938–39): 50–61. In 1948 Gretchen Fraser won a gold medal, as did Andrea Mead Lawrence in 1952.

56. Dot Brewer broke her back in 1936; Hannah Locke broke a hand and a foot in 1937; Lilo Schwarzenbach broke a leg in 1938.

57. Craig Burt to C. Minot Dole, 18 January 1949, cited in Mazuzan, "Skiing in Vermont," 61; *The Ski Bulletin*, 13 March 1936, 11; *Ten Winters*, 52; C. Minot Dole, *Adventures in Skiing* (New York: Watts, 1965), 50–61.

58. Peabody interviewed by Stearns; Ted Cooke interviewed by Janet Young. Insurance advertisements may be found in *The Ski Bulletin*, 27 January 1933, 4; and 10 February 1933, 8, for example.

59. The questionnaire is in *The Ski Bulletin*, 27 March 1936, 8. See also ibid., 13 January 1939, 7; Dole, *Adventures*, 51.

60. *The Ski Bulletin*, 14 February 1936, 8–9; and 13 March 1936, 11.

61. *The Ski Bulletin*, 23 February 1940, 6. Maybe those recuperating from broken bones played Otto Schniebs's "Ski Game" while recovering. The game can be played at the New England Ski Museum.

62. Clapp interviewed by Noble; Al Sise interviewed by Nick Brewster.

63. J. S. Apperson to Harold Goddard Rugg, Schenectady, N.Y., 13 April 1914, Apperson Papers no. 14   036, Adirondack Research Center. Henry Baldwin, "The Skiing Life," MS, 18. *Ski News, New Hampshire Supplement*, 15 January 1946, 1. Charles N. Proctor, talk at Hanover, N.H., 23 September 1981. See also Proctor, "History and Development of Skiing in America," 53–78, and his interview by Moulton for film *Legends of American Skiing*. John Holden, "Spectacular Schuss of 'Headwall' Told by Amazed Witness," *Ski*, February 1954, 22–23.

64. Arthur C. Comey, "Skiing in Inferno," *Mountain Magazine*, October–November 1929, 7–8.

65. For representative contemporary literature on the Inferno, see *Appalachia*, December 1932, 472; and June 1934, 121; and "Suicide Race," ibid., December 1932, 528.

66. Sise interviewed by Brewster.

67. The New England Ski Museum holds a tape of Toni Matt's own version of the

run, recorded in North Conway in 1984. See also his telling of the run in film *Legends of American Skiing* which accompanies a short excerpt of this most famous Inferno.
68. *Appalachia,* December 1932, 472.

10/ Western Idylls

1. Church, "Lake Tahoe in Winter," 274–76.
2. Otto Barkan, "Skiing in California," *Sierra Club Bulletin,* February 1931, 40–41; Morison, "Ski-ing in California," 513.
3. O. R. Lirsch, "Dope about Ski Dope," *Winter Sports,* November 1932, 4.
4. Walter Mosauer, "Skiing on the East Side of the Sierra," *Sierra Club Bulletin,* February 1936, 55.
5. David Brower, "Skiing Development in Yosemite," *American Ski Annual* (1937–38): 201.
6. In film *Legends of American Skiing.*
7. See the photo in Vandenbusch, *The Gunnison Country,* 398.
8. Strom, *Pioneers on Skis,* 19; G. C. Torguson cited in "Ancient and Exhilarating Sport of Skiing," *Literary Digest,* 14 February 1920, 112, 115.
9. Strom, *Pioneers on Skis,* 26–34.
10. Carpenter, "Civic Commercial Organizations," 207–10.
11. *Sierra Club Bulletin,* December 1928, 133–34; Don Tressider to W. E. C., 28 January 1929, in ibid., April 1929, 108.
12. *American Ski Annual* (1935): n.p.; (1936): [15]; (1937–38): [23].
13. Carpenter, "Civic Commercial Organizations," 203–4.
14. Bestor Robinson, "An Appraisal of the Ski Terrain of the Sierra Nevada of California," *American Ski Annual* (1935): 53; Don Tressider, "Ski-ing in California," *British Ski Year Book* (1931): 36; "Far West Kandahar," *The Ski Bulletin,* 24 March 1939, 11.
15. Otto Schniebs cited by F. Martin Brown, "Let's Aspen," *American Ski Annual* (1937–38): 82; Roch report cited by Queal, "Colorado Skiing—A Century of Sport," 13. For a recent view see André Roch, "A Once and Future Resort," trans. Ernest Blake, *Colorado Heritage* 4 (1985): 17–23. A progress report to 1939 of the Mt. Hayden project may be found in T. J. Flynn, "Mount Hayden to Date," *The Ski Bulletin,* 8 December 1939, 6.
16. Lee Ashley interviewed at Berthoud Pass by Moulton. USEASA, *The Ski Annual* (1934): 126; Richard H. Tompkins, "Notes from the Western Division," *American Ski Annual* (1937–38): 194.
17. Graeme McGowan, "A Diagnosis of Colorado Skiing," *Appalachia,* December 1934, 256–57.
18. Frank M. Ashley, "Colorado Skiing," *American Ski Annual* (1936): 110.
19. Tompkins, "Notes," 193–94.
20. Brown, "Let's Aspen," 82; O'Rear and O'Rear, *The Aspen Story,* 62.
21. Norman C. Barwise, "The Rocky Mountain Ski Association Downhill Cham-

pionship Races at Aspen February 26–27, 1938," *American Ski Annual* (1938–39): 200–201; Ashley, "Colorado Skiing," 113.

22. Tom Cabot, "Notes on Skiing in Colorado," *Appalachia*, June 1931, 316.

23. In film *Legends of American Skiing*.

24. Ben Thompson, "Ski-Scraping Mt. Baker," *American Ski Annual* (1935): 68; Fritz Hagist, "A New Ski Country," ibid. (1935): 78–79; Fred H. McNeil, *Wy'East "The Mountain"* (Portland, Oreg.: Metropolitan Press, 1937), 230–31, 234, and his remarks in "1845–1939," *The Ski Bulletin*, 17 March 1939, 7.

25. *The Skisport* (1910–11): 64; (1911–12): 71–72; (1913–14): 49. Photograph in *Sierra Club Bulletin* 9 (1912): facing 83; (1913): 200. Newspaper clipping from 1916 in scrapbook, "Early Skiing in Western North America," in Western Skisport Museum. See also Marion R. Parsons, "A Snowshoe Trip to Mt. Hood," *Outers-Book Recreation*, February 1918, 129. John McCrillis, a transplanted Dartmouth skier, attracted notice when he took a party of schoolboys up Mt. Rainier in 1923 and 1924 (*Seattle Post Intelligencer,* 1 April 1923, and *Seattle Daily Times,* 23 March 1924). I am grateful that the late Mr. McCrillis allowed me to see his photographic record, which remains with his estate. For a historical view of early skiing in the Northwest, see Joseph T. Hazard, "Winter Sports in the Western Mountains," *Pacific Northwest Quarterly* 44, no. 1 (1953): 9–11.

26. Veida S. Morrow, "Skiing America First," USEASA, *The Ski Annual* (1934): 13–14.

27. *Sierra Club Bulletin* 13 (1928): 89; Boyd French, "From Roses to Skis in Ninety Minutes," *American Ski Annual* (1935): 77; Hagist, "A New Ski Country," 78; McNeil, "1845–1945," 7, 14–15.

28. George M. Henderson, "Developments in the Pacific Northwest," *American Ski Annual* (1939–40): 188–89; *The Ski Bulletin*, 8 December 1939, 11.

29. Advertisements may be found in *American Ski Annual* (1938–39): [18, 19]; (1939–40): [40]; (1940–41): [40].

30. Elkins, *The Complete Ski Guide* (1940), 158.

31. David Niven, *The Moon's a Balloon* (New York: Putnam's, 1973), 233, 235, 242–45. Averell Harriman interviewed by Richard W. Moulton, Washington, D.C., April 1981, for film *Legends of American Skiing*. See also Averell Harriman to Carl R. Grey, New York, 2 October 1935, cited in Taylor, *Sun Valley,* 9. Other accounts of Sun Valley are Doug Oppenheimer and Jim Poore, *Sun Valley: A Biography* (Boise, Idaho: Beatty Books, 1976), and Peter J. Ognibene, "Schussing at Sun Valley," *Smithsonian*, December 1984, 108–19. For Hannigan's role, see also Donald J. Mrozek, "The Image of the West in American Sport," *Journal of the West* 17, no. 3 (1978): 6–9.

32. Cited in Taylor, *Sun Valley,* 28.

33. J. McLaughlin to Betty Woolsey, cited in Woolsey, *Off the Beaten Track,* 109.

34. "East Goes West to Idaho's Sun Valley, Society's New Winter Playground," *Life,* 8 March 1937, 20–27. Hans Hauser, ski school director, was featured on the cover of *Scribner's Magazine* in January 1938 to enhance the article on p. 4.

35. Kelner, *Skiing in Utah,* 120–21.

36. Wallace Dickson, "New England, a Playland for Skiers," in *The Ski Guide for 1938,* ed. Frank Elkins (New York: Greenberg, 1937), 41.

11/ The Economics of Pleasure

1. Stephen Hardy, "Entrepreneurs, Organizations, and the Sport Marketplace: Subjects in Search of Historians," *Journal of Sport History* 13, no. 1 (Spring 1986): 14–33. Although not relating to skiing, the following have been most useful for their analyses of leisure: Arthur H. Cole, "Perspectives on Leisure-Time Business," *Explorations in Entrepreneurial History* 1 (Summer 1964): Supplement; 1–38; Fritz Redlich, "Leisure-Time Activities: A Historical, Sociological and Economic Analysis," ibid. 3 (Fall 1965): 3–23; Robert Goldman, "'We Make Weekends': Leisure and the Commodity Form," *Social Text* 8 (Winter 1984): 84–103.

2. *Troubadour,* February 1933, 14. Winston Pote cited in Tom Eastman, "An Interview with Winston Pote," *Powder,* February 1986, 49. The 1922 brochure for the Lincoln Hotel, for example, does not mention skiing as a winter activity for visitors but *Pycolog,* January 1923, 2–3, the magazine of the resident paper manufacturing company, Parker Young, mentions an interest in skiing and particularly in ski jumping.

3. Elkins, *The Complete Ski Guide,* viii.

4. The graph is adapted from material in Julius Weinberger, "Economic Aspects of Recreation," *Harvard Business Review,* September 1937, 456.

5. USEASA, *The Ski Annual* (1934): ix; "Winter Ski-scape," *House Beautiful,* January 1937, 68; John Kieran, "The Ski's the Limit," *American Magazine,* February 1937, 95; "The Ski Cruise," (brochure in New England Ski Museum); Lowell, "Bright Idea," 9.

6. *Boston Evening Transcript,* 14 December 1934; *Boston Herald,* 5 December 1935.

7. Bramhall, "The History of Skiing," 169.

8. *The Ski Club Hochgebirge* (1938), 11ff. [a printed booklet].

9. *American Ski Annual* (1935): facing 145.

10. Roger Clapp interviewed by Susan Noble, 11 November 1980.

11. For Count de Pret see *Ski Illustrated,* February 1938, 33; February/March 1939, 27.

12. "One Million Schussers," *Time,* 8 March 1940, 62–64; *Appalachia,* June 1936, 95; Bramhall, "The History of Skiing," 126; "Skis Aid Boom: Railroads Rejoice over Growing Popularity of Snow Trains," *Literary Digest,* 5 December 1936, 39; Boston and Maine, *Annual Reports* (1931–40).

13. Roger Peabody, executive director of USEASA, cited by Hook, "Ski Clubs Boom throughout America," 13.

14. Information on the Syracuse club comes from account books and miscellaneous correspondence of the Onondaga Ski Club, Syracuse, N.Y., held by Gene Beckeman of DeWitt, N.Y., to whom I am indebted.

15. Account books and miscellaneous papers of the Plymouth Ski Club, Plymouth, N.H. are held by the New England Ski Museum. I would like to thank Robert Rand of Plymouth for his help.

16. Wheaton H. Brewer, "Winter Fun and Business," *California Journal of Develop-*

ment, December 1933, 27; H. H. Roberts, "Winter Sports—How Do We Stand?" *California—Magazine of the Pacific,* December 1949, 21.

17. Fred Pabst cited in Ezra Bowen, *The Book of American Skiing* (New York: Bonanza Books, 1963), 163. For Pabst, see Carlton C. Buckman, "Pabst of Big Bromley," *Ski Magazine,* 1 February 1950, 15, 19.

18. Two years before the Games began, "roadsides of northern routes were dotted with sign boards" and an "elaborate pre-Olympic program of entertainment and sport" was under way. In summer more than ten thousand were expected to view the winter facilities. Otis P. Swift, "Lake Placid, Ready for Olympics Offers Regal Sport Program," *Motordom,* 24, no. 7 (1930): 6; George M. Lattimer, "Sport's Enthusiasts Will View the Great Olympic Facilities at Lake Placid," ibid., 25, no. 1 (1931): 34.

19. Palmedo's book was reviewed by Minot Dole, a fellow member of the Amateur Ski Club of New York, in *New York Herald Tribune,* 9 June 1938.

20. USEASA, *The Ski Annual* (1934): v, and inside back cover. For Lund's Northland factory in Laconia, N.H. see *Laconia Evening Citizen,* 31 August, 1 October, and 29 November 1937; 14 and 20 January, 19 February, and 23 April 1938.

21. Laminated skis were first experimented with in Norway. In 1932 there was a Canadian model on the market and this was followed by the Anderson and Thompson ski (*Canadian Ski Annual* [1932]: 44).

22. Spalding had been manufacturing skis at least as early as 1913 when they advertised in *Spalding's Winter Sports* "Red Cover" series of Athletic Handbooks. In spite of the obvious effort to attract domestic customers, the eight pages devoted to "The Norwegian Ski" depicted the sport of the European elite in the 1917 edition. By 1932 in the company's Athletic Series, *Winter Activities in Snow and Ice,* skiing for women was given equal space in the various athletic events.

23. Advertisements in *American Ski Annual,* 1934 through 1937.

24. *The Ski Bulletin,* November 1939, 5. Everett Hunt of Newport, Vermont, filed a patent application for the manufacture of skis "from metal, preferably sheet metal" on 19 May 1924. He was granted patent no. 1,552,990 on 8 September 1925. See also John Auran and Martin Luray, "What Hath Head Wrought," *Ski Magazine,* January 1967, 77.

25. Department of Commerce, *Bureau of Census Report,* 3 January 1941, cited in Langley, "Survey of Skiing," 5. The various prices throughout this chapter are drawn mostly from contemporary advertisements in ski publications and newspapers and will not be footnoted individually.

26. William Mason interviewed by Dale Rodgers, Waterbury, Vt., 2 November 1981, New England Ski Museum, Oral History Archive.

27. Diettrich, *Skis and Skiing,* 16.

28. Rockwell Stephens interviewed by Dale Rodgers, Woodstock, Vt., 11 December 1980, New England Ski Museum, Oral History Archive.

29. Diettrich, *Skis and Skiing,* 17.

30. *The Ski Bulletin,* 4 December 1934, 6.

31. Fritz von Allmen to June B. Simonton, Gwatt, Switzerland, 13 April 1977; copy in author's possession. I would like to thank Helen McAlpin for sending me the letter.

32. For Hambro see the *Boston Herald,* 28 December 1934; 3 December 1937; *Boston Evening Transcript,* 22 December 1933; 1 March 1935; *The Ski Bulletin,* 13 February 1942, 5.
33. Stephens interviewed by Rodgers. Charles Proctor interviewed by Moulton.
34. USEASA, *The Ski Annual* (1934): xvi.
35. *New York Times,* 12 January and 27 November 1937.
36. See, for example, the drawing in *The Ski Annual* (1915–16): 38, and the advertisement for Northern Wool Products in *The Skisport* (1923–24): 1.
37. *World Traveler,* January 1928, 36.
38. "America Takes to Skis," *Publishers Weekly,* 12 December 1936, 2288; Kieran, "The Ski's the Limit," 29; "Compass Pointers: Ski-Minded," *House Beautiful,* December 1937, 118.
39. Cited in Roland Palmedo, "Rediscovery of Snow," *Country Life in America,* January 1935, 88. See also the *New York Evening Journal* cited in *The Ski Bulletin,* 31 December 1937, 13.
40. *Mt. Mansfield Ski Club Bulletin,* 15 February 1935, n.p. The question of color in clothing for skiing was influenced by the subtle British upper class, particularly those at Mürren. As early as 1924 the Dartmouth community was advised against wearing colorful clothes. (Diettrich, *Skis and Skiing,* 20).
41. *Boston and Maine Snow Train* (1936): 10, 22, 27.
42. *Troubadour,* December 1933, 3.
43. *Boston Herald,* 2 December 1937. Maria Springer, "Making the Snow Fly," *Collier's,* 11 December 1937, 67–68. White Stag also used Hollywood advertising in *Ski Illustrated,* December/January 1937–38, 5. For the men's show, see ibid., 42. The Ski Alliance Show is covered in *New York Times,* 24 June 1936.
44. *Ski Illustrated,* December/January 1937–38, 26–27.
45. The lobbying by automobile clubs for snow removal in New York State may be followed in "State Highways Open," *Motordom,* February 1929, 12–13; "State Must Provide Money for Snow Removal," ibid., December 1929, 18; "Automobile Clubs Promote Winter Travel," ibid., 24; James E. Cutlip, "'Snowbound' Becomes a Legend," ibid., January 1930, 3; "Storm Warning," ibid., January 1931, 6; "Hamilton County Extends Welcome," ibid., December 1931, 4. The quote is from Cutlip's article. For the later 1930s, see *New York Times,* 3 January 1937.
46. Roberts, "Winter Sports—How Do We Stand?" 24; Wheaton H. Brewer, "Winter Sports Review," *California—Magazine of the Pacific,* December 1940, 45.
47. Boston and Maine, *Annual Reports* (1931–40). The chairman's remark is in the 1934 report, page 7. For the snow train tie-in with a shop, see *New York Times,* 12 July 1936.
48. Account books of the Gunstock Ski Hoist in the New England Ski Museum; Ted Cooke interviewed by Janet Young. The film is in the New England Ski Museum's film archive. The museum also holds the patent documents for Cooke's rope-tow gripper.
49. McDill, "Woodstock, Cradle of Winter Sports," 16. But see also the letter of Barklie McKee Henry, one of the three sponsors of the tow who remembered the cost as $75, in *Time,* 23 February 1959, 6. I find $500 the more likely figure.

50. Cooke interviewed by Young. Interview by author with Weston Blake, Hanover, N.H., 5 February 1981, and with Charles Beebe, Wilton, N.H., 20 February 1986.

51. Langley, "Survey of Skiing," 173.

52. *Manchester* [N.H.] *Union Leader,* 17 May 1934; *New York Times,* 23 August 1934; State of New Hampshire Archives and Records, Concord, N.H., Box 14070: House Judiciary; MSS of minutes for 7, 14, and 19 February, 20 March, and 13 June 1935, Box 14066: Senate Committee, Revision of Laws; MS of minutes for 20 April 1937. See also *Journal of the House of Representatives, January Session of 1935* (Concord: Rumford Press, n.d.), 99, 425, 935–51, 1026, 1035, 1067–68, 1106, 1116, 1124–28, 1172, 1183; *Journal of the Honorable Senate, January Session of 1935,* 421, 423, 427, 441–2, 445; *Laws of the State of New Hampshire, passed January Session, 1935, Legislature Convened January 2, Adjourned January 21* (Concord, 1935), 186–90, 295–98. The progress of the tram was frequently commented on in *Appalachia* from 1934 onward. See also the remarks in *The Ski Bulletin,* 12 January 1934, 7; Arnold Lowell, "The Bright Idea," ibid., October 1935, 9; USEASA, *The Ski Annual* (1934): 33, 106–7; *American Ski Annual* (1937–38): 152–53; (1939–40): 136–37. For a negative view of the proposed tram, see "The Aerial Tramway," *Exeter News-Letter,* 21 September 1934, and correspondence from Philip W. Ayres, Forester for the Society for the Protection of New Hampshire Forests, to Nathaniel Goodrich and Alexander Bright, 2 January 1935, TLS in Goodrich Archive.

53. *Boston Herald,* 20 December 1935.

54. For Plymouth, N.H., see ibid., 13 December 1935; for Fryeburg, Maine, see ibid., 24 January and 30 November 1936.

55. Ibid., 3 December 1937.

56. William Putnam, *Joe Dodge—One New Hampshire Institution* (Canaan, N.H.: Phoenix, 1986).

57. *American Ski Annual* (1937–38): 36–41.

58. *The Ski Bulletin,* 1 February 1935, 7–8.

59. *Ruth V. Morse vs New York State,* accident at Bear Mountain, N.Y. on 29 January 1939 (*The Ski Bulletin,* 27 March 1942, 14).

60. *Boston Herald,* 10 January 1936.

61. For an official slope photographer, see *Boston Herald,* 10 January 1938; for night skiing, ibid., 20 December 1935, and see also John Hitchcock, "Bousquet Is Where Lighting All Began," *Ski Area Management* 9, no. 2 (1970): 56.

62. For Bertram, see the *Boston Herald,* 17 February 1939, and for Franconia, ibid., 7 February 1936.

63. Langley, "Survey of Skiing," 163.

64. Brewer, "Winter Sports Review," December 1940, 42; A. E. Goddard, "Good News for Skiers!" *California—Magazine of the Pacific,* December 1941, 28; Roberts, "Are Winter Sports Slipping?" ibid., December 1948, 26; idem, "Winter Sports—How Do We Stand?" ibid., December 1949, 23.

65. Circulation figures may be found in *The Ski Bulletin,* 11 January 1935, 6; 29 March 1935, 8; 20 March 1936, 7; November 1939, 1.

66. *Ski Illustrated,* December/January 1937–38.

67. All these misrepresentations were criticized in *The Ski Bulletin,* 22 January

1937, 4. The last reference I have found to skiing with a single pole is in 1933; see Hastings, "Winter Sports in Yosemite," January 1933, 15.

68. *Sierra Club Bulletin*, June 1939, 132–42.

69. Otto Schniebs and John W. McCrillis, *Modern Ski Technique* (Brattleboro, Vt.: Stephen Daye Press, 1937). *Modern Ski Technique* first appeared serially in the *Dartmouth Alumni Magazine* (December 1931; January and February 1932).

70. *Boston Herald*, 3 January 1936. See also the comments on Station WABY in Albany, N.Y., in *The Ski Bulletin*, 5 February 1937, 4.

71. Lowell Thomas interviewed by E. John B. Allen, Charles Morrissey, and Richard W. Moulton, Woodstock and Stowe, Vt., and Pawling, N.Y., 17 and 18 March, 26 August 1981 for film *Legends of American Skiing*.

72. See the film clips in *Legends of American Skiing*.

73. On the ski shows, see *The Ski Bulletin*, 9 December 1938, 4; *Time*, 21 December 1936, 31–32; *Boston Herald*, 5, 6, and 9 December 1935; *American Ski Annual* (1937–38): 178–79; "America Takes to Skis," *Publishers Weekly*, 12 December 1936, 2,289. In 1939 there were the New York World's Fair in the East and the western equivalent on Treasure Island, San Francisco. See Marjorie Walsh, "Summer Skiing at the Fairs, I: On Treasure Island," and E. Dubois, "Summer Skiing at the Fairs, II: New York," *The Ski Bulletin*, October 1939, 5, and November 1939, 5.

74. An American had seen such a slide in Berlin, Germany, and suggested it to Saks. The slides could be moved and Saks's was used indoors at the third annual conference on Outdoor Recreation in March 1936 at Massachusetts State College (*The Ski Bulletin*, 6 March 1936, 12). One slide was put on the oceanliner *Paris*, which Saks sponsored for its "Snow Boat Cruise" from New York to St. Moritz, Switzerland (*New York Times*, 28 September 1936).

75. *The Ski Bulletin*, 3 January 1936, 10.

76. *Newsweek*, 26 December 1936, 18–19; *New York Times*, 5 April 1936; "America Takes to Skis," 2,287.

77. Roberts, "Are Winter Sports Slipping?" 24.

78. For figures on 1940, see *New York Times Magazine*, 11 February 1940, 9. See also Langley, "The Present Status of Skiing in America," 10. In 1937, in spite of a lack of snow, one department store reported doing ski-related business at six thousand dollars a day for a week's total of thirty-six thousand dollars: $6,000 skis; $8,800 women's clothing; $3,000 shoes; $4,500 men's clothing; $1,000 poles, bindings, wax; $7,200 girls' clothing; $2,100 boys' clothing (*New York Times*, 10 January 1937).

79. "Selling Snow," *California—Magazine of Pacific Business*, December 1936, 15.

12 / Epilogue

1. J. R. Tunis, *Sport for the Fun of It* (New York: A. S. Barnes, 1940), 241.

2. *Boston Herald*, 3 March 1939.

3. Otto Lang, *Downhill Skiing* (New York: Henry Holt and Company, 1936), 76.

4. Capt. Howard C. Crawford, "Fifteenth Infantry Ski Patrol," *The Ski Bulletin*,

14 March 1941, 5–6; *Christian Science Monitor, Weekly Magazine,* 8 March 1941; "Army's New Ski Patrol on the Snowy Slopes of Mt. Rainier," *Life,* 20 January 1941, 78, 81; Lt. Charles C. Bradley, "A Mountain Soldier Sings," *American Ski Annual* (1945): 37–48. An account of filming the recruiting film is in John Jay, *Skiing the Americas* (New York: Macmillan, 1947), 208–17.

5. Torguson, "Skiing: A Wonderful Winter Sport," 109.

SELECTED BIBLIOGRAPHY

The four major repositories of skiing material in the United States are the Western Skisport Museum (WSSM), Boreal Ridge, California; the Colorado Ski Museum (CSSM), Vail, Colorado; the National Ski Hall of Fame (NSHF), Ishpeming, Michigan; and the New England Ski Museum (NESM), Franconia, New Hampshire. Each contains an excellent collection of regional artifacts and a growing number of documents, papers, magazines, films, and, except for Colorado, each has a substantial library.

In published material, information on American skiing may be found in the contemporary press, in the sports magazines, and in books written for popular consumption. There is very little serious history. This bibliography lists many of the available unpublished sources as well as the important printed material. Titles that contain few references to skiing are included only when their importance is justified. The oral history collections at the National Ski Hall of Fame and the New England Ski Museum are varied in their quality.

The following abbreviations have been used:

ALS	Autograph letter signed
AMs	Autograph manuscript
TD	Typewritten document
TL	Typewritten letter
TLS	Typewritten letter signed
TS	Typewritten manuscript

UNPUBLISHED MATERIAL

Manuscripts, Letters, Diaries, Photographs, and Scrapbooks

APPERSON, John S. Papers and photographic collection. ALS, TLS. Adirondack Research Center, Schenectady, N.Y.

BARBIN, Henry J. Scrapbook, 1925–1937. NESM.

BALDWIN, Henry I. Letter to author, December 1986, ALS. Allen Collection: NESM.

———. "The Skiing Life, 1986." TS. Held privately.

BERRY, Bill W. On Californian Skiing. Untitled TS. Held privately.

BLAIR, Charles H., [?], to Charles A. Proctor, 13 January 1937. ALS. With photostat of an article by Blair in *Harper's Young People,* 12 January 1892. Special Collections, Baker Library, Dartmouth College, Hanover, N.H.

BROWN Company, Berlin, N.H. Photo archive, Plymouth State College, Plymouth, N.H.

CARPENTER, J. E. "Truckee, Pioneer in Winter Sports." TS of talk 1960. Allen Collection: NESM.

CORNWALL, Harry C. "The Gunnison Country, 1879–1886." 1928 TS. Western State College Library, Gunnison, Colo.

FERRILL, Will. Scrapbook. 3 vols. Denver Public Library, Denver.

GOODRICH, Nathaniel L. Correspondence and papers, 1920s–1930s.

HARRIS, Fred H. Diaries, 1904–11, AMs. Held by Helen Harris, Brattleboro, Vt.

———. Papers, AMs and various. Held by Helen Harris.

———. Photo albums (black); scrapbook (green); Memory Books 1, 2, 3. NESM.

HIRSCH, Harold S. "If I Had to Do It All Over Again." TS of talk to Ski Business Week Panel, Vail, Colo., 1 December 1979. Allen Collection: NESM.

HOLT, Herman, III. Diaries, 1896–97, AMs. Held by Barbara Holt, Dover, N.H.

HOOKE, David O. "Dartmouth Outing Club History," 1984. TS. Dartmouth College.

HOYT, Natalie. Letters, 1931–32. ALS. Held by Natalie Hoyt, Hopkinton, N.H.

KELLOGG, Dr. Clarence W. Diary with additions, late 1800s to 1940s. Copy TD. Plumas County Museum, Quincy, Calif.

MORGAN, John E. P. [?], to Charles H. Bell, 26 October 1966. Copy TL. Allen Collection: NESM.

NATIONAL Ski Patrol System, including the Minot Dole Papers, 1938–Present. 14 boxes. Western History Collections, University of Colorado, Boulder, Colo.

PALMEDO, Roland, to Helen Boughton-Leigh. 19 June 1934; 14 December 1934. Copy ALS. Allen Collection: NESM.

———, to Arnold Lunn. 24 October 1934. Copy ALS. Allen Collection: NESM.

PERKINS, Henry J. Scrapbook. NESM.

PERRY, John C. Diaries, 1885–1888. AMs. New Hampshire Historical Society, Concord, N.H.

PROCTOR, Charles N., to author. 12 January 1985. ALS. Allen Collection: NESM.

———. Scrapbook. NESM.

SCHNIEBS, Otto, [?] to Dick [Emerson]. 21 February 1971. ALS. NESM.

SLUYTER, Robert J., and Grace J. Sluyter. "Historical Notes of the Early Washington, Nevada County, Californian Mining District." Collected by Robert J. and Grace J. Sluyter. TS. WSSM.

TAYLOR, James P. Document Box T 4, Folder 7; Document Box T 7, Folders: Green Mountain Club 1911–21; Document Box T 11, Folder: Vermont Academy. Vermont Historical Society, Montpelier.

TELLEFSEN, Carl. At the annual meeting of the Ishpeming Ski Club. 18 April 1904. TD. NSHF.

YELLOWSTONE National Park. Photo Archive. Yellowstone, Wyo.
YOSEMITE Winter Club Scrapbook, 1927–39. WSSM.

Oral Histories, Films, and Interviews

ORAL HISTORIES

DEPOSITED at NESM: Henry I. Baldwin, Edward Blood, David Bradley, Arthur Callan, Dorothy Clay, Ted Cooke, Arthur Doucette, Helen McAlpin, Fred Nachbaur, Carroll Reed, Rockwell Stephens, Edward Wells, Betty Whitney.

CONDUCTED for documentary film, *Legends of American Skiing* (to be deposited at NESM): Lee Ashley, Bill Berry, Thomas Cabot, Abner Coleman, Richard Durrance, Alf Engen, Don Fraser, Selden Hannah, Averell Harriman, Charles Lord, Toni Matt, Helen McAlpin, John McCrillis, Barney McLean, Janet Mead, Perry Merrill, Charles N. Proctor, Sepp Ruschp, Ted Ryan, Al Sise, Lowell Thomas, Gordon Wren, Mary Bird Young.

FILM ARCHIVE, NESM

COOKE, Ted. On Gunstock Ski Hoist. 7 minutes. 1935.
MCCRILLIS, John W. *Skiing on Mt. Moosilauke.* 7 minutes. 1931.
MOULTON, Richard W. *Legends of American Skiing.* Produced and directed by Richard W. Moulton. 78 minutes. Keystone Productions, 1982.
WARE, W. P. On Peckett's Inn and Ski School. 12 minutes. 1932.

INTERVIEWS

Bill Berry, Dorothy Clay, Otto Mason, Lyman Johnson, Douglas Philbrick. Notes in Allen Collection: NESM.
"Welch Nossamen's Life Story of Pioneer Life in Iowa and Colorado related at the insistence of Carl Weeks to I. E. Carlin, 1851–1937." TD. 1933. Denver Public Library, Denver.

Institutional Records

AURORA Ski Club, Red Wing, Minn. Constitution and Minutes, 1886–1892. AMs microfilm. Minnesota Historical Society Archives, St. Paul.
DARTMOUTH Outing Club, Hanover, N.H. Minutes. File I-10-5 in Box 10. DOC Collection, Special Collections, Baker Library, Dartmouth College.
FIRST Kingdom of the Ski, Utica, N.Y. Constitution, 10 December 1902. Copy TD. Allen Collection: NESM.
GUNSTOCK Ski Hoist Account Book. NESM.
ISHPEMING Ski Club, Ishpeming, Mich. Organized 18 April 1901. AMs. NSHF.
NANSEN Ski Club, Berlin, N.H. Grunlove Skiklubben "Fridtjof Nansen," and Minutes, 1907–17. AMs. Held privately.
NATIONAL Ski Association. Minutes, 1932–36. TD. NSHF.
ONONDAGA Ski Club Accounts and Correspondence, 1937–39. Syracuse, N.Y. AMs and TD. Allen Collection: NESM.
PLYMOUTH Ski Club Accounts and Correspondence, 1930s. Plymouth, N.H. AMs and TD. NESM.
UNITED States Eastern Amateur Ski Association. Minutes, 1923–33. TD. NESM.

Theses

BORMAN, Bill. "The Birth and Development of Competitive Skiing at Dartmouth College: 1910–1930." Thesis, Dartmouth College, [1952?].

BRAMHALL, Lawrence H. "The History of Skiing in New England and the Lake Placid, New York Region." M.A. thesis, Boston University, 1946.

JACOBS, Janis Gayle. "Tin Cup, Colorado: A Cup Full of Dreams." M.A. thesis, Western State College, Gunnison, Colo., 1974.

LANGLEY, Roger F. "A Survey of Skiing in the United States." M.Ed. thesis, State Teachers College of Fitchburg, Mass., 1946.

MAZUZAN, George T. "Skiing in Vermont: Four Case Studies." M.A. thesis, University of Vermont, 1964.

PUBLISHED MATERIAL

Primary

BOSTON and Maine Railroad. *Annual Reports,* 1931–40. B & M Historical Collection, Center for Lowell History, University of Lowell, Lowell, Mass.

GOULD, Helen Weaver, compiler. *La Porte Scrapbook.* La Porte, Calif., 1972.

RUBIEN, Frederick W., ed. *Report of the American Olympic Committee.* New York: American Olympic Committee, [1936].

U.S. Government. *Census.* Ninth to Fourteenth (1870–1920). Washington, D.C.: Government Printing Office, 1872–1922.

The Winter Sport of Skeeing: Theo. A. Johnsen Company, Manufacturers of Sporting "Tajco" Sporting Goods. Portland, Maine, 1905.

Secondary

ALLEN, E. John B. "The Development of New Hampshire Skiing: 1870s–1940." *Historical New Hampshire* 36, no. 1 (1981): 1–37.

———. "The Making of a Skier: Fred H. Harris 1904–1911." *Vermont History* 53, no. 1 (1985): 5–16.

———. "'Millions of Flakes of Fun in Massachusetts': Boston and the Development of Skiing." In *Sports in Massachusetts: Historical Essays,* ed. Ronald Story. Westfield: Institute for Massachusetts Studies, 1991.

———. "The Modernization of the Skisport: Ishpeming's Contribution to American Skiing." *Michigan Historical Review* 16, no. 1 (1990): 1–20.

———. "'Skeeing' in Maine: The Early Years, 1870s to 1920s." *Maine Historical Society Quarterly* 30, no. 3, 4 (1991): 146–65.

———. *Teaching and Technique: A History of American Ski Instruction.* 2d ed. Latham, N.Y.: EPSIA Educational Foundation, 1987.

AMATEUR Ski Club of New York. *Ten Winters, 1931–1941.* New York: Amateur Ski Club, 1942.

BENSON, Jack A. "Before Aspen and Vail: The Story of Recreational Skiing in Frontier Colorado." *Journal of the West* 22 (January 1983): 52–61.

———. "Before Skiing Was Fun." *Western Historical Quarterly* 8 (1977): 431–41.

BERRY, Bill. "The Dopemaker Is King." *Ski Illustrated,* November 1938, 11–13, 32, 34.

———. "Into the Ski Cradle." *Ski Illustrated,* December–January 1938–39, 14–15, 26–28.

———. *Lost Sierra: Gold, Ghosts and Skis.* Ed. Chapman Wentworth. Boreal Ridge, Calif.: Western America Skisport Museum, 1991.

———. "The Romance of the American Ski Cradle." *Ski Illustrated,* February– March 1939, 14–17, 34–35.

BJORK, Kenneth. "'Snowshoe' Thompson: Fact and Legend." *Norwegian-American Studies and Record* 19 (1956): 62–88.

BRADLEY, Captain Alfred E. "The Ski, and Its Use for Military Purposes in Yellowstone National Park." *Proceedings of the Association of Military Surgeons* 9 (1900): 403–13.

BRADLEY, David. "Dartmouth in the Old Days." *Ski Magazine,* January 1959, 17– 19, 68–75; February 1959, 22–25, 64–69.

BREWER, Wheaton H. "Winter Sports Review." *California—Magazine of the Pacific,* December 1940, 20–21, 42–46.

BURT, Craig O. "How Skiing Came to Stowe." *Mt. Mansfield Skiing* 28, no. 4 (1962).

CARLSON, Albert F. "Ski Geography of New England." *Economic Geography* 18 (July 1942): 307–20.

CARPENTER, Delphine. "Is Your Wife a Ski Widow?" *Leisure,* January 1935, 26–27.

COMEY, Arthur C. "Skiing in Inferno." *Mountain Magazine* 8, no. 1 (1929): 7–8.

"Crossing the Sierras." *Hutchings' California Magazine,* 8 February 1857, 349–54.

DUDLEY, Charles M. *60 Centuries of Skiing.* Brattleboro: Stephen Daye Press, 1935.

DYER, John L. *The Snow-Shoe Itinerant: An Autobiography of the Rev. John L. Dyer.* Cincinnati: Cranston and Stowe, 1890.

EGGER, C. "England und Amerika." *Ski* [Swiss] 5 (1909): 144.

FAIRLIE, Gerard. *Flight without Wings: The Biography of Hannes Schneider.* London: Hodder and Stoughton, 1957.

FAY, Abbott. *Ski Tracks in the Rockies: A Century of Colorado Skiing.* Cordillera, Colo.: Cordillera Press, 1984.

FULLER, Z. "Rocky Mountain Snow-Shoeing." *Midland Monthly* 9, no. 3 (1898): 204–8.

GRINDEN, Harold A. *History of the National Ski Association and the Ski Sport in the United States of America, 1840–1931.* Np.: Duluth, Minn. [1931].

GUTTMANN, Allen. *From Ritual to Record: The Nature of Modern Sports.* New York: Columbia University Press, 1978.

HARRIS, Fred H., ed. *Dartmouth Out O'Doors.* Boston: Crosby, 1913.

———. "Skiing and Winter Sports in Vermont." *The Vermonter* 17, no. 11 (1912): 677–81.

———. "Skiing Over the New Hampshire Hills." *National Geographic Magazine,* February 1920, 136–64.

———. "The Splendid Sport of Ski Jumping." *Country Life in America,* February 1924, 48–50.

HAYNES, Jack Ellis. "The First Winter Trip through Yellowstone National Park." *Annals of Wyoming* 14 (April 1942): 89–97.

HAZARD, Joseph T. "Winter Sports in the Western Mountains." *Pacific Northwest Quarterly* 44, no. 1 (1953): 7–14.

HENDEL, Charles W. "Snow-Shoeing in the Sierras." *Mining and Scientific Press,* 3 January 1874, 1, 9.

HIGHAM, John. "The Reorientation of American Culture in the 1890s." In *Writing American History: Essays on Modern Scholarship,* ed. John Higham. Bloomington: Indiana University Press, 1972.

HOFER, Elwood. "Winter in the Park." *Forest and Stream,* 17, 24, 31 March; 7, 14, 21, 28 April; and 5 May 1887.

HOVELSEN, Leif. *The Flying Norseman.* Ishpeming: National Ski Hall of Fame Press, 1983.

HOWE, Nicholas. "Skiing's Man For All Seasons." *Skiing,* December 1981, 165–66, 169.

JAY, John. *Ski Down the Years.* New York: Universal Publishing, 1966.

KELNER, Alexis. *Skiing in Utah: A History.* Salt Lake City: Alexis Kelner, 1980.

KNUDSON, John. "The Birth of New England Skiing." *Skiing* (Spring 1974): 117–18E, 121–22E.

LATTIMER, George M., compiler. *Official Report III Olympic Winter Games: Lake Placid 1932.* Lake Placid: III Olympic Winter Games Committee, 1932.

LEARS, T. J. Jackson, *No Place of Grace: Antimodernism and the Transformation of American Culture 1880–1920.* New York: Pantheon, 1981.

LIVERMORE, R., Jr. "Notes on Olympic Skiing: 1936." *Atlantic Monthly,* May 1936, 617–22.

MARDEN, B. J., Captain. "Wanderings Through Eastern America." *British Ski Year Book* (1928): 359–65.

MAZUZAN, George T. "Skiing Is Not Merely a Schport: The Development of Mt. Mansfield as a Winter Recreation Area: 1930–1955." *Vermont History* 40, no. 1 (1972): 47–63.

MCCRILLIS, John W. "Skier's Album—Winter Trip 66 Years Ago." *Forest Notes* 151 (Winter 1983): 5–7.

MCGOWAN, Graeme, assisted by Garrat B. Van Wagenen. "The First Chapter in the History of Ski-ing in Colorado." *British Ski Year Book* (1930): 503–6.

METZLER, P. W. "Third Winter Olympics." *Conservationist* 34, no. 3 (1979): 12–16.

MORISON, Duncan M. "Ski-ing in California." *British Ski Year Book* (1926): 510–14.

MOSAUER, Walter. "Ski Mountaineering in Southern California." *American Alpine Journal* 3, no. 3 (1935): 325–30.

MROZEK, Donald J. "The Image of the West in American Sport." *Journal of the West* 17, no. 3 (1978): 3–15.

NANSEN, Fridtjof. *Paa Ski over Grønland: En Skildring af den Norske Grønlands-Ekspedition 1888–89.* Kristiania: Aschehoug, 1890.

PALMEDO, Roland, ed. *Skiing: The International Sport.* New York: Derrydale, 1937.

PATTERSON, Steve, and Kenton Forrest. *Rio Grande Ski Train.* Denver: Tramway Press, 1984.

PROCTOR, C. A. "Notes on Ski-ing in the United States." *Ski Notes and Queries,* May 1931, 150–52.

QUILLE, Dan de. [William H. Wright]. "Snow-Shoe Thompson." *Territorial Enterprise* [Virginia, Nev.], 13 February 1876.

ROCH, André. "Un hiver aux Montagnes Rocheuses du Colorado." *Der Schnee-Hase* (1937), trans. Ernest Blake. "A Once and Future Resort." *Colorado Heritage* 4 (1985): 17–23.

SARAH Platt Decker Chapter of the D.A.R., Durango, Colorado. *Pioneers of the San Juan Country.* 2 vols. Colorado Springs: Old West Printing and Stationery Company, 1946.

SCHNIEBS, Otto, and J. W. McCrillis. *Modern Ski Technique.* Brattleboro, Vt.: Stephen Daye Press, 1937.

SELIGMAN, R. "United States and Canada." *British Ski Year Book* (1905): 34–35.

SERAFINI, Enzo. "First American Intercollegiate Ski Meet." *Skier,* February 1965, 27–30.

The Ski Club Hochgebirge. [Boston]: By the Ski Club Hochgebirge, 1938.

SQUIER, H. G. "Snow Shoers of Plumas." *California Illustrated Magazine,* February 1894, 318–24.

STONE, Robert G. "The Distribution of the Average Depth of Snow on the Ground in New York and New England: Curves of Average Depth and Variability." *American Geophysical Union, Transactions* (1940): 672–92.

SVAHN, Åke. "Idrott und Sport. Eine semantische Studie zu zwei schwedischen Fachtermini." *Stadion* 5, no. 1 (1979): 20–41.

TAYLOR, Dorice. *Sun Valley.* Sun Valley: Ex Libris, 1980.

WARREN, E. R. "Snow-shoeing in the Rocky Mountains." *Outing,* January 1887, 350–53.

WATTERS, Ron. *Ski Trails and Old Timers' Tales in Idaho and Montana.* Moscow, Idaho: Solstice Press, 1978.

WEINBERGER, Julius. "Economic Aspects of Recreation." *Harvard Business Review,* September 1937, 448–63.

WHITE, Helen M. *The Tale of a Comet and Other Stories.* St. Paul: Minnesota Historical Society Press, 1984.

WHITE, William M. "Mount Marcy—Winter 1911." *Adirondac,* January 1984, 3–5.

WORCESTER, William E. "The Early History of Skis in Vermont." *Vermont Life* 34, no. 2 (1979): 2–5.

WORMINGTON, Sam. *The Ski Race.* Sandpoint, Idaho: Selkirk Press, 1980.

Periodicals and Newspapers

Alpine Chronicle [various] (1873–92); many issues missing
American Ski Annual (1935–49)
American Skiing Annual and Skiing Journal (1950–57)
Annual Report of the National Ski Association of America (1906); name changes but generally called *The Skisport*
Appalachia (1887–1940)
Boston Evening Transcript (1922–40)
Boston Globe (1926–37)
California Journal of Development (1928–33)
Christian Science Monitor Weekly Magazine (1926–41)
Daily Alta California [San Francisco] (1849–57, 1861–75); some issues missing

The Dartmouth (1909–20)

Dartmouth Alumni Magazine (1923–50)

Downieville [Calif.] *Mountain Messenger* (1865–88); some issues missing

Eastern Ski Annual (1957–58)

Eastern Ski Association Echoes (1926–29)

Iron Ore [Ishpeming, Mich.] (1899–1908)

Lake Placid Club News (1927–30)

Lake Placid Club Notes (1905–33)

The Mazama (1927; 1937–38)

Mining Journal [Marquette, Mich.] (1883–88; 1901–06)

Motordom (1912–33)

National Ski Association of America, Inc. *Year Book* (1930–31)

New York Times (1900–40)

Sacramento Daily Union (1851–90), issues missing

Sierra Club Bulletin (1900–40)

The Skisport (1906–25)

Snow and Ice. [Yosemite Park, Calif.] (Winter Season 1933–34)

Troubadour (1930–40)

United States Eastern Amateur Ski Association. *The Ski Annual* (1934)
———. *Year Book* (1928, 1929)

Winter in New England and the Snow Train. Boston: Boston and Maine Railroad, 1936.

Winter Sports (1931–34)

INDEX

Accommodations, 82–83, 102, 116, 119, 137–38, 140–44, 147, 162–64, 167
Air travel, 109, 147
Albizzi, Marquis d', 114, 147
Alpine racing, 98–99, 116, 123–26, 139, 141. *See also* Collegiate skiing
Artists: Adrian Allinson, 97; Tyler Micoleau, 120; Dwight Shepler, 130

Baillets, Ernest des, 138
Berry, Bill [William B.], 41
Boughton-Leigh, Helen [McAlpin], 128
Bradley, David, 122
Bright, Alexander H., 113, 123, 125, 126, 127, 147
British influence, 10, 97, 98–102, 132, 152, 214 n.40
Buchmayr, Siegfried, 119, 140, 145, 165, 169

Carleton, John, 79, 91, 114–15, 132
Civilian Conservation Corps (CCC), 114–15, 140, 141–42, 149, 164
Climbing mountains on skis, 78, 102, 132
Club organization, 53
Clubs, in general, 64
Clubs, regional: California and Northwest, 84, 121, 138, 141, 149; Midwest, 47, 49, 50, 52–54, 60; New England and New York, 64, 104, 107, 117, 147, 149; Rocky Mountains, 8, 46, 84, 139, 144
Clubs, selected: Amateur Ski Club of N.Y., 107–8, 111, 116, 130–31, 147; Appalachian Mountain Club (AMC), 81, 98, 100, 102–8, 114, 119, 127, 133–34, 157; Alturas Snow Shoe Club (Calif.), 14, 21, 22; Aurora SC (Minn.), 50, 53, 57–58, 60, 74; Hochgebirge SC of Boston, 111, 117, 123, 125–27, 132–34, 139, 147; Norden, later Ishpeming SC (Mich.), 50–51; Sierra Club, 81, 83, 138, 166, 169; Skiklubben, later Nansen SC (N.H.), 47, 49, 50, 54, 79, 133; White Mountain Ski Runners (Mass.), 98, 111, 147, 161; Woodstock Ski Runners (Vt.), 115–16; Yosemite Winter Sports Club, 137
Club uniforms, 53
Cochand, Emil, 102
Collegiate skiing: Alpine skiing, 101–2; at Dartmouth College, 5–6, 9, 33, 45, 75–79, 89, 91, 98, 100–102, 106, 109–11, 115–17, 119, 123, 125, 127, 157, 162–64; Dartmouth College and founding of Dartmouth Outing Club (DOC), 75–78; at eastern colleges, 73, 75–76, 79, 104, 117; at midwestern colleges, 54, 75; at western colleges, 141
Collegiate skiing, coaches: Diettrich, Anton, 73, 101, 152; Prager, Walter, 119; Schniebs, Otto, *see* Schniebs, Otto Eugen
Cooke, Ted [Theodore], 113, 130, 161–62
Cross-country racing, 47, 54–55, 62, 76

Dewey, Godfrey, 69–70, 92–93, 95
Diettrich, Anton, 73, 101, 152
Dole, Minot, 130–31
Dope (ski wax), 13, 26, 28, 135
Durrance, Richard, 125, 129, 133, 144
Dyer, John L., 35, 37

Elmer, R.S., 90
Equipment: bindings, 33, 36, 42, 43, 44, 71, 72, 73, 136, 152; boots, 44, 73–74, 136, 152–53; clothes, 156–58, 165–66, 169, 172; poles, double, 73, 153, 156; poles, single, 40, 43–44, 73, 135, 136; skins, 8, 44. *See also* Skis

Fédération Internationale de Ski (FIS), 69–70, 95, 126, 128

Goodrich, Nathaniel, 98, 100
Gunderson, Oscar, 67
Guttmann, Allen, 4–5, 50, 171

Hall, Henry, 84
Harriman, Averell, 113, 143
Harris, Fred H., 9, 12, 45, 69, 76, 78, 90
Haugen, Anders, 70, 84, 91–92
Haugen, Lars, 84, 137, 172
Health, 3, 75, 78–79, 80, 96, 98, 103, 106–7
Hemmetsveit brothers, 56–60, 62, 70–71
Hendel, Charles W., 8
Holter, Axel, 11–12, 51–54, 61–62, 63, 66, 67–68, 71
Hovelsen, Karl, 53, 83–84

Idraet, 4, 10–12, 14, 28, 41, 47–62, 64–65, 67–68, 74, 79, 84–85, 89, 91–92, 96, 98, 102, 107, 109–10, 121, 132, 137, 138, 154–55, 171
Inferno race, 132–34
Instruction: Arlberg, 96–98; pre-ski school, 102, 105, 107, 119, 141; professional, 119–23, 138, 163, 166, 169

Jeldness, Olaus, 46
Jumping, 52, 55–59, 63, 64–70, 74, 76, 78–79, 84, 91–96, 109–10, 142, 172, 192 n.52

Lake Placid Club, 81–83, 102, 121, 123, 138, 159; and antisemitism, 83; Olympic Games, 92–96
Lang, Otto, 120, 142, 171, 173
Langley, Roger F., 118, 131
Laugen, Gullik, 30
Lunn, Arnold, 90, 96, 98–100, 101, 128–29, 139

McCrillis, John, 123–24, 166
Mail delivery. *See* Utilitarian skiing

Matt, Toni, 134
Mikkelsen, Strand, 102
Monson, Rolf, 92
Mt. Washington, 78, 132–34, 163, 165, 167, 201 n.43
Muir, John, 20, 45, 83

Nansen, Fridtjof, 11, 47–49, 102, 171, 201 n.43
National Ski Association of America (NSA), 27–28, 63, 84, 89, 90–92, 131, 137; affiliation with FIS and IOC, 68–69, 90; control of member clubs, 64–65, 74, 89, 90, 165; founding, 11, 47, 50–52; and jumping, 49, 58–62, 65–69; Olympic Games, 91–96, 127; regional associations, 90, 117–18, 123–24, 137; sanction of Alpine races, 123–24; strike, 61
National Ski Patrol System, 129–32

Oimen, Casper, 95, 127
Olympic Games of the North, 68
Olympic Winter Games: 1924 (Chamonix, France), 64, 68, 79, 89, 90–92, 150; 1928 (St. Moritz, Switzerland), 70, 92–93, 101, 150; 1932 (Lake Placid, N.Y.), 14, 69, 92–96, 132, 137, 150, 155, 166, 192 n.52; 1936 (Garmisch-Partenkirchen, Germany), 126–29, 141, 147, 150, 153, 167; 1940 (canceled), 125; 1960 (Squaw Valley, Calif.), 17
Omtvedt, Ragnar, 68, 84, 92
Oyass, Oscar, 90

Palmedo, Roland, 113, 116, 128, 129, 131, 140, 147, 150, 169
Prager, Walter, 119
Prizes: goods, 22; money, 21–22, 25, 59–62, 64
Proctor, Charles A., 101
Proctor, Charles N., 70, 92–93, 101–2, 108, 114–15, 132, 138, 143, 155–56
Publications, 12, 14, 78, 83, 98, 114, 132, 149–50, 165–67; *American Ski Annual,* 122, 131, 138, 147, 156, 163, 165, 169; *The Ski Bulletin,* 104, 107, 125, 131; *The Skisport,* 11, 12, 49, 52, 62, 64–65, 71, 79, 90, 165

Railroads, 6, 59, 104–9, 113, 148, 160; Boston & Maine (B&M), 104–7, 147, 149, 158, 160–61; Denver & Salt Lake, 139–40; Union Pacific, 112–13, 143, 167; others, 107–9
Roosevelt, Theodore, 5, 8, 51

Ruschp, Sepp, 115
Rybizka, Benno, 119–21, 142

Scandinavian immigrants, 8–9, 10–11, 14, 28, 29–35, 41–42, 48, 54–55, 84, 91, 179n.6, 188n.1, 199n.24
Schneider, Hannes, 96–98, 100, 119–20, 128, 142, 152, 153, 163, 172
Schniebs, Otto Eugen, 102–3, 119, 121, 125, 139, 140, 151, 166
Ski centers, 115–16, 140, 141–42, 159–65, 171–72
Ski films, 97, 123–24, 135–36, 141, 144, 167, 172, 173
Skis: factory made, 63, 70; Darby & Ball, 151–52; Excelsior, 70–71; Groswold, 150; Holter, 63, 71; Johnsen, 9, 73–74; Lund (Northland), 72–73, 150–55, 172; Strand, 71–74, 150–51, 153–55; Tubbs, 150; Wold, 74; homemade, 8, 15, 21, 25–26, 30, 33, 35–36, 40–44, 45, 63–64, 135, 137; of unequal length, 8
Ski shops, specialist: Carroll Reed, 163; Hambro, 151–57; Osborn, 145, 155–56; Ski Sport, 152, 153, 155–56; others, 107, 151–53, 156–58, 163, 167, 169
Ski shows, 167–69
Ski terminology: English, 3, 7–12, 121, 176nn.13, 17; German, 107, 118–19, 121–23; Scandinavian, 9, 49–50, 56, 58, 121
Ski tows, 109–114; aerial tram, 113–14, 147, 162; California, 21, 109–10, 135; chairlifts, 112, 113, 116, 142, 144, 162, 167; rope tows, 104, 109–11, 140, 145, 147, 150, 161–62, 163; safety, 130; wire cable lifts, 111–14, 138, 140, 162–63
Ski trails, 10, 103–4, 114–16, 126, 132, 133, 164
Ski venues: Alta (Utah), 35–36, 136; Aspen–Mt. Hayden (Colo.), 34, 46, 139, 140, 143, 145, 166, 173; Berkshires (Mass.), 107–8; Berthoud Pass (Colo.), 109, 139–40; Brattleboro (Vt.), 92, 115;

Cannon Mtn. (Franconia, N.H.), 113–15, 160–62, 166; Eastern Slopes (N.H.), 112, 160–61, 163–64; Hot Sulphur Springs (Colo.), 83–84; Lake Placid Club (N.Y.), 83, 92–96, 102, 121, 123, 137, 150, 159; Mt. Hood (Oreg.), 140–42, 164; Mt. Rainier (Wash.), 127, 140–41, 173; Norfolk (Conn.), 107; Poconos (Penn.), 108; Steamboat (Colo.), 84, 137; Stowe (Vt.), 33, 108, 113, 115, 116, 129, 131, 152, 158, 166; Sugar Hill (N.H.), 82; Sun Valley (Idaho), 6, 108, 112, 113, 139, 143–44, 158, 167, 173; Truckee/Lake Tahoe (Calif.), 109–10, 135; Woodstock (Vt.), 82, 110–11, 115–16, 132, 162; Yosemite (Calif.), 113, 137–38, 143
Ski wax. See Dope
Spectators, 23–25, 51, 59, 62, 65, 79, 83, 95, 131
Strand, Martin A. See Skis
Straumann, Dr. Reinhard, 69
Strom, Erling, 121, 137

Tellefsen, Carl, 50–51, 61
Thompson, John A. "Snowshoe," 16–19, 26
Torguson, G. C., 84, 137
Tricks on skis, 62, 79
Tuckerman Bowl and Ravine, 132–34, 163, 165

United States Eastern Amateur Ski Association (USEASA, Eastern), 89, 90, 100, 101, 104, 117–19, 124, 148–49
U.S. Military, 39–40, 74
Utilitarian skiing, 8, 9, 12, 14–16, 28, 30–37, 83; mail delivery, 14, 16–20, 34, 37–39, 83

Women on skis, 15–16, 46, 53–54, 62, 73, 79, 80, 105–7, 112, 118–19, 135; races, 24–25, 150; at 1936 Olympics, 127–29